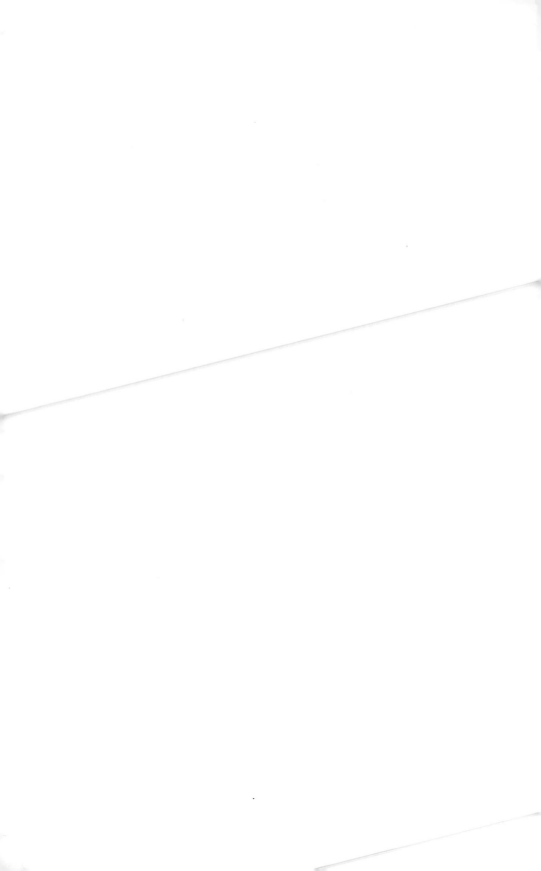

Schools and the Problem of Crime

Schools and the Problem of Crime

Stephen Boxford

WILLAN
PUBLISHING

Published by

Willan Publishing
Culmcott House
Mill Street, Uffculme
Cullompton, Devon
EX15 3AT, UK
Tel: +44(0)1884 840337
Fax: +44(0)1884 840251
e-mail: info@willanpublishing.co.uk
website: www.willanpublishing.co.uk

Published simultaneously in the USA and Canada by

Willan Publishing
c/o ISBS, 920 NE 58th Ave, Suite 300
Portland, Oregon 97213-3786, USA
Tel: +001(0)503 287 3093
Fax: +001(0)503 280 8832
e-mail: info@isbs.com
website: www.isbs.com

Hardback
ISBN-13: 978-1-84392-178-3
ISBN-10: 1-84392-178-2

British Library Cataloguing-in-Publication Data

A catalogue record for this book is available from the British Library

Typeset by GCS, Leighton Buzzard, Beds
Project management by Deer Park Productions, Tavistock, Devon
Printed and bound by T.J. International, Padstow, Cornwall

Contents

Acknowledgements

I would like to thank the Economic and Social Research Council who funded my Doctorate and my Postdoctoral Fellowship (award number PTA-026-27-0182), both of which I completed at the Institute of Criminology, University of Cambridge.

Without the support and help of Cardiff's headteachers this research would not have been possible. I would like to thank them, Cardiff's teachers and Year 10 pupils for their assistance in this research endeavour.

Professor Per-Olof Wikström proved to be a first-class PhD Supervisor and I would like to thank him for both his academic and social support.

This book and the work that went into it would not have been possible without the encouragement of my family (Mum, Dad and James, in particular) and all my friends. Thanks everyone!

List of figures and tables

Figures

Tables

Chapter 1

The Cardiff School Study

Crime reduction and improving educational standards are grails sought by politicians across the spectrum and by governments across the world. In the UK, like elsewhere in the world, news and politics are dominated by daily developments in policy and stories relating to both crime reduction and education. The ability of society to deal effectively with crime and education directly affects the nation's youth and ultimately all our futures. Countries strive for low crime rates and highly educated populations. Achieving these goals improves living standards and helps to secure economic competitiveness.

In criminological research there is a history of recognising the importance of schools in influencing juvenile delinquency and offending (see Wilson and Herrnstein 1985; Gottfredson and Hirschi 1990; Gottfredson 2001). Very few studies, however, have attempted to understand offending in the school setting, which of course may set precedents and affect people's propensity to offend outside the school setting and in later life. Educational research has recognised that pupil misbehaviour and delinquency affect the ability of schools to function successfully, pupils to learn effectively, and affects the life chances of pupils both involved in delinquency and those not involved (see, for example, Hargreaves *et al.* 1975; Willis 1988). Examples of research that seeks to investigate the causes of crime in schools, which may inform policies that address societal crime rates and educational standards, are few and far between. In the UK, over the last 30 years, little empirical research focusing on crime in schools has been produced (see Rutter *et al.* 1998). This is surprising for several reasons:

1   *Political agenda*: The issues of education and crime have been
    at the top of the political agenda for decades. Government at
    all levels appears to strive to improve education and reduce
    crime. It seems remarkable that little has been done regarding
    investigating crime in schools, when schools are often seen as
    breeding grounds for criminals and that criminality in schools
    may reduce the educational efficacy of schools.

2   *Media issue and reality*: The media are fond of reporting cases that
    illustrate the problem of crime in schools, which bring the issue
    to the public's attention. The shootings at Dunblane, the murder
    of the headteacher Philip Lawrence and recent stabbings (such
    as that of Luke Walmsley) in several schools in England, have
    highlighted the fact that crime in schools is an important issue in
    the UK. These cases may be at the extreme, but have brought the
    issue of crime in schools to the public sphere. In the USA, films
    such as *Bowling for Columbine* and *Elephant* have illustrated the
    problem of gun crime in schools.

    A report by the Department for Education and Skills (2004)
    indicated that during the summer term of 2003 there were
    336 expulsions for pupils attacking other pupils and 12,800
    suspensions. This all occurred during just one term, which gives
    an insight into the extent of the issue.

3   *Crime prevention*: Schools both in the UK and elsewhere have
    long been seen as potential arenas where crime prevention
    efforts should be focused (see Hawkins *et al.* 1992; Herrenkohl
    et al. 2001; Cowie *et al.* 2003). However, if the mechanisms that
    generate crime in schools are poorly understood it is difficult
    to understand how crime prevention programmes can be truly
    effective both in the short term regarding juvenile delinquency
    and in terms of long-term crime prevention.

4   *Educational efficacy*: If schools are to be truly effective in educating
    the nation's youth intellectually and morally their task will be
    made more straightforward if pupils behave well in school. Pupils
    who are delinquent in school not only adversely affect their life
    chances, but also affect the life chances of other pupils.

5   *Explanation of the crime phenomenon*: Explaining and understanding
    juvenile delinquency has been an obsession of criminologists.
    Indeed, why people offend is one of the most important
    criminological questions – if not the most important. However,
    in the last 30 years or so UK criminologists have undertaken

only a sparse amount of empirical research seeking to explain juvenile delinquency generally, let alone explaining specifics like crime in the school context. School, after the family, is probably the most important arena of socialisation for the nation's young people. Schools provide a context where pupils from a variety of backgrounds, with a variety of behavioural and cognitive dispositions, mix together on a daily basis. Young people in the school context are subject to the control of the school, but also have access to numerous opportunities to commit crimes and deviant acts. As probably the most important arena of socialisation after the family for most young people, schools may be very important in affecting crime. Understanding the influence of schools on crime is a crucial part of the explanation as to why people offend.

In an environment where raising standards in education and reducing juvenile delinquency and crime are priorities it seems strange that crime in schools has been under-researched.

6   *A 'school effect' or pupil composition?* Very little research in the UK has been undertaken regarding whether schools themselves make a difference regarding juveniles' delinquent or criminal behaviour, or whether it is a compositional effect of the pupil population. Graham (1988: 3) made the following fundamental distinction: 'It has yet to be established whether the variations between schools in their delinquency rates are due to differences in the schools themselves or merely their pupil intakes.'

The Cardiff School Study (the study that forms the empirical basis for this book) was conducted in response to the inadequate attention that has been given to the causes of offending in secondary schools in the UK since the seminal British study, *Fifteen Thousand Hours*, was published in 1979 by Rutter *et al.* (see Rutter *et al.* 1998 and Chapter 3 for a discussion). In the UK there has been little aetiological research exploring the issue of pupils' offending behaviour in secondary schools since *Fifteen Thousand Hours.*

The Cardiff School Study is also a response to the lack of current research on young people's offending in the UK in general. The most recent, important, cross-sectional study concerning adolescent offending in the UK was based in the English city of Peterborough and examined 1,957 14–15-year-olds. This was an aetiological investigation of their offending and victimisation experiences (Wikström 2002). As well as this study, the only other recent studies of adolescent offending are the national self-report studies conducted by Graham and Bowling (1995) and Flood-Page *et al.* (2000), the 'Cautionary Tales' study of approximately 1,200 11–15-year-olds, from four selected schools in Edinburgh (Anderson *et al.* 1994), and the Edinburgh-based 'Youth in Transition Study', which is an ongoing longitudinal study of 4,300 juveniles covering most schools in that city (Smith *et al.* 2001; Smith and McVie 2003). McDonald (1969) conducted a self-report survey of nearly 1,000 adolescent boys in 12 schools (ranging from grammar to secondary modern) in London. The main aim of this study was to investigate the link between social class and delinquent behaviour. (The prominent recent self-report studies in the UK are shown in Table 2.3 in Chapter 2.) As well as these studies, there is also the important longitudinal 'Cambridge Study in Delinquent Development' (in the rest of the book referred to as the Cambridge Study), which has followed a male cohort from 1953 onwards (see West and Farrington 1973, 1977). The Cardiff School Study includes both males and females.

Contribution to knowledge and research aims

The Cardiff School Study is a cross-sectional, self-report study of 3,103 adolescents, who started Year 10 (ages 14–15) in autumn 2001 in the 20 state comprehensive schools in Cardiff. The present study contributes to knowledge regarding the aetiology of pupil offending in schools. It investigates the extent to which pupils offend in schools. The study explains why pupils offend in the school context, specifically taking an integrative analytical approach in investigating the factors that cause and predict pupil offending in schools. The two main research questions are thus:

1   Do schools vary in offending rates among pupils?
2   What factors cause and predict offending by pupils in the school context?

The main aims of the study are to:

• explore the nature and extent of offending behaviour among pupils in schools;
• provide an aetiological investigation of pupil offending in school; and
• examine the relative influences of and interactions between explanatory factors which include individual pupil characteristics,

lifestyles, pupils' family social position, community context and school context in investigating the causes of pupil offending in schools.

Analytical framework

The following outlines the analytical framework of the book by describing what each of the chapters focuses on.

Chapter 2 examines the research design and methods, outlining why Cardiff is an ideal research site and the key characteristics of the education system. This chapter illustrates how the research was conducted and discusses the response rates achieved. It discusses the key methodological issues – in particular, the reliability and validity of the research tools employed. A comparative exploration of general offending rates between the Peterborough Youth Study (Wikström 2002) and the Cardiff School Study are presented which, it is argued, suggest the reliability of the research methodology employed.

Chapter 3 discusses previous research as it pertains to the present study. The chapter introduces the aims of education and schooling with reference to Aristotle. Specifically, it presents a state-of-the-field review of criminological and educational research focusing on crime in schools. It examines previous integrative analytical approaches in criminological and educational research and suggests how they can be strengthened as well as illustrating weaknesses. An agenda for future research is presented based on previous literature. There is a discussion regarding the importance of causes and causal mechanisms for social science research and this book in particular. The chapter explores previous research undertaken, focusing on crime in schools. It reviews research that has been done in the UK, the USA and also in continental Europe on the subject of crime in schools. The final part of the chapter explores a theoretically grounded analytical framework, which forms the basis for the empirical investigation in the chapters that follow.

Chapter 4 provides a detailed presentation of prevalence and frequency rates of offending behaviour in schools in Cardiff among the Year 10 population. The chapter discusses pupil offending in the pupil population as a whole, as well as examining sex differences[1] and between-school differences in rates of offending. The nature of pupils offending behaviour is examined in relation to where it takes place, versatility or specialisation in offending, what the offences consist of and whether offenders are caught or reported to the school authorities and/or the police. The relationship between offending and victimisation is explored. This represents one of the most detailed examinations of pupil offending behaviour undertaken in the UK.

Chapter 5 examines the role of pupils' area of residence structural risk in relation to offending prevalence and frequency in the school context. A measure of pupils' area of residence structural risk is created using official deprivation data and then discussed and analysed in relation to young people offending in the school context.

Chapter 6 investigates the relationship between family social position (including measures of family socioeconomic status, family structure (parental composition), family size (siblings) and family ethnicity) and pupils' offending prevalence and frequency in schools. This chapter examines each of these explanatory factors independently in relation to pupil offending in schools. A risk score is created combining these explanatory factors and its efficacy in predicting individual offending behaviour is tested. Regression-based analyses examining which of these factors have the most predictive power regarding pupil offending in schools are presented. The aggregate level is explored in relation to between-school differences in pupils' family social position and pupil offending rates.

Chapter 7 examines the relationship between pupils' school context and offending behaviour in school. A series of innovative key constructs is introduced and related to pupils' perception of school ethos, pupils' social capital, respect for school authority, school disorder and parental school interest. Two school context risk scales are created based on these constructs – one measuring school climate and one measuring pupil relations in schools. These are analysed in a series of regression-based models to examine how predictive the school context measures are of pupil offending, when controlling for pupils' area of residence structural risk and family social position.

Chapter 8 concerns the pupils' individual social situational (bonds to society and parental monitoring) and dispositional characteristics (self-control, pro-social values and (sense of) shaming) in relation to pupils' offending prevalence and frequency in schools. An overall individual risk-protective scale is created based on the constructs mentioned. Analysis is carried out regarding which of these factors is the strongest predictor of pupil offending in schools. Relationships between pupils' family social position and pupils' individual social situation and dispositional characteristics are explored. Regression-based analysis examines how powerful individual characteristics are, regarding predicting pupil offending behaviour in schools when controlling for pupils' family social position, area of residence structural risk and school context.

Chapter 9 explores the relationship between pupils' lifestyle and offending behaviour in schools. An exploration of how lifestyles, area of residence structural risk, individual characteristics and family social position affect offending behaviour in schools, particularly examining their relative predictive powers and in terms of any interaction effects, is presented. As part of this exploration there is an analysis concerning the interaction between lifestyles and individual characteristics, on which a typology of pupil offending in schools is identified which is very similar to that identified and proposed by Wikström (2002). Pupils' family social position, area of residence structural risk and individual risk-protective characteristics (based on Chapter 6) are explored in relation to their lifestyles.

Chapter 10 explores between-school differences in pupils' offending prevalence and frequency. This was achieved by categorising schools by pupils' mean composition regarding pupils' individual characteristics, lifestyles, family social positions, area of residence structural risk, school climate and pupil relations, which it is argued combine to create a measure of school context. This showed significant between-school differences in prevalence and frequency for various types of pupil offending. An analysis is then reported which investigates the interaction between school context and pupils' individual risk-protective characteristics. This analysis suggests the importance of school context in relation to different groups of individuals and their offending behaviours.

Chapter 11 concludes the book by providing a summary of the key findings in terms of their empirical, analytical and theoretical importance. The chapter suggests ideas which have great importance for policy-makers, educationalists, criminologists and all who are interested in factors that affect young people in today's society.

Through gaining an understanding and providing explanation as to why young people offend in school and what factors cause schools to differ in offending rates, it is hoped that policy solutions can be developed which will have a real impact in enhancing pupils' life chances.

Note

1 Throughout the book sex differences are examined as they pertain to offending in schools.

Chapter 2

The Cardiff School Study: research design and methods

This chapter discusses the research design, methodology and approaches taken in the Cardiff School Study. The first section introduces the city of Cardiff, discusses why Cardiff was chosen as a research site, and describes the school system in Cardiff. The second section discusses how access to the schools was gained, the period in which the research took place, the piloting of the questionnaire and how the main study was achieved, including a discussion regarding sample size and the response rate. The third section discusses the rationale for the self-report design in reference to the major research questions and introduces the constructs and variables included in the principal research instrument. This section includes a discussion relating to the reliability and validity of measures used in the research. It also discusses in what ways the data will be analysed and presented in later chapters. The fourth section investigates a comparison of prevalence of adolescents' general offending rates between the Peterborough Youth Study (Wikström 2002) and the present study, which shows similarities that support the reliability of the research methodology used in the present study.

The city of Cardiff

The site chosen for this research is Cardiff, the capital city of Wales. Cardiff has a population of 305,340 people according to the 2001 census. Approximately 7 per cent of the population was born outside the UK, and approximately 92 per cent of the population class themselves as white, with the largest ethnic minority group being Asian (approximately 4 per cent) (see www.cardiff.gov.uk 28 July 2003). Cardiff is situated on the southeast coast of Wales and has largely been reshaped following the Second World War. Cardiff's initial growth was due to the economic development of the South Wales valleys in the nineteenth century, which centred on the coal, iron and, more recently, the steel industries. The city acted as a port for these heavy industries. Cardiff grew in importance as a centre for administration with the growth in population that industrialisation sparked, but only in 1955 did it become the Welsh capital.

Cardiff is an ideal site to study what factors cause and predict pupil offending in schools, both focusing on individual differences and between-school differences. The city varies widely in terms of advantage and disadvantage. For instance, of the 28 urban electoral wards in Cardiff, 4 are in the 100 top most deprived areas in Wales (865 wards in total) – these are Butetown, Ely, Splott and Caerau. At the other end of the spectrum, Cardiff is home to the least deprived ward in Wales (Cyncoed). Such variations in neighbourhood disadvantage make Cardiff a particularly interesting site because the schools serve pupils from varying social contexts and socioeconomic backgrounds, which will provide differing challenges for the schools involved in the study.

Cardiff has a fairly 'comprehensive' (at the time of writing and research) school system with 20 state-funded schools serving the population. There are no major public (fee-paying) boy's schools, although there is a public school for girls. Cardiff no longer has any grammar schools (selective schools usually based on selecting approximately the top 5 per cent of pupils in terms of academic ability from an area). Among the 20 comprehensive schools in Cardiff there is, however, some variation in levels of pupil selection and, since parental choice legislation, there is movement of pupils between schools, meaning that young people do not necessarily attend the schools nearest to them. There are two Welsh-speaking schools, three Roman Catholic schools and two Church in Wales schools. Thus, out of the 20 schools there are seven schools that may, to a degree, be able to select their intake. For example, the Welsh schools require Welsh speakers to attend them, while the faith schools may vet parents and pupils on the grounds of religion.

In Cardiff, there are also three special schools and six independent schools. The three special schools cater for pupils with learning difficulties. This population was not included in the study because the pupils would have had great difficulty in filling out the survey, and confidentiality for them may have been breached. The number involved in total in this population, when the survey was conducted, is approximately 30 pupils in Year 10. The independent schools were not approached. The number in this population is approximately 175 pupils in Year 10.

Conducting the research

Piloting the questionnaire

After successfully negotiating and gaining access to conduct the questionnaire survey in the 20 schools in Cardiff, the focus moved to piloting and refining the principal research instrument – the questionnaire. Before entering the field, the questionnaire was tested in focus group meetings involving senior academics and doctoral researchers. The questionnaire and its content were also discussed with headteachers and teachers so that account could be taken of practitioners' views.

The questionnaire was piloted in September 2001, with a group of seven lower-ability Year 10 pupils from a secondary school in Cardiff. Once the pupils had filled out their questionnaires, they were asked their opinion regarding the questionnaire to ensure that they understood the questions as intended. The pilot study indicated that 50 minutes was sufficient time for the questionnaires to be completed and that the pupils understood the questions as intended.

The main study

The main study was conducted between the end of September 2001 and April 2002. The fact that 20 schools were involved, comprising 3,103 pupils, meant that this time period was essential due to the limitations of resources. For those surveyed after Christmas 2001, the time period was adjusted in the questionnaire to 'the Christmas before last' so that pupils would still answer in terms of a time period of approximately one year (more will be said regarding this later in this chapter).

The pupils who were taking part in the questionnaire were assured of anonymity and confidentiality before they completed the questionnaire. They were also given a brown envelope with the questionnaire, so that they could place the completed questionnaire in the envelope and seal it once the questionnaire was complete. This was done to reassure pupils of the anonymity of the questionnaire.

Such a strategy was decided on because it was not possible in some instances for the researcher to be present in the classroom, in which case a well briefed teacher administered the questionnaires. The teachers who did this were well aware of the nature of the questionnaire and had a set talk to present to the pupils regarding the anonymity and confidentiality of the questionnaire. The teachers were also told not to influence pupils and to try to keep a distance from those filling out the questionnaire. However, if pupils could not understand a question, teachers were encouraged to provide assistance. The need for silence while completing the questionnaire was strongly asserted to both pupils and teachers. The survey, thus, provided teachers with an hour of silence while the pupils were completing the survey!

Response rates and the population

In order to gain a thorough knowledge regarding the offending behaviours of pupils in Cardiff, it was essential to include as many schools and as many Year 10 pupils in Cardiff as possible in the survey. This was so that pupils from different backgrounds and schools could be examined in relation to their offending behaviours. Such a methodology allows analyses that can take account of individual and contextual differences (for example, family, school and neighbourhood) in relation to offending behaviour. Farrington and Wikström (1994) inform the rationale for selecting the Year 10 population (pupils aged 14–15) as they showed that the rate of offending (among males) has an initial peak between the ages of 13 and 15 and that the ages of 13–15 also seem to be a period where there is an initial peak in the prevalence of offenders (approximately 7–8 per hundred males in both London and Stockholm). However, the present author notes that at the age of 17 in the London sample there is a peak of just over 10 offenders per 100; this is not true for Stockholm. This research also indicated (in the Stockholm sample) that the offending frequency of individuals' peaks between the ages of 14 and 15.

All 20 schools agreed to participate in the study and, out of a possible Year 10 population of 3,900 pupils, 3,103 pupils participated in the study. The tables indicate the response rates for the total population (Table 2.1) and by school (Table 2.2).

Table 2.2 indicates the response rates gained in each school and overall. The overall response rate is 80 per cent. However, some schools have better response rates than others. To a degree, this

Table 2.1 Questionnaire response rate in the Cardiff School Study

	No.	Percent	Comment
Questionnaire			
Sample	3,900	100	All Year 10 pupils in Cardiff
Included in study	3,103	80	
Non-responses	797	20	
Thereof absentees	797	20	

Table 2.2 Response rates by school

School**	Year 10 population*	No. surveyed	Response rate (%)
Henson	159	122	76.7
Luscombe	168	124	73.8
Parker	137	120	87.6
Shanklin	214	189	88.3
Williams	234	187	79.9
Robinson	172	136	79.1
Peel	400	323	80.7
Jones	278	247	88.9
Bennett	172	115	66.9
Cockbain	115	101	87.8
Llewellyn	199	190	95.5
Davies	198	104	52.5
Charvis	221	197	89.1
Owen	197	169	85.8
Phillips	208	154	74.0
Jenkins	247	155	62.8
Sweeney	175	161	92.0
Ruddock	187	154	82.4
Morris	107	85	79.4
Thomas	112	70	62.5
Total	3,900	3,103	80.0

Notes:
 * *Source*: Cardiff County Council Schools Service (2002).
** The schools' original names have been replaced with the names of players
   and the coach of the Wales Rugby Union squad, which beat Argentina
   35–20 in Buenos Aires in 2004.

reflects reality as schools will vary in their absentee and truancy rates. In individual schools the response rate varies from a high of 95.5 per cent to a low of 52.5 per cent. This latter result is a low response rate and is disappointing. When the school was initially surveyed there was a nasty viral outbreak that hit the whole of the UK and affected numbers participating in the study from this school dramatically. Attempts were made to survey more but these were unsuccessful. Some of the lower response rates (i.e. those in the 60–70 per cent region) are in some of Cardiff's schools situated in more disadvantaged areas. However, 16 of the 20 schools have response rates over 70 per cent, with 11 schools having response rates of 80 per cent or more.

All the schools in Cardiff are co-educational. The sample contains 1,606 (52 per cent) males and 1,497 (48 per cent) females. In comparison with previous similar research in the UK, this sample size is large and also has a high response rate. This is indicated by Table 2.3, which shows previous self-report research of a cross-sectional nature that has been undertaken in the UK.

Non-respondents and missing data

Of the total Year 10 population enrolled in Cardiff's schools at the time of the survey, 20 per cent did not complete the questionnaire. This was due to absenteeism on the day that the questionnaire was conducted in their school. It is likely that the non-responses may include a higher number of pupils with different kinds of social problems and that, as a result, there may be some underestimation of some rates in this study. However, it can be argued that on any given day, approximately 10 per cent of the school population will be absent. In one of the last readily available statistical reports on absenteeism in Cardiff (School Information Booklet, Welsh Office 1998), schools reported authorised absence rates ranging from 7.3 per cent to 19.9 per cent for the year 1997–8. As such, reporting of offending in schools may not be affected that greatly by the 20 per cent who were absent on the day the questionnaires were conducted because it is usual for schools to have a proportion of their pupils absent, as indicated above. The pupils also had no forewarning that the questionnaire was going to take place, making truancy or absence due to the questionnaire unlikely. It should also be noted from an examination of Table 2.3 that an 80 per cent response rate compares favourably with previous UK research in this vein, as does the number of pupils surveyed.

Table 2.3 Self-report studies in the UK

Researcher and date of survey*	Description of main sample	Type of survey	Response rate (%)
Willcock (1963)	808 males aged 15–21 from England, Wales and Scotland	Individual interview	71.0
Belson (1967)	1,425 males aged 13–16 from London	Individual interview	86.0
Mawby (1975)	327 males and 264 females aged 12–15 from one Sheffield school	Group self-completion	80.0
Riley and Shaw (1983)	378 males and 373 females aged 14–15 from England and Wales	Individual interview	71.0
Anderson (1989)	465 males and 427 females aged 11–15 from four Edinburgh schools	Group self-completion	Not stated
McQuoid (1990)	149 males and 161 females aged 14–21 from Belfast	Individual interview	95.0
McQuoid (1992–3)	456 males and 427 females aged 14–21 from Belfast	Individual interview	92.0
Graham and Bowling (1992–3)	738 males and 910 females aged 14–25 from England and Wales	Individual interview	64.0
Flood-Page et al. (1998–9)	4,848 persons aged 12–30 from England and Wales	Computer interview	69.0
Wikström (2001)	2,118 Year 10 pupils (boys and girls), aged 14–15, from the 13 state-funded schools in Peterborough	Class-room self-completion	92.4

Note:
* Date of survey refers to when this was carried out and not necessarily when reports, articles or books based on the survey were published.
Source: Adapted from Farrington (2001).

Missing data are a problem experienced by most self-report, self-completion surveys. In this study the effort that was made in designing and piloting the questionnaire aimed at minimising this problem. However, there are missing data in the final data set. These data are retained as missing data. No estimation of values for missing data has been done.

The exception to this rule regards frequency of offending behaviour and victimisation (see Chapter 4). There was a minority of cases where an adolescent has reported offending (in terms of prevalence) but not answered the follow-up question regarding how many times they had committed the offence. In these cases the adolescents were assumed to have offended once and this was included in the frequency rates. This was done so that the prevalence and frequency rates correspond with each other.

The research design

Rationale for a self-report survey

There were several reasons why a cross-sectional, self-report research strategy was deemed the best and most efficient way of addressing the study's main research questions. First, the self-report survey methodology has great utility in measuring offending validly and reliably (as discussed later) and for achieving an aetiological investigation that can help our understanding of the offending phenomenon (more will be said regarding this below). Secondly, the self-completion method was chosen because it provides anonymity to respondents, providing a high likelihood of honest responses. It was felt that 14–15-year-olds would be more truthful if they could fill out the questionnaire on their own as opposed to the researcher asking pupils questions face to face. Confidentiality would lessen the respondents' possible embarrassment when discussing delinquent acts and would more likely result in more dependable and truthful answers. Thirdly, the self-report methodology allows a large and detailed survey to be gained in a time-efficient way. The survey was administered in schools, and large numbers of pupils could complete the questionnaires in silence at the same time. Fourthly, the fact that pupils could complete the questionnaire in school meant a higher response rate was achieved in comparison with other possible methods such as postal surveys or telephone interviews, for example, which may have lead to a lower response rate. It also ensured that no third parties could influence the subjects' responses (for example, no parents were present during the survey, which could skew respondents' answers). For these reasons the self-report survey was seen as the best possible way (both methodologically and practically) to conduct the research.

Self-report methodology and criminological research

According to Hagan (1993), the self-report method is now the most commonly used method in criminology. Junger-Tas and Marshall (1999: 293) sum up the importance of the self-report research design to criminological research: 'Self-report studies have two main goals: to establish prevalence and incidence rates of crime and delinquency of specific populations that have higher validity than do official delinquency measures, and to search for correlates of offending and test etiological theories of crime.'

Thornberry and Krohn (2000: 71) state that self-report methodology 'is now a fundamental method of scientifically measuring criminality and forms the bedrock of etiological studies'. Junger-Tas and Marshall (1999: 292) argue the background to this rise in its popularity can be attributed to numerous factors, including dissatisfaction with official crime statistics: 'researchers long ago came to realize that their findings would be limited to what official statistics allowed them to see ... as long as their studies were based on official statistics.' Junger-Tas and Marshall (1999) see official statistics as management tools that are devised by government agencies to assist them with solving policy questions. They argue that police statistics, for example, have numerous problems including, first, that police activity tends to be reactive and dependent on people's willingness to report offences. They suggest that police detection of offences is rare (for example, many shoplifters may never be caught). Secondly, there is wide variation in reporting of offences to the police. This may be dependent on such variables as the nature and the seriousness of the offence, insurance requirements or the victim's perception of police effectiveness. Crimes in which the victim is also the offender may not be reported at all. Thirdly, recording of crimes by the authorities is often far from perfect and can be dependent on such issues, for instance, as offence seriousness, the probability of clearance by arrest and police priorities.

As well as these general problems with official statistics there are other reasons why self-report methodology may be a stronger research tool. In this book the subject is that of juvenile crime and delinquency. The age of the subjects is 14 or 15 and, as such, they may be under-represented in official statistics. Much delinquency will not be reported and it can be argued that crime and delinquency at school may not be treated in the same manner as that outside school. For example, the school may have its own disciplinary processes and punishments and not report crime to the police or the authorities. Indeed, some headteachers may be reluctant to report pupil crime to the police for fear of losing the trust of pupils and the community. The self-report survey may give a more accurate picture of the delinquency of juveniles than will official statistics. Shapland (1978: 255) argues that 'using the self-reported delinquency method with younger children enables a very much fuller picture of the delinquency of that age-group to be obtained than if the source of the data were official statistics'. Junger-Tas and Marshall (1999: 291) argue that self-report tries 'to measure behaviour that is punishable by law, usually hidden, socially unacceptable and, morally condemned'. Therefore, self-report methodology is ideally suited to measuring the criminal and delinquent activity of a juvenile population.

Reliability and validity of self-reports

The Cardiff School Study takes a scientific approach seeking to measure adolescents' offending behaviour and its possible causes. Reliability and validity of measurement are intrinsically linked to the success of answering the research questions. Thornberry and Krohn (2000: 44) state: 'For any measure to be scientifically worthwhile, it must possess both reliability and validity.' Reliability can be defined as the extent to which a measuring procedure achieves the same results across tests in relation to both space and time. Validity can be defined as the extent to which the measure measures the concept one sets out to measure and nothing else. Validity concerns the relationship between the theoretical concept one sets out to measure and the concept one actually measures (Thornberry and Krohn 2000).

Reliability

There are two main ways of ensuring the reliability of a measure in self-report surveys. These are 'test-retest' reliability and internal consistency measures. Internal consistency means that multiple items, which make up a scale used to measure a theoretical concept, should be highly intercorrelated. In this study, this is addressed by reporting Chronbach's alpha, which indicates the level of internal consistency of the scale.

Huizinga and Elliot (1986) argue that test-retest validity is the best way of gaining confidence in the reliability of a measure used in self-report surveys. In this method a sample of respondents is administered a self-report scale and then after a short interval the same scale is re-administered. This test should use the same questions and refer to the same reference period on both occasions. A number of studies have used this method regarding testing the reliability of self-report scales and have shown that self-report methodologies are reliable (see Hindelang *et al.* 1981; Huizinga and Elliot 1986). In the present study there were not the resources to perform a test-retest reliability check on the scales used. However, it is interesting to note the similarity in Chronbach's alphas between the scales used in this study and those that have been used in previous research. For example, the measure of family bonds used in this study has an alpha of 0.63. The same scale was used in the Peterborough Youth Study and Wikström (2002) reports its alpha as 0.64. This goes some way to indicating the reliability of the tool used across samples. Thornberry and Krohn (2000: 49) argue that previous research indicates that the self-report methodology possesses acceptable reliability for most analytic purposes. They state: 'Test–retest correlations are often 0.80 or higher, and self-reported delinquency responses are no less reliable than other social science measures.'

Validity

Most criticism of self-report studies has centred on how valid their measures are regarding criminality. Farrington (2001: 13) states: 'the key issue is validity: how far do self-reports produce an accurate measure of the true number of offences committed? How accurately do self-reports measure the prevalence, frequency and seriousness of offending?' Junger-Tas and Marshall (1999) argue that validity of self-reports can be measured in terms of the following four concepts of validity. The first is *theoretical or construct validity*. This can be gained through assessing how the variable in question ought to relate to other variables theoretically. *Concurrent validity* examines whether results from self-reports are consistent with results from other sources of knowledge about delinquent behaviour. *Predictive validity* assesses the relationship between report scores and one or more criterion variables, such as arrests, future criminal involvement or convictions. *External validity* refers to the generalisability of the sample's self-report results to the research population.

Regarding concurrent validity, previous research has illustrated that the self-report method is valid. West and Farrington (1977: 20–6) found that, at the age of 18, 94 per cent of convicted boys admitted that they had been convicted, while only 2 per cent of unconvicted boys claimed to have been. More importantly with regards to the present research, Gibson *et al.* (1970) found that 91 per cent of offences leading to convictions were admitted on a self-report survey for juveniles aged 14 – the same age group as that used in the present research. More recently, Farrington *et al.* (2003) in a comparison of court records and self-reports in a prospective longitudinal study following boys and girls through adolescence in Seattle came to the conclusion that self-reports and court referrals identified the same people as the worst offenders to a considerable extent.

Farrington (2001) argues that predictive validity is more impressive than concurrent validity, because a person who has been convicted may more readily admit to delinquent acts. This may be because a person may assume that the researcher will know about convictions and thus concealment may be futile. This may or may not be the case in the present research. However, as a methodology, it is interesting if similar surveys have predictive validity as this may add to confidence when considering the present research. Farrington (2001) cites two studies of predictive validity that have been carried out in the UK among unconvicted people. Both are part of the Cambridge Study. He states: 'among unconvicted boys, a measure of self-reported variety of offending at age 14 significantly predicted convictions in the next 3 years' (2001: 14). This was later replicated for specific types of offences. Farrington (1998, cf. 2001) found that, among boys not convicted for burglary up to the age 18, 20 per cent of those self-reporting burglaries had convictions for burglary up to the age of 32. This is compared with only 2 per cent of men who denied burglary up to the age of 18 but who up to the age of 32 had convictions.

The present study does not address levels of predictive validity, but the fact that other studies such as those mentioned have shown predictive validity indicates that a self-report methodology such as the one in this research is likely to be valid. External and construct validity all can be addressed in the present research. Predictive validity may be readily assessed in a longitudinal study such as the Cambridge Study. Cross-sectional research, like the present study, makes measuring predictive validity very difficult, as there may be no follow-up research. In sum, the conclusion of Hindelang *et al.* (1981: 114) appears reasonable when considering the validity of self-report measures: 'Reliability measures are impressive and the majority of studies produce validity coefficients in the moderate to strong range.'

Questionnaire design

The Cardiff School Study is based predominantly on the successful design and execution of the questionnaire survey. Other data sources were used, including the 1991 census and data from the 2000 index of multiple deprivation (National Assembly for Wales 2000; Cardiff Research Centre 2002). The questionnaire employs questions that are original to this study, that are based on questions from other surveys carried out previously, and questions that have been taken directly from other research. Major self-report study questionnaires that were consulted included the Peterborough Youth Study (Wikström 2002); the Victimisation in Schools Study (Gottfredson and Gottfredson 1985); the questionnaire used by Lindström (1993) in his study of school context and adolescent delinquency; and the Pittsburgh Youth Study (see Loeber *et al.* 2002). From these questionnaires, ideas were gained as to what questions were to be included in the questionnaire used in this study.

Central aspects of creating a successful questionnaire are, first, that the questions measure what you intend them to measure and that they are reliable and valid (see above discussion); and that, secondly, the people who are going to answer the questions understand them and can answer them in a timely manner. For the purpose of this study it was decided that the questionnaire should be made up mostly of closed questions, which would give pupils clear choices that could be answered just by ticking a box. This is, arguably, a superior method than open questions when dealing with young respondents, who may not be so keen to answer open questions that require essay-style answers. The language used in the questionnaire was purposely as simple as possible. As well as this, cues were employed to help the children think about their replies. There is an issue of memory regarding self-report methodology. By giving the pupils a cue such as 'since last Christmas' rather than 'in the last year', it may help the juveniles to think more clearly as it gives a referencing point. A factor in designing the questionnaire was to understand that pupils work at different speeds, and that they may also get tired of completing the questionnaire. Also pupils would probably get no longer than an hour to complete the questionnaire. Thus, the length and content of the questionnaire were carefully considered, in order to make the questionnaire as interesting as possible for pupils to complete and also to ensure that the slowest pupils would still be able to complete the whole questionnaire in under an hour.

Variables in the survey

Dependent (outcome) variables

The dependent (or outcome) variables examined are primarily concerned with adolescents' offending behaviour. In the following chapters there is a distinction made between general offending and offending in schools. In the questionnaire a series of questions were asked regarding whether or not the subject had: 1) taken something from a shop without paying; 2) beaten up someone; 3) stolen a car or something from a car; 4) broken into a house to steal something; 5) broken into a non-residential building to steal something; and 6) vandalised something. These acts all relate to what is referred to as general offending. However, some of these acts may have been committed in schools (for example, beating someone up, vandalising something and breaking into a non-residential building may also include breaking into a school). The distinction was not made clear in this question. Thus, general offending refers to having committed the said act at any time in any space (in the year time period).

The offending in schools category includes acts which specifically occurred in school or on the school premises. Five categories are included: 1) having stolen something from school or from somebody in school (theft); 2) beating up or hitting someone in school (assault); 3) purposely damaging or destroying property not belonging to you in school (vandalism); 4) using a weapon or force to take money or things from other people at school (robbery); and 5) breaking into school in order to steal something.

General offending thus refers to adolescent offending that can take place anywhere (including as stated above in schools), whereas offending in schools refers to acts that specifically take place in schools. It is recognised that, particularly for the categories of assault and vandalism, there may be some overlap between those who report having done this generally, because they may be referring to an act committed in school. However, the focus is primarily on offending in schools and the questions employed for offending in schools specifically measure pupil offending prevalence and frequency on the school premises.

Explanatory variables

Explanatory variables used relate to improving our understanding of the aetiology of offending behaviour in schools and concentrate mainly on contextual and individual factors. Community-level variables are based on the index of multiple deprivation (Cardiff Research Centre 2002). Family social position for each individual in the survey is measured by items including parental composition, ethnic background, immigrant status, socioeconomic status and family size that are included in the self-report questionnaire. School contextual variables are measured in the questionnaire. Constructs used include the pupils' respect for authority, school ethos (for example, whether the pupils think they are supported in school), pupils' social capital in school (based on friendship and support) and pupils' view of school disorder. Another factor at the school level is that of parental interest in schooling.

At the individual level, factors can be divided between dispositional, situational and lifestyle based. Dispositional characteristics measured include self-control, pro-social values and pupils' sense of shame. Social situational factors include measures of school bonds, family bonds and parental monitoring. Lifestyle factors include delinquent peer measures both in and out of school and substance use.

These explanatory factors are assessed in relation to pupil offending behaviour in schools. The research is particularly concerned to see how different factors interact in the prediction of offending behaviour in schools with a view at investigating cross-level interaction. This is a particularly pertinent issue in criminology, as Wikström and Loeber (2000: 1118) state: 'Our theoretical and empirical understanding of offending behaviour as related to the individual–community interaction is rather rudimentary.' One of the aims of the present research is to gain a greater understanding regarding individual–social contextual interactions in explaining pupil offending behaviour in schools.

Risk-Protective factors

A series of risk scores are created (for example, area of residence structural risk, school climate risk, pupil relations risk, family social position risk, individual risk-protective and lifestyle risk). These are measures that are composed of constructs pertaining to a particular theoretical construct. Wikström and Loeber (2000) recognise there is a debate among scholars on how risk and protective factors are conceptualised. In this study their conceptualisation is utilised. The terms 'risk' and 'protective' will refer to different ends of the distribution of a single variable, construct or composite construct. The assumption is made that the strength of the association between an independent (explanatory) factor and the dependent (outcome) factor can be concentrated anywhere on the continuum of the independent (explanatory) factor. The utility of such an approach allows another assumption to be made, which is that single factors with different risk and protective characteristics operate jointly in complex ways and that classifying, for example, individuals by their set of risk and protective characteristics will allow certain essentials to be captured regarding individual differences. The analytical approach utilised focuses on a person-oriented approach, whereby constructs are analysed that take account of factors pertaining to the individual as opposed to a variable-focused approach.

Statistical techniques
Statistical analyses performed in the following chapters include tests of statistical significance regarding group differences. Unless otherwise stated, the findings referred to as statistically significant are so at the 5 per cent level or better. The tests used when referring to group differences in prevalence rates are chi-square, and when analysing differences in mean frequencies *F*-tests (ANOVA) are used. In cases where significant group differences are found for prevalence rates the gamma measure of association is reported. Where significant group differences are found for mean frequencies the eta^2 measure is reported, which indicates the variance explained by the independent variable in relation to the change in the dependent variable.

Other statistical analyses performed include factor analysis, logistic regression (prevalence) and ordinary least squares (OLS) regression (frequency). These regression-based analyses are performed to see which variables are most important in predicting offending behaviour, both independently and in interaction with others.

A comparison of adolescents' general prevalence of offending between the Cardiff School Study and the Peterborough Youth Study

Previously in this chapter the issues of validity and reliability were discussed in relation to self-report methodology. This section illustrates the reliability of the research tool used in the present research by comparing self-reported offending prevalence rates among adolescents in general between the present study and the Peterborough Youth Study (Wikström 2002), which was conducted during 2000–1, a year before the present research which was conducted during 2001–2. It is argued that the similarity between prevalence of general offending rates between the two studies suggests the reliability of the research tool used in both studies – i.e. that they are measuring offending in general among the two adolescent populations. This comparison is achievable because of the similarity in questions relating to general offending prevalence employed in the two studies.

Table 2.4 shows a comparison of general offending prevalence rates between the Year 10 pupils in Cardiff and the Year 10 pupils in Peterborough. The table reports information regarding the total population (boys and girls) in the studies and a breakdown by sex.

Table 2.4 shows that:

- One third of the pupils have offended generally, at least once, both in Peterborough and in Cardiff.

- One in 15 has committed a serious crime of theft in Peterborough and in Cardiff.

- Approximately one in five have assaulted somebody in Cardiff in general, compared with one in four in the Peterborough Youth Study.

- Approximately one in four have vandalised something in Cardiff, compared with one in five in the Peterborough Youth Study.

- In general, self-reported offending seems to be very similar between the two populations, especially when looking at the 'All crimes' category and the categories of serious theft, non-residential burglary, residential burglary and theft of or from cars.

The fact that such similar patterns of general offending prevalence rates are found between the Peterborough Youth Study and the Cardiff School Study respondents may give an indication of the reliability of the self-report methodology employed. In terms of other UK studies, the Edinburgh Youth in Transition Study (Smith *et al*. 2001; Smith and McVie 2003) found that 13-year-olds reported the following rates in these categories: 26.6 per cent shoplifting, 15.9 per cent vandalism and 46.1 per cent assault. The pupils in the Edinburgh survey were a year younger, but it can be seen that the rates are similar for vandalism between all three studies. However, assault prevalence in Edinburgh is substantially higher. It is possible that wording differences between the Edinburgh study and the Peterborough and Cardiff studies could account for this variation.

Table 2.4 General self-reported offending prevalence: a comparison between the Cardiff School Study and the Peterborough Youth Study

General offending	Prevalence (%) in Cardiff School Study	Prevalence (%) in Peterborough Youth Study
Population		
Shop lifting	16.4	13.9
Non-residential burglary	4.0	3.1
Residential burglary	2.4	1.3
Thefts of or from cars	4.1	3.2
Vandalism	22.6	17.0
Assault	18.2	24.0
Serious theft*	6.4	6.8
All crimes**	*36.6*	*37.7*
Males		
Shop lifting	20.0	11.8
Non-residential burglary	6.6	4.8
Residential burglary	3.9	2.2
Thefts of or from cars	7.0	4.5
Vandalism	29.3	22.7
Assault	26.3	32.2
Serious theft*	10.4	9.8
All crimes**	*45.6*	*44.8*
Females		
Shop lifting	12.8	16.1
Non-residential burglary	1.4	1.5
Residential burglary	0.8	0.5
Thefts of or from cars	1.2	2.0
Vandalism	15.7	11.3
Assault	9.8	15.7
Serious theft*	2.2	3.8
All crimes**	*27.2*	*30.6*

Notes:
* 'Serious theft' is non-residential burglary, residential burglary and theft of or from cars all combined.
** 'All crimes' is a composite measure of all the general offending types.

Table 2.4 also shows the prevalence of general offending categorised by sex (i.e. males and females). It can be seen that more boys than girls commit offences. For instance, 45.6 per cent of boys have committed one or more offence in comparison with 27.2 per cent of girls in Cardiff (compared with 44.8 per cent of males and 30.6 per cent of females in Peterborough). Again the results are very similar in comparison with the Peterborough Youth Study, suggesting the reliability of the methodology employed.

In comparison with Flood-Page *et al.* (2000), there are some differences. Flood-Page *et al.* report that 33 per cent of boys, aged 14–15, reported offending, while 18 per cent of girls in that age group report offending. The reason for lower offending rates in their study may be due to 1) lower response rates than achieved in the Cardiff and Peterborough studies; 2) a differential methodology regarding surveying (Flood-Page *et al.* 2000 used interviews often in the presence of significant others); and 3) the fact that Flood-Page *et al.* employed a more complex sampling system (see Wikström 2002, for a full discussion of these differences).

However, Table 2.4 illustrates the similarity in offending prevalence rates between the Cardiff School Study and the Peterborough Youth Study, indicating the reliability of the methodology employed.

Summary

This chapter has indicated the suitability of Cardiff as a research site for investigating pupil offending in schools particularly with reference to contextual and individual differences. The comprehensive school system and the range of backgrounds of pupils make Cardiff ideally suited to a study of this kind. The self-report methodology employed has been shown to be both reliable and valid as shown by previous research and an indication of the reliability of the questionnaire survey is shown by the Cardiff–Peterborough comparison in rates of general offending. The study itself on pupil offending in the school context draws on one of the largest cross-sectional self-report surveys ever accomplished in the history of British criminological research, with a wide and detailed data set that allows the investigation of the effects of both individual and contextual-level explanatory factors and their interaction on pupil offending behaviour.

Chapter 3

Offending in schools: key issues

Schools are central to the efficient and successful functioning of society. In the UK, the government recognises the importance the education system plays in building a competitive economy and inclusive society. To this end the government states its number-one priority is raising standards in education (Department for Education and Skills 2002). One of the government's central aims is to 'enable all young people to develop and to equip themselves with the skills, knowledge and personal qualities needed for life and work' (Department for Education and Skills 2002: 4). Schools play a major role in producing well-socialised and educated adults. Education empowers people and enables them to make informed decisions which impact on their ability to have successful pathways through life and work. Hand (2004: 27) states:

> We educate children not just to promote a flourishing economy, or to broaden their repertoire of pleasures, or to make them more fully human, but to do all these things and more. We educate children because the goods of learning are too many and varied for their achievement to be left to chance.

Hargreaves (2001) argues that schools should focus on producing, principally, two outcomes in educating their pupils. These outcomes are both cognitive and moral. Drawing on an Aristotelian view, Hargreaves argues that the purposes of education are intrinsically linked to the functioning of the state. Aristotle viewed the purpose of the state, and therefore of its institutions (i.e. schools), as enabling its citizens to lead a good life. In the Aristotelian view the purpose of life is to achieve *Eudaimonia* (a Greek word meaning happiness or well-being) (see Lear 1995). Hargreaves argues that *Eudaimonia* is not a set of feelings or a state of mind but a quality of conduct, or disposition, to act in a certain way. He argues that schools are crucial in helping people achieve *Eudaimonia*. They can do this by promoting two main virtues or excellences (from the Greek, *Arete*). These excellences are both intellectual (such as science, art and practical wisdom) and moral (such as courage, self-control and justice). Hargreaves (2001: 488) states that: 'A person's excellences are not so much a matter of his or her capacities as how they have chosen to be and act.'

It is the role of education to initiate the nation's youth into these excellences, through which the young acquire the disposition to make sound moral and intellectual choices and judgements. Hargreaves (2001: 489) states: 'The principal outcomes of schooling, both intended and unintended, are thus assumed to refer to the quality of the intellectual and moral life of students.' In order for pupils to achieve well-being (the Aristotelian aim), it is essential that they be given every opportunity so that they can learn how to pursue these excellences.

Pupils' offending behaviour in schools will adversely affect the chances of some pupils achieving *Eudaimonia* – both for those who offend and for those who are affected by the offending behaviour of others in schools. Schools are critical in the development of pupils' moral lives and their behaviours. Research is therefore needed to understand what factors cause individuals to offend in schools so that initiatives can be pursued that will enhance the life chances of would-be offenders in schools and those who would be affected by the offending behaviour of other pupils.

Offending in schools can disrupt pupils' learning by increasing fear in school communities, by disrupting lessons and by concentrating key resources on dealing with crime as opposed to focusing on education. Pupils who offend in schools can spread fear among fellow pupils and staff, disrupt learning for others and cost schools in terms of both human and financial resources, meaning that not all pupils will have access to as fair a playing-field for progress and education as others. Those in high-crime schools may not have the same environment for learning, development and progress as those who attend low-crime schools. Pupils' offending behaviour in school can disrupt both their (those who offend) and others' development of moral and intellectual excellences and ultimately pupils' chances of achieving well-being in life.

At present in the UK, schools operate in a particularly challenging environment. MacBeath and Mortimore (2001) argue that, since 1979, the number of people living in poverty has increased threefold in the UK. There has been a widening inequality between rich and poor, privileged and underprivileged. In the UK, MacBeath and Mortimore (2001) state that the proportion of children living in poor households is 32 per cent, compared to the European Union average of 20 per cent. As well as a widening background of wealth inequality, there have been increasing concentrations of disadvantage in urban areas. The UK population is also becoming more diverse in terms of religion and ethnicity. Those from socially disadvantaged and excluded backgrounds have fewer opportunities and, as a result, restricted life chances. It is the job of schools in this challenging environment to educate the nation's youth and to aspire to strive to give every child equal opportunities regardless of the community they serve and the family backgrounds of the children who attend. In order to achieve this, it is essential for schools to provide safe and secure learning environments, where pupils and school staff feel comfortable, for the process of education to be successful and thus society in general to be successful.

This chapter will investigate how criminological and educational research and theory can help us understand and explain pupil offending in schools, focusing on communities and crime research, and individual and family research concerning offending behaviour. It will also explore previous research that takes an integrative approach. The review discusses the importance of causes and causal mechanisms in social science research. The first section will investigate what research has previously been done regarding crime in schools. It will examine the scarcity of previous research, particularly regarding pupil offending as the outcome variable and also in the UK. The review will illustrate the lack of a focus on pupils' individual characteristics (i.e. social situation and dispositions) and lifestyles in the explanation of crime in school, and also the rare attention given to explaining between-individual differences in offending behaviour in schools. These limitations will be addressed in the second section, which will seek to explicate a theoretically based analytical framework that will be empirically tested in the remaining chapters of the book.

Crime in schools: a review of previous research

The following review examines the state of the research field concerning offending and victimisation in schools. It illustrates the limitations and strengths of research in this sphere in terms of definitions, approaches taken, outcome measures and explanatory constructs used. At a time when education and crime are key political issues it is shown that the UK lacks research on crime in schools, whereas US researchers have paid more attention to the issue, but still more comprehensive research is needed. Previous research, which employs self-report methodologies, observational techniques and official data (whether from schools, courts or the police), is reviewed. A starting point for scientific inquiry concerns how the dependent (or outcome) variable is measured. How pupil offending in school is measured is, therefore, critical.

Outcome measures: how has crime in schools been measured?

Many studies of juvenile offending use school samples but few investigate crime in schools and the school as a context for pupil offending and victimisation specifically. Very little is known regarding pupils' offending and victimisation in the school context, especially in the UK context (see Rutter *et al.* 1998). McPartland and McDill (1977: 3) state: 'We have a vast literature on juvenile offenses, but we have little direct information about the independent role schools may play.' One reason for this is possibly the relative difficulty of gaining reliable information and measures regarding pupils' offending and victimisation experiences on the school premises. Three main tools have been used in gaining this information in the past. These are 1) self-reports of pupils or teachers (sometimes in combination); 2) using data from official sources such as the courts or the police; and (3) direct observational studies. Official data have significant problems gaining reliable records of pupils' offending and victimisation in schools (as discussed in Chapter 2). A lot of juvenile delinquency and crime that takes place in school will never be reported to the police, meaning that a self-report methodology may provide one with a clearer picture of reality. Espiritu *et al.* (2001: 47) argue: 'Previous research using self-report measures indicates that young people are willing to report accurate information about their delinquent acts – both minor and serious.'

What exactly constitutes a crime or delinquent act in school? In previous research this outcome variable varies quite widely. Some research has used proxy measures such as suspension rates for delinquency (see Hellman and Beaton 1986). Other researchers have focused on truancy rates and minor disorder measures of offending, and some researchers have incorporated more serious offences into their research (for victimisation, see, Gottfredson and Gottfredson 1985).

In this book, offending in schools is measured using a self-report methodology, which focuses on specific acts that in everyday life would be deemed acts that break the law. Thus, the categories include assault, theft, vandalism, robbery and breaking into the school. These acts are often not treated as criminal in the school context, but the argument is that they would be treated as criminal if they occurred outside the school environment. Within the school, these acts are still treated as rule or norm breaking and are sanctioned and treated by the school authority often without a need for the intervention of outside social agencies. The measure of pupil offending regards examining acts which the pupils know to be norm or law breaking within the school. In this book, explaining pupil offending is therefore ultimately about explaining why pupils break a rule of law, or rule in the school context.

It is vital to explain the act of crime (or the offence), rather than the propensity an individual has to commit acts of crime or offending. As Wikström (2004: 3) states: 'Propensity may be part of the explanation of why an individual may commit a crime (he or she may have a propensity to break moral rules) but it is not the same as an act of crime.' In the analytical framework that follows in this chapter, the aim is to provide explanations of pupil offending (acts) in schools. Part of this explanation concerns individual characteristics and experiences which influence propensities, and part regards the contexts in which pupils find themselves, including the school and neighbourhood context and their family background. It is the interaction between individual (*propensity*) and the contexts, in which the individual acts illegally, which is of critical interest to developing criminological theories further.

Crime in schools: approaches taken

Studies that fail to measure and separate school from community contextual effects provide only a combined estimate of the two effects. This imprecision applies to most studies of community and school contextual effects (Gottfredson 2001: 68).

Studies that are concerned with school crime outcome variables, particularly offending in schools, are the primary concern of this review. The author recognises that there is a wider body of research that has also looked at school effects on outcome measures such as pupils' achievement (see Coleman *et al.* 1966; Jencks *et al.* 1972; Hauser *et al.* 1976; Smith and Tomlinson 1989; MacBeath and Mortimore 2001), which is also referred to. The body of research concerning deviant outcome measures in school is complex in that studies take a wide variety of approaches and measure numerous outcomes. The discussion will focus on studies that looked specifically at the effects of schools on deviant outcome measures, as well as those that attempt multi-level analysis, in order to disentangle the effects of schools in relation to other constructs.

One of the key limitations of this body of research is that it rarely, if ever, controls for both pupils' dispositional and social situational characteristics (e.g. social bonds to family, school, etc.). It is a central argument that, to gain an understanding of school effects, this is essential. Research that focuses solely on individual or contextual explanations fails to provide us with satisfactory explanations.

UK school-level studies

Although the relationship between schools and juvenile crime has been a source of some debate, there has been very little empirical research on the precise nature of this relationship, and what research has been done is far from unequivocal (Graham 1988: 5).

As is all too evident, the question of school influences (for better or worse) on young persons' antisocial behaviour has received very little systematic attention in school effectiveness studies over the last 15 years. The evidence is sufficient to indicate that schools do exert an effect, but much has still to be learned about how the effect operates and the circumstances under which it is most likely to be critical (Rutter *et al.* 1998: 235).

Very few studies have been carried out investigating adolescent offending in schools in the UK as the above quotations from two leading UK researchers demonstrate. The independent influence of schools on juvenile crime has also been under-researched (Rutter *et al.* 1998). One of the earliest studies undertaken in the UK investigated the influence of schooling on official juvenile crime. Power *et al.* (1972) studied 20 secondary modern schools in Tower Hamlets, London. They focused on offending which was measured by juvenile court appearances. They found a wide variation in delinquency rates between schools (which they argued were not related to variations in district rates), and schools that had not been reorganised during the study period showed 'remarkably consistent rates' (1972: 130). They argued that once school size, school building age and delinquency rates of the schools catchment area were controlled for, the school's themselves seemed largely responsible for the variations. This study was crude in terms of analysis used but as Gottfredson (2001: 69) notes, 'although largely inadequate for assessing the unique contribution of schools beyond those of families and communities from which students are drawn', it was useful in showing the existence of a wide variation in school-level outcomes, which were not comprehensively accounted for by the characteristics of the communities in which the schools were located. However, the fact that this study focused on juvenile court appearances indicates that it did not focus on crime in schools. The study, rather, focused on the issue as to whether or not schools were home to individuals who had offended or not. Does school context contribute to causing individuals to offend? The conclusion of Power *et al.* (1972) would suggest that they could be a contributory factor in explaining why some individuals offend and others do not.

The issue as to whether it was the school characteristics (as suggested by Power *et al.*) or the intake of the schools that were responsible for variations in school crime rates was further debated in 1973, when West and Farrington, in the Cambridge Study, a longitudinal study of delinquent development, illustrated that much of the variation in delinquency rates between schools can be attributed to intake differences (see also Farrington 1972). They showed that high delinquency schools take a higher proportion of pupils with records for troublesomeness, as rated by teachers and classmates. Such a finding suggests that school contexts have little influence on delinquency. These early studies began the ongoing debate in the UK as to whether schools do influence delinquency. However, the amount they contribute to knowledge regarding offending and victimisation in schools, in the UK, is questionable, because neither study directly measured offending and victimisation among pupils in the school context. Both studies focused solely on boys, thus ignoring any possible sex differences.

UK multi-level studies

Rutter *et al.* (1979) conducted an impressive systematic study of the influence of school effects on children's attendance, attainment and behaviour. Their work indicated that there were substantial school effects associated with these outcome measures in the 12 inner-London schools that were studied. However, this study did not look at offending and victimisation of the children specifically. The study contained two measures of behaviour. The first of these measures was an aggregate measure based on a mixture of pupil reports (in the third year; the equivalent today is Year 9) gained from the schools and direct observations of pupils in lessons, assemblies and playground activities, by researchers who helped conduct the study. Most of the scale related to direct observation of bad behaviour, such as shouting out in class or needing a pencil to fill in the questionnaire. They also observed fights in playgrounds, pupil violence and graffiti. These measures were based on researchers' observations over an average period of three weeks. The pupil questionnaire measures of behaviour related to missing lessons, absconding, truanting and the wearing of school uniform. There are arguably some issues with this outcome measure of school behaviour. First, as Rutter *et al.* (1979) acknowledge, it is an aggregate measure, which does not allow for individual differences in behaviour to be assessed (a shortcoming which this book seeks to address by focusing on both individual differences and between-school differences). Secondly, in this scale there are some items which may only be partially due to pupil misbehaviour. For instance, damage of chairs is included in the scale as observed by the investigators (in terms of number of damaged chairs per room) or cracked windows. A similar measure of graffiti and anorak wearing in class was taken. These factors may be more to do with adequate funding and resourcing in schools (i.e. whether the school has funds to remove graffiti, repair chairs and heat the school (so anoraks do not have to be worn)). These factors are also likely to vary by the time of year the investigators conducted the study. Thirdly, the self-report questions were based on mild types of misbehaviour. Fourthly, it is questionable whether researchers are likely to pick up all misbehaviour that may occur through direct observation – their presence may also have meant pupils behaved differently from the norm. Thus, a fair indication of pupil offending may not have been derived from observations.

The second behavioural measure used in the study is that termed delinquency. This measure was based on data collected from the Metropolitan Police Juvenile Bureaux (when the pupils were in their 18th year) for all pupils who had been on roll at any of the 12 secondary schools at the age of 14. These data concerned whether the pupil had been officially cautioned or found guilty of any offence in a juvenile court on at least one occasion. This measure is based on official data recorded until the age of 18, and is a measure of problem behaviour outside the school premises, in the main (as relatively few crimes are likely to be reported to the police if they take place on the school premises). It is questionable as to whether this measure gives an outcome measure relevant for the independent variables used in the study (which focused on measures of school context), as the behaviour may not have occurred in school. Another factor related to this is that, according to the age crime curve, criminality is likely to peak initially at around the ages of 13–15 (see Farrington and Wikström 1994). It may be the case that a large proportion of the pupils labelled as delinquent in this study (i.e. according to court appearances at the age of 18) may in fact have left school when they committed their first and subsequent officially recognised offences.

Rutter *et al.*'s (1979) study did, however, indicate that school effects were important when composite individual intake variables were controlled for (i.e. secondary school intake measures from primary school transfer, parental occupation, ward-level information relating to deprivation). They found that children's observed behaviour in the school was particularly associated with what they termed 'school process' variables (these are discussed below). They concluded: 'of all the outcomes considered, this is the one for which the child's personal characteristics, his home background and the balance of intake to the school were least important' (1979: 175). Rutter *et al.* (1979) did recognise that other aspects of children's behaviour may be strongly influenced by personal, family and social variables, but suggest that the behaviours under scrutiny in their study had developed as a response to the school environment the pupils encountered. Interestingly, as they put it, their delinquency measure was the 'odd man out' in their four outcome measures. Delinquency was found to be influenced by the child's ability level, but unlike the other measures was equally influenced by parental occupation. The biggest difference was that school process had a very small effect, but the academic balance (the mix of school pupils) had a very large effect: 'The implication was that peer group influences of some kind were serving to shape children's behaviour. It is interesting in this context to note that it was *academic* balance which was crucial rather than any mix of socio-cultural backgrounds from which the children came' (1979: 176). This conclusion may be unsurprising because, first, their delinquency measure related to official offences up to the age of 18 and, secondly, these offences probably did not occur in school and, as such, may not be influenced particularly by school processes.

Rutter *et al.*'s (1979) study showed that schools did influence pupil behaviour. This finding was controversial at the time in the UK. Reynolds (1992: 2) argues that the findings of the Rutter *et al.* study challenged the intellectual hegemony of traditional British educational research. The paradigm at the time was psychologically determined relating to the primacy of individual, family and community-based influences on children's 'educatability'. Indeed, the Plowden Committee (Department of Education and Science 1967) argued that there was little differential effect of schools on pupils, and parental factors, including social class and attitudes, were the key determinants. Thus, *Fifteen Thousand Hours*, in many respects, was a groundbreaking study, which showed that schools did affect student outcomes, in terms of behaviour, attainment, attendance and, to a lesser extent, delinquency. The study suggested that there were several elements of schools that contributed to influencing the outcome measures they examined. These were as follows:

1 *Academic balance*: this related to the balance regarding intellectual ability of the school's intake. It was suggested that a large proportion of intellectually less able pupils would influence the formation of peer-group cultures and an anti-academic or anti-authority emphasis.

2 *Reward and punishment systems.*

3 *A positive school environment*: this consists of good working conditions, responsiveness to pupils' needs and well maintained buildings.

4 *Involvement of pupils* in the running of the school and encouraging pupils to take responsibility.

5 *Clear academic goals*, involving the good use of homework and an environment that instils confidence in pupils' abilities.

6 *Good teacher behaviour*: this sets a role model for pupils regarding time-keeping. Also teachers should be willing to deal with pupil problems.

7 *Good classroom management*: for example, keeping the attention of the whole class.

8 *Firm school leadership*: a decision-making process where teachers feel their views are represented.

Generally, these factors were found to be related to each of the four outcomes Rutter *et al.* examined. However, as stated, their relationship with delinquency was a lot weaker. This study inspired several school effects studies that took place in the UK during the 1980s. Mortimore *et al.* (1988) examined data regarding junior schools in inner London and found that individual information regarding sex, social class, attainment and race were poor predictors of pupils' progress over four years, without the addition of information regarding school organisation. Smith and Tomlinson (1989) and Nutall *et al.* (1989) have also reported that school effects influence pupil outcomes, even after multiple factors were measured relating to pupil intakes. Smith and Tomlinson (1989) studied approximately 3,100 students from the ages of 11 to 15 and found substantial differences between schools in examination scores at the end of secondary school, controlling for academic performance at intake. The importance of these studies is that they illustrate that schools matter in affecting student outcomes. One of the problems, in terms of comparisons with the present research, is that they do not focus specifically on problem behaviour, deviancy, offending and victimisation; rather, they focused on intellectual outcomes of pupils. However, *Fifteen Thousand Hours,* the most comprehensive study to date on the topic of school influences on adolescent behaviour in the UK, suggests that schools do have an effect on pupils' behaviour, despite some of the weaknesses highlighted in outcome measures relating to this.

US school-level studies

Crime in the schools does not occur in isolation from crime in the rest of society (Wilson 1977: 48).

Coleman *et al.* (1966) conducted one of the earliest studies investigating school contextual effects. This study involved some 645,000 students in 4,000 elementary and secondary schools. They found that individuals' outcome measures (which were not measuring delinquency but, rather, achievement test scores) were not really explained by between-school differences (these school characteristics included class size, level of teacher qualification and per-pupil expenditure). Rather, test scores were explained more by student background characteristics. Although not specifically looking at crime in schools, this study, similarly to its early British counterparts, raised the issue of whether school differences could affect differences in pupils' outcomes. Other early US studies and reviews conducted by Jencks *et al.* (1972) and

Hauser *et al.* (1976) all indicated that school effects were not primarily responsible for differing outcome measures of pupils between schools – a conclusion similar to Farrington (1972) and West and Farrington (1973) in the UK. Gottfredson (2001) believes that this early research led many leading scholars to conclude that manipulating school organisational characteristics or process variables would be fruitless in affecting delinquency rates in schools. However, following these early forays into the study of school effects, later scholars started to apply more sensitive measures both in terms of outcome (dependent) measures and independent variables employed.

Hellman and Beaton (1986), in research in public schools in Boston, used suspension rates as a proxy measure of school crime. This may not be an ideal proxy measure, because schools may suspend pupils for various reasons, which may vary over time and between and within schools. The study measured both school and community characteristics and found that, for middle schools, school crime was a function of the school environment, not of the community. However, for high schools they found that 'while suspensions tend to be higher in schools with low academic quality and high student instability, the community exerts a strong independent influence' (1986: 102). This study used fairly crude measures of school characteristics including building characteristics, teacher demographics and school size. The study used aggregate variables of community and school but, like many studies in research on crime in schools (including the majority of early UK studies, including Rutter *et al.* 1979), failed to control for individual social situational, dispositional and lifestyle characteristics of pupils, which may be important in determining offending in schools – i.e. schools that have a high proportion of pupils with high-risk lifestyles, with high-risk social situational characteristics and who display poorly adjusted dispositions may experience higher delinquency rates.

US multi-level studies

Over the last 20 years or so the Gottfredsons have dominated research concerning crime in schools in the USA. Much of their work focuses on student and teacher victimisation. Although this book focuses primarily on pupils' offending behaviour, issues and approaches used to study student victimisation are of interest, because they may highlight innovative methods that could be employed to investigate offending in schools. Gottfredson and Gottfredson (1985) reanalysed Safe School Study data and attempted to relate school disorder (measured by student and teacher victimisation) to various factors internal and external (i.e. community) to schools. They found that schools with the worst discipline problems shared similar organisational characteristics. Rules tended to be unclear, unfair or inconsistently enforced. Schools used ambiguous or indirect responses to student behaviour. For example, some schools lowered grades in relation to school misconduct. Rules were not fully understood by teachers and administrators and, thus, they could not coherently respond to situations. In some instances, students lost belief in the legitimacy of the rules. Their study also found several other predictors of school misconduct. These included poor teacher–administrator co-operation and inactive administrations. Structural predictors included school size. Large school size was found to increase the chances of misconduct. High student/staff ratio was also found to increase the likelihood of misconduct, as were low school budgets for learning materials.

Gottfredson and Gottfredson (1985) measured elements of the community (community poverty and disorganisation, for example), as well as the socio-demographic characteristics of the students in the school and the characteristics of the school environment, as mentioned above, from student, teacher and principal surveys. The results indicated that community context, the demographic characteristics of the students enrolled in the school and the way the school is organised all contribute in explanation of their measure of student disorder. They also found that the schools with the least effective policies tended to be located in the most disorganised communities. In terms of teacher and student victimisation, both community and school effects (once community was controlled for) were found to be influential. This study, however, failed to control for individual characteristics of pupils in terms of social situation, dispositions and lifestyles. It failed to account for and predict why individual outcomes may differ as individual-level data were aggregated to the school level – thus individual differences were ignored. However, the study was informative regarding the fact that schools could affect student outcomes on an aggregate level when community factors were controlled for. This study, and the work of Rutter *et al.* (1979), gave support for the view that schools and the way they are run and organised could be successful sites for crime prevention initiatives.

During the late 1980s and 1990s, Bryk and his associates published a wide array of studies investigating school effects in relation to educational and student outcomes (for example, Bryk and Driscoll 1988; Bryk and Thum 1989; Bryk *et al.* 1993; Bryk and Schneider 2002).

Although not specifically researching crime in schools, these studies did investigate the influence of schools on school drop-out rates and behavioural problems of students, which included absenteeism, class cutting (truancy), and classroom disorder. The research used hierarchical linear modelling as a main analytical tool, and the data used in the 1988 and 1993 study were based on administrator and teacher surveys, in 357 schools which took part in the High School and Beyond Survey (which was a nationally representative sample), and official data. The research illustrated the fact that important features of school composition (for example, school social class, minority concentration and average academic background) were correlated with important aspects of school organisation. The findings suggest that school organisation had a significant effect in reducing problem behaviour and improving academic outcomes. The research showed that the effects of composition and school size tended to diminish once the communal organisation variable was controlled for. This suggests that school processes (in this study including expectations for learning, expectations for student achievement and behaviour, and an 'ethos of caring', for example) are more important in influencing academic and behavioural outcomes than the structural composition of schools. However, the analysis did not control for social situational and dispositional characteristics, nor did it focus particularly on offending in schools. It did, though, provide further evidence for a 'school effect' that operated independently of school compositional and community characteristics.

Felson *et al.* (1994) examined a 'subculture of violence' thesis using data on 2,213 young males across 87 high schools. The data gathered were from the Youth in Transition data set, a multi-wave panel study of high-school boys. Personal interviews and questionnaires administered to students and principals were the main data sources for the research. They analysed the three following outcome variables: 1) interpersonal violence (e.g. whether the respondent had got into a serious fight at school, hit a teacher, etc.); 2) theft and vandalism index (based on responses regarding theft and vandalism on the school premises); and 3) the school delinquency index (based on items such as cheating and truancy). The key independent variable in the study regarded the respondent's individual adherence to a subculture of violence. These responses were aggregated in order to create a score for each school. They found that school norms (the aggregate of the pupil responses) regarding violence significantly predicted individual violence, theft, vandalism and school delinquency. Laub and Lauritsen (1998: 144) ague that this study was important in two main ways:

'First, by summarising the information provided by students within each school, they found peer group cultures concerning academic achievement and approval for the use of violence differed from school to school.' Felson *et al.* found that schools in which students valued academic success tended to be those where pupils were anti the use of violence. Laub and Lauritsen (1998: 144) comment further: 'Second, these dimensions of a school's culture affected each student's risk for violence, over and above the risk associated with the student's own values regarding violence.'

Welsh and his colleagues (Welsh *et al.* 1999, 2000; Welsh 2000, 2001) have recently made an attempt to study crime in schools in a multi-level perspective. Welsh *et al.* (1999) studied 11 middle schools in Philadelphia, which involved surveying some 7,583 students (aged 12–15). The sample was selected from a total of 43 middle schools on the basis of school disorder (based on official records) and community-level factors. The researchers selected a sample that would include a spread of schools across low, medium and high risk in terms of disorder and community disadvantage. The response rate in the 11 schools was 65 per cent. Some 7,583 pupils answered the surveys, but after a list-wise deletion of missing variables, 6,693 students were included in the subsequent analysis. This, therefore, represents less than a 65 per cent response rate. This means, in a similar vein to many self-report surveys, that there is likely to be an under-reporting of crime, as offenders are probably the ones to be most likely to be absent, or who do not fully complete the questionnaire (for a discussion of this, see Wilson and Herrnstein 1985). High response rates in self-report surveys are beneficial.

The research included five individual-level student characteristic scales, which concentrated more on the population characteristics of the school; that is, they describe a school by the people who inhabit it. The five scales used in the study correspond to Hirschi's (1969) control theory. The scales are school involvement (involvement in school activities); positive peer associations (the degree to which students have friends who value school and avoid trouble); belief in school rules (the extent to which students believe in the validity of conventional social rules); school effort (how much care and effort students devote to school work); and school rewards (how much students are rewarded for good behaviour). As well as these measures, they included pupil age, sex and race in the analysis. Community characteristics, including community poverty and stability, were also analysed and their effects on a measure of school misconduct were analysed. This measure of school misconduct included four dichotomous variables assessing student misbehaviour during the current term. The measure included items concerning whether the student was sent out of class for punishment, was suspended from school or had a fight to protect him or herself.

Welsh *et al.* (1999) used hierarchical linear modelling to analyse their data. This analysis suggested the primacy of the individual characteristics measured as predictors of school misconduct in comparison with community and institutional-level factors. The measures of school and community were based on community characteristics. They focused on imported community characteristics of the school (i.e. the characteristics of where the pupils lived in terms of community) and the community in which the school was located. Hoffmann and Johnson (2000) criticise Welsh *et al.* for not considering cross-level interactions, which may provide information regarding how communities interact with individuals in explaining delinquency. It is, however, an example of a multi-level approach in investigating school misconduct, which suggests the primacy of individual bonding (social situational) characteristics over community explanations.

Welsh (2000) examined the influence of school climate on school disorder. This study was based on the same sample as the 1999 study. However, in this study five different measures of school disorder were obtained. These were school safety (perceptions of pupils' safety); student victimisation (assaulted by other students or robbed at school); avoidance (this was a measure of fear of certain places in school); offending (assaulting other pupils, theft, for example); and student misconduct (same definition as in the 1999 study). These dependent measures were compared with the same individual characteristics scales described above. However, a measure of school climate was added. This was based on pupils' perceptions using five psycho-social climate scales. These included measures of school safety, clarity of rules, fairness of rules, respect for students, student influence on school affairs, and planning and action (student reports of the degree to which the school undertakes efforts to plan and implement school improvement). Welsh found that the 11 schools in the sample differed significantly on all five measures of school climate and these climate factors were significant predictors of pupils' outcome measures. He found that teacher respect significantly predicted avoidance, victimisation, safety, offending and misconduct. Planning and action significantly predicted victimisation and safety. Fairness of rules significantly predicted victimisation, offending and misconduct. Clarity of rules significantly predicted avoidance, victimisation, safety and offending. Student influence significantly predicted avoidance, safety and offending. However, other school bond variables and community structural variables also predicted these outcomes. In this investigation there was no attempt at disentangling effects across levels. Nor was there an attempt made to see which variables were the strongest predictors of the outcome measures selected. However, the study was useful in reopening the debate concerning whether school climate could influence offending and victimisation in schools. These two papers are of particular interest because they actually analysed offences, misconduct and victimisation that take place on the school premises. The research did not take into account frequency of the outcome measures on the school premises. Welsh (2001: 938) further examined the data set used in the previous two studies and states: 'I find a clear need to distinguish more explicitly between individual and institutional influences of school disorder, especially for students' misconduct and offending.' He found that both student characteristics in terms of the school bond and school climate variables provided significant explanatory power regarding the five measures of school disorder he used in the study (i.e. avoidance, victimisation, offending, misconduct and safety).

Welsh *et al.* (2000) studied school climate theory and social disorganisation theory in relation to school disorder in Philadelphia's public schools. This study included all 43 middle schools, and relied heavily on official data. They measured community in two ways. First, local, which was the census tract around the school and, secondly, imported, which was the aggregated measure of where the students actually lived. This is the same as in the previous two studies reviewed. On the school level, measures regarded school size and school stability (a factor score based on student attendance and turnover). School disorder was a factor score based on school incident data and pupil dismissal rates. This study could be argued to suffer from an over-reliance on official data, especially in terms of the dependent variable. It is more than likely that school policies will vary with how to record incidence rates and when dismissals should be employed. However, the study reported that community poverty exerted strong indirect effects on school disorder in both the local and imported community PATH models. It was found that the effects of community variables were strongly mediated by school stability. Thus it would appear that a study of institutional processes might add to an understanding of school crime.

These four studies, although having shortcomings, have opened up a debate regarding the importance of school effects in US schools. The multi-level approaches taken are commendable, but it is the view of this author that there is much still to be done. These studies did not focus on individual social situational (although the school bond was examined) and dispositional factors (thus failing fully to control for individual pupil characteristics), nor did they analyse interaction effects between levels, which could help to inform regarding aspects of school or community influences on pupils. None the less, in their ambition these studies are pointing in a direction that will have great utility in unravelling the factors that cause and predict crime in schools.

Recently the Gottfredsons have presented initial findings regarding the US National Study of Delinquency Prevention in Schools. Gottfredson *et al.* (2002b) investigated school climate predictors of school disorder. This study encompasses data from 254 public, secondary schools. The mean response rate of students in this survey was 75 per cent with a range of 16–100 per cent. The teacher survey response rate had a mean of 75 per cent, with a range of 12–100 per cent. School disorder was measured using three scales: teacher victimisation, student victimisation and student delinquency. The last measure focused on delinquency that occurs in schools. This was made up of four items relating to vandalism, assaulting or threatening a teacher or adult, theft or assaulting and threatening a fellow student. The recall period for these items was 12 months. In terms of independent variables, the research focused on school climate measures (including scales relating to fairness of rules, clarity of rules, organisational focus, morale, planning and administrative leadership) and so-called 'exogenous variables'. These include poverty and disorganisation, percentage students and teachers of African-American origin and residential crowding, for example. The analysis indicated that school climate explained a greater percentage of the variance than community or student composition in terms of student delinquent behaviour and teacher victimisation. However, student victimisation was more strongly influenced by community and student compositional characteristics. They found that schools in which students perceived greater fairness and clarity of rules had less delinquency and student victimisation.

Gottfredson *et al.* (2002a) investigated community characteristics, staffing difficulty and school climate in relation to school disorder. In this study, school disorder was measured in terms of teacher victimisation and classroom orderliness. The investigation showed that community-concentrated disadvantage leads to difficulty in recruiting teachers and disorderly schools. They found that school-staffing advantage leads to more school order whereas black predominance (teachers and students) leads to less school order. The central implication of the research was that solving school staffing difficulties would increase school orderliness.

Continental European studies

Swedish and Dutch scholars have made important contributions to knowledge regarding crime in schools. Baerveldt's (1992) study sought to measure the delinquency of low-stream third-year pupils, in 14 secondary schools in the Netherlands. The measure of delinquency was gained from self-report studies and was a scale involving 26 items of minor delinquency. The study used hierarchical linear modelling techniques to separate the effects of school-level, class-level and individual-level factors on delinquency and also on a measure of pupil integration into school. This last scale was made up of factors such as low truancy in schools, positive school attitudes and little punishment in school. Variables in the study were gained from a variety of methods including the pupils' survey, interviews, observations, teachers' survey and an observers' survey. The research found that features of the school, teachers' attitudes and lessons did not predict delinquency. The study found that, rather than school organisation, the most important predictor of between-school delinquency differences was a measure of pupil bonding to school, in terms of pupil integration. Thus, the individual-level measure of school bonding was the most important predictor of between-school delinquency rates. This is a finding that is of considerable interest because in the later school studies in the USA, reviewed above, between-individual differences in school bonding features were found to be important predictors of offending in school. It could, thus, be argued that more research regarding individual differences of pupils, in terms of their social situations (such as school bonds) and also dispositions (such as self-control levels), would provide a fruitful area of analysis when studying what factors cause crime in schools.

In Sweden, Lindström has carried out a number of studies regarding school context and delinquency. Lindström (1993) examined whether the social context of the school affected adolescents' anti-social behaviour, once individual-level characteristics had been controlled for. He examined this by carrying out a self-report survey of 800, 15-year-old students in Stockholm (this was part of the Stockholm Project – see Wikström 1990 for an overview of the project). The response rate in the project was 95 per cent. This study did not, however, focus on crime and delinquency in schools, but on the influence of schools, parenting and individual bonds to schools regarding general delinquency (which does not necessarily occur in the school context). The main findings of the study showed that parental involvement both at the individual level and at the aggregated school level generates a social capital, which is of importance when preventing school adolescents from engaging in delinquent behaviour. This finding was replicated in Lindström's (1995) study, in which he argues that the internal characteristics of the schools made no significant contribution to adolescents' general delinquent behaviour. However, perhaps if the influence of the school on school-based delinquency had been measured this finding may differ. In terms of the school context measure, Lindström concentrated on aggregate structural measures such as socioeconomic status of pupils' families, family size, disrupted families and family interaction. Lindström did include a measure of school climate based on a five-item scale of pupils' perception. Following the use of a regression model, Lindström (1993: 117) stated: 'When using relative family interaction and family disruption at the individual level and aggregated relative family interaction, students' perception of school, the proportion of qualified teachers and number of students per teacher in a contextual analysis it was found that none of the school internal characteristics were statistically significant.' However, the interesting findings in the study of the influence of bonds between pupils and schools and families, and of parental monitoring, suggest that school studies in the future should investigate and control for individual characteristics of pupils' social situation when investigating whether schools or, indeed, community contexts, have a separate and important influence.

Lindström (2001) investigated school violence in a multi-level perspective. He found wide variations between schools in violent victimisation rates. In the least violent school, 8 per cent of students were victimised, whereas in the most violent school 30 per cent of students indicated they had been victimised. The data used in this study came from more than 2,000 students in the seventh grade in 26 schools in Sweden, who took part in the Drug Abuse Resistance Education Survey (Project DARE). The schools were mainly located in large urban areas. Lindström investigated the effects of: 1) the proportion of students living in broken families; 2) the proportion of students with at least one parent born in a country other than Sweden; 3) family interaction; 4) academic climate (based on three items measuring self-perceived attainment, number of times students skipped classes, and whether or not pupils do homework); and 5) deviant values (four items measuring whether or not the students think it is alright to use drugs and commit violent crimes). On the basis of a weighted least-squares regression model Lindström concluded that there was a clear pattern of more violence in schools with a disadvantaged student population, in terms of their home situation and academic background. Lindström executed a hierarchical regression model that indicated individual-level characteristics, including sex, self-esteem and school involvement, are all significantly related to victimisation. At the aggregate level, Lindström found that in schools where students in general have low family interaction, the victimisation rate is higher. He showed that neither academic climate nor deviant values at the school level have statistically significant effects on violent victimisation. Thus, contrary to early studies, when one controls for individual characteristics of social situation, the influence of school climate diminishes.

Crime in schools: a research agenda

Some key themes can be drawn from this review of the research field regarding crime in school. More rigorous research following the agenda discussed below should in the future contribute to a better understanding of crime in schools and the factors that cause it. This can only produce a sound basis on which to base policy solutions that should make schools safer places to be and more effective deliverers of education for all.

(a)   *Much more research regarding crime in schools, particularly regarding offending and victimisation among pupils, is needed in the UK.*

It can be seen from the review that, in the UK in particular, there has, since 1979, been little research conducted in the sphere of crime in secondary schools. This is a surprising conclusion when one considers the importance the media put on crime in school, and the costs both socially and economically inflicted by school crime in the UK.[1] It is also surprising because education is a top priority for governments and parents, yet little has been researched regarding behavioural aspects in secondary schools, which may have an impact on pupils' successful intellectual and moral outcomes and, thus, on society.

(b)   *Research concerning crime in schools needs further to refine multi-level approaches, particularly regarding the measures of school context, community context and types of individual characteristics employed.*

The review illustrated that the approaches used to investigate the issue of crime and delinquency in schools have evolved in countries, other than the UK, during the 1980s, 1990s and early 2000s. Researchers in the USA, Sweden and Holland have begun to investigate the issue in a more sophisticated manner. No studies have, as yet, fully controlled for individual dispositional characteristics and lifestyle characteristics of pupils, and few have controlled sufficiently for individual social situational characteristics. More rigorous measures of school context and community are also needed, as previously stated.

In terms of investigating the influence of school context on offending and victimisation in schools, there is little coherence in the measures of schooling used. In the future it is essential to develop tools that effectively measure aspects of school context. This is similar to the call for a more sophisticated way of measuring community contexts – ecometrics (see Raudenbush and Sampson 1999). This research seeks to develop some pupil-based measures of school context. These measures will be based on previous research that has been reviewed above.

It is also of prime importance to develop analytical techniques that can disentangle different levels of explanation. Within this it is essential to handle data carefully so that factors are not over controlled for. In studies examining the importance of contextual and individual characteristics, it must always be remembered that individuals develop in their contexts and environments and these develop and shape individual characteristics. This is an issue that statistical techniques cannot yet sufficiently account for and thus findings and interpretations must be treated sensitively and with this in mind.

(c) *In order for comparative research to be undertaken in a national and international perspective, outcome measures of school crime need to be refined. Measures are needed that accurately measure levels of offending and victimisation among pupils in schools.*

Many studies that have been reviewed do not specifically study offending in schools. Studies often focus on school misconduct in terms of truancy, being sent out of class, answering teachers back and disrupting the class. Very few studies actually extend to studying pupils who violently assault, who thieve, who vandalise, who rob and who break into the school. This behaviour occurs in schools and should be measured. A plethora of self-report studies in the USA and in the UK indicates that adolescents are actively involved in these offending habits. However, for some reason there appears to be little research that explores these behaviours in schools. Schools are a vital arena of socialisation and bad behaviour can disrupt learning and, as such, the life chances of pupils.

(d) *Longitudinal research regarding pupils' offending behaviour and victimisation risk in schools is needed, to disentangle comprehensively the influences of community context, family context, school context, and individual social situational, dispositional and lifestyle characteristics.*

Most of the research regarding offending and victimisation among pupils in schools is cross-sectional in nature. However, it is argued that to understand and explain offending and victimisation more fully among pupils in schools, both in terms of *between-individual pupil differences* and *between-school differences*, a longitudinal research design would be beneficial. Such research designs should be more sophisticated in dealing with the evolution of individuals in their contexts.

Towards a theoretically grounded analytical framework

Short of a social experiment in which individuals are randomly assigned to live in different communities and attend different schools, the ideal study of school effects would employ individual-, school-, and community-level data for a large number of social areas. Further, it would measure the specific characteristics of community and school context as well as the specific individual-level factors thought to contribute to the behaviour of interest. No study has yet accomplished this combination of measurements and sample size (Gottfredson 2001: 68).

Previous research regarding crime in schools has been reviewed and an agenda for future research has been identified. The review illustrated some central limitations of previous research, including 1) measurement of the outcome (dependent) variable; 2) a lack of attention to individual differences; and 3) ignoring some possible key explanatory variables such as pupils' individual characteristics, lifestyles and also some more basic pupil information regarding family background, among other factors.

This section will explore theoretical perspectives which have great utility in the investigation and explanation of individual differences in pupil offending in schools, as well as between-school differences in offending rates. After this chapter, the book focuses on an empirical investigation, which looks at exactly what factors cause and predict offending in schools.

Causes and causal mechanisms

Causality is of fundamental importance in social science research. In order to understand and improve the social world, it is important to understand how outcomes (such as crime) are affected by possible causes. If causes are understood, then it is possible to alter outcomes – ideally for the better! Notions of cause and effect are commonly used without much attention to what they mean. Indeed, an extensive philosophical debate concerns the issue of causality (see, for example, Hellevik 1984). Greenberg (1979: 2) defines a causal effect in the following manner: variable A will be seen as a cause of B if there are circumstances under which a change in A is followed by a change in B. He also states that causation does not necessarily imply determination or that causation is unidirectional (i.e. if A causes B, it is not excluded that B may also be a cause of A). In assessing whether an independent variable causes an outcome (dependent) variable to change there must be some time ordering (i.e. at time X, there is a change in variable A, which causes a change in variable B at time Y). The present research is cross-sectional in nature, meaning that it is not possible to take account of time ordering which notions of causality imply. Therefore, it is necessary for causal variables to be based on theoretical constructs, while also applying several rigorous tests which help the scientist to be confident that the independent variables employed do or will cause changes in the dependent variable (if manipulation could be achieved).

When testing for causal variables in cross-sectional research there are several basic tests which indicate causal relevance. First, the variable concerned should co-vary with predictors of the outcome. Secondly, the variable should co-vary with the outcome itself. Thirdly, the association with the outcome should persist once other potentially important causes have been controlled for (Halpern 2001). Within this third point, one must be careful not to over-control for variables (see Chapter 11 for a discussion). Fourthly (and a point sometimes overlooked), there must be a plausible theoretical explanation as to why the variable may cause the outcome under consideration. The empirical chapters later on in the book will indicate causes of pupil offending in schools based on these four important tests.

Criminological research has shown a wide variety of risk factors that are associated with offending. These factors are not necessarily, in themselves, direct causes, though. Farrington (2000: 7) states, concerning criminological research: 'a major problem of the risk factor paradigm is to determine which risk factors are causes and which are merely markers or correlated with causes.' As well as the problem of identifying whether factors are causative or merely correlative with offending behaviour, there can be instances where several factors, which independently may not operate as a cause, act together to become a causal influence. Research has shown that thresholds exist in terms of risk factors. For instance, two risk factors may not have a significant effect on individuals' behaviour or performance but the operation and presence of three or more, for example, may make a significant difference (see Sameroff *et al.* 1987). There is also discussion regarding whether certain risk factors are additive in nature or whether factors interact with each other to affect an outcome. An interaction effect occurs when the effect of $A1$ (independent variable 1) on B (outcome variable) depends on the value of $A2$ (independent variable 2) (Greenberg 1979). Such interaction effects concerning pupil offending in the school context become particularly relevant in later chapters.

Wikström and Sampson (2003) argue that, in order for social science to offer explanation for patterns in social life, it is necessary to map out these risk factors or correlates of human social action and then to understand the underlying causal mechanisms at work. An understanding of risk factors, correlates and their operation is essential in this process of understanding and explanation. Much work is still to be done in this arena alone. However, Wikström and Sampson argue, based on Hedström and Swedberg (1998), that criminological research should pay more attention to gaining an understanding of causal mechanisms. A causal mechanism may be defined as a plausible (unobservable) process that links a cause to an effect. Wikström and Sampson (2003) argue that an important task is to evaluate correlates for their potential as representing causal mechanisms in relation to what constitutes social action.

Wikström (2002) argues that a possible causal mechanism for social actions, like pupil offending, is that social action is a result of individual choice and perception of alternatives. Wikström (2002: 7) states:

> the key challenge for social science research is to understand how individual characteristics and contextual factors, independently and in interaction, influence individual perception of alternatives and processes of choice. This is of course a monumental task, and no single research project can hope to be able to provide more than a small contribution to this goal.

51

Although not specifically focusing on the causal mechanism suggested by Wikström (2002), this author recognises the importance of the notion of causal mechanisms (see Hedström and Swedberg 1998; Bunge 1999, 2004) regarding criminological inquiry and, indeed, the possible importance of the proposed mechanisms in providing a link between contextual and individual levels. An understanding of social action of individuals may add a significant contribution in the understanding of the mechanisms that link contextual levels of analysis to individual levels (for a discussion of social action and its importance to criminological research, see Wikström and Sampson 2003).

Contextual and individual explanation

Structure: social disorganisation

Schools do not operate in isolation from the rest of society in aiming to deliver the key, Aristotelian-based, goals of education. Schools are affected by the communities that they serve, and also by the pupils' backgrounds and the individual characteristics of the pupils who attend the schools. Criminological theory has long recognised the importance of neighbourhood and community differences in explaining differential offending rates both between communities and effecting differential rates between individuals (see Bottoms 1993). The social disorganisation thesis, first proposed by Shaw and McKay (1969), identified a relationship between offending patterns and the features of neighbourhoods. Shaw and McKay proposed that social disorganisation might explain how structural characteristics could determine differential offending patterns between neighbourhoods. They argued that low economic status, high residential mobility and high ethnic heterogeneity lead to disruption of community social organisation, which in turn accounts for variations in delinquency and crime rates. Communities that are socially disorganised would have a lesser prevalence and interdependence of social networks. Social ties in the community may be disparate. These disorganisation characteristics would diminish collective supervision of anti-social and criminal activity. Gottfredson (2001: 3) suggests: 'according to this perspective, schools are only part of a larger community disintegration process that allows delinquency to flourish.' Schools that serve communities which are socially disorganised may have to educate pupils who are less well supervised and as a result may be more problematic, resulting in a higher likelihood of offending.

Process

The social disorganisation perspective, which originally focused on structural characteristics, has developed by focusing on community processes (e.g. Kornhauser 1978; Sampson and Groves 1989; Coleman 1990; Sampson *et al.* 1997). Such community processes contribute to theories relating to why some schools experience higher pupil offending rates than others and what factors cause and predict pupil offending in two main areas. First, as has been noted, schools do not operate in isolation from the rest of society. What happens in the community outside school may affect how pupils behave in school. Where communities display criminogenic processes that allow adolescents to offend, these may spill over into the school environment. Secondly, such community processes that are identified in criminological theory may also be applicable to the school community or environment.

Recent community process research and theory, which may be of importance when considering pupil offending in schools, includes socialisation, informal social control, social cohesion, social integration, social capital and 'collective efficacy' (e.g. Kornhauser 1978; Sampson and Groves 1989; Coleman 1990; Sampson *et al.* 1997). These processes, it is argued, mediate structural characteristics of communities (and argued here, schools) and thus contribute to an understanding of variations in offence rates. It can be hypothesised that schools serving communities, which have high levels of social control, social cohesion, social integration, social capital and collective efficacy, may have a less problematic intake of pupils than schools that serve communities with the opposite characteristics. This is because these processes will operate to prevent pupils from offending generally. However, it is also postulated that schools promoting high levels of social control, social cohesion, social integration, social capital and collective efficacy within their school community may be able to reduce pupil offending rates. This could mean that effective schools, in terms of these crime-reducing processes, may help prevent offending in schools. For example, if an effective school (in terms of operating processes that reduce pupil offending) is located in a socially disorganised community, where community processes operate poorly in terms of reducing individuals' propensity to offend, the school may help prevent crime among pupils, thus in some way balancing processes and structural characteristics external to the school.

Theories that have developed from the social disorganisation perspective have been criticised over time, in particular for not taking account of individual differences in offending propensities. Indeed,

Farrington (1993: 16) has criticised the original thesis of Shaw and McKay on the following grounds:

> The key problem with Shaw and McKay's research is that it is impossible to know how far varying delinquency rates of different areas reflect variations in neighbourhood factors such as physical deterioration or social disorganisation and how far they reflect variations in other factors, such as individual characteristics or family influence.

Through focusing on communities' structural characteristics and community processes, community theories have tended to overlook the individual compositional characteristics of communities. A point eloquently made by Kornhauser (1978: 114):

> How do we know that area differences in delinquency rates result from aggregative characteristics of communities rather than the characteristics of individuals selectively aggregated into communities? How do we even know that there are any differences at all in delinquency rates of communities once their differing composition is taken into account?

It would seem reasonable to hypothesise that both the general characteristics of communities and schools (in terms of social disorganisation and social processes) and the composition of communities and schools in terms of individuals may affect the proportion of pupils who offend in schools. Of major importance is how individuals interact with their environment.

In explaining the causes of pupil offending in schools it is necessary to pay attention to both community and school contextual characteristics and the processes that may affect pupil offending, as well as paying attention to the individual characteristics of pupils. The next section will identify some of the key individual characteristics which may contribute to individual pupil differences in offending in schools. Such differences may also, to a large degree, affect whether some schools experience more pupil offending than others. For instance, if a school has a high proportion of pupils who display high-risk individual characteristics, the school may experience high pupil offending rates due to the composition of the pupil population.

Individual factors
Criminological research, as well as developing community and context-

based theories, has also developed theories relating to individual and individuals' family characteristics, which may have great utility in helping to understand and explain offending in schools. It can be hypothesised that those individual characteristics (both in terms of individual social situation and disposition) that cause adolescents to offend generally will also operate to cause individuals to offend in schools.

A multitude of individual and family correlates of offending have been identified by criminological research. The Gluecks, in their seminal study of 500 delinquent and 500 non-delinquent boys, indicated numerous significant differences between delinquents and non-delinquents in terms of individual and family factors. Glueck and Glueck (1950) found that at the age of six the most important family predictors of delinquency were poor supervision of the boy by the mother; erratic or over-strict discipline of the boy by the father; low family cohesiveness; and hostile or indifferent attitudes of the mother and father to the boy. Individual factors included adventurousness or risk-taking, extraversion, being easily led, stubbornness and emotional instability. Farrington (1993) recognises that both Shaw and McKay's and the Gluecks' legacy to modern criminology is great. He argues, though, that the Gluecks and Shaw and McKay suffer from the same inability to take account of cross-level influences. Of the Gluecks' research he argues 'the possibility remains that their observed individual and family differences between delinquents and non-delinquents were confounded with and a consequence of neighbourhood differences. The delinquents lived in worse areas on average' (1993: 21). Integrative analytical approaches would allow account to be taken of cross-level interactions between contextual factors of schools and communities and individual characteristics.

Farrington (1992) reviewed the most important individual and family predictors of offending (both juveniles and adults, based on official records and self-reports). He reported that high impulsivity (low self-control), low intelligence and attainment are the most important individual predictors of offending. Regarding family predictors, poor parental monitoring, large family size, harsh parental discipline, parental conflict, criminal parents or siblings and disrupted families are the most important factors in terms of predicting offending. It would seem reasonable to hypothesise that such individual factors predict individual offending in schools. Such factors may also be responsible for some schools experiencing higher pupil offending rates than others, if some schools serve pupils who have more risk factors for offending than others.

Integration

Community and individual theories, developed in criminology, can have great utility in explaining what factors cause and predict individual pupil offending in schools and in answering why some schools may experience more pupil offending than others. However, research in both traditions is open to the criticism that they largely ignore the other perspective. Thus, research regarding individual and family characteristics often ignores community factors, and research regarding community factors often fails to take account of individual characteristics. If knowledge of the causes of pupil offending in schools is to advance, it is necessary to include community factors and pupils' individual characteristics, thus taking account of both traditions which, as argued above, have much to offer in terms of explanation regarding pupil offending in schools.

This goes hand in hand with one of the major themes in recent criminological debate. There have been numerous calls to integrate individual and contextual approaches to aid explanation in criminology (see, for example, Tonry *et al.* 1991; Farrington *et al.* 1993; LeBlanc 1997). Wikström and Sampson (2003) argue, based on Reiss (1986), that much more is to be gained from integrating individual and environmental approaches than from their continued separate development. In terms of criminological research, in general, Farrington (1993: 30) states: 'Researchers interested in neighbourhood influences have generally not adequately measured individual and family influences, just as researchers interested in individual and family influences have generally not adequately measured neighbourhood influences.' Sampson *et al.* (1997: 32) argues: 'few studies have successfully demonstrated a unified approach to the individual- and community-level dimensions of crime.'

Although these observations are pertinent to general criminology, they are also of great importance to the study of pupil offending in schools. It is essential to take into account contextual and individual aspects that influence pupil offending behaviour. It is one of the aims of this study to integrate knowledge regarding community factors, family factors, school factors and individual social situational, dispositional and lifestyle factors to increase and improve knowledge regarding the causes of offending in schools. Criminological inquiry generally has not focused on the school environment, which may be a grave omission, because, as Gold (1978) has argued, the school after the family is a child's second most important sphere of socialisation. Most calls for theoretical and analytical integration have focused on integrating knowledge regarding community and individual approaches. Including schools can only enhance this integration.

Multi-level studies

No study has, as yet, adequately measured individual dispositional, social situational and lifestyle characteristics, family factors, school factors and community factors and successfully disentangled the relative effects of these influences regarding offending behaviour. Studies have, however, attempted to investigate the relative predictive powers of community and individual factors in relation to crime. Very few studies have included the school in this analysis.

As science has advanced, more sophisticated analysis and methodologies have been employed so that over the last 15 years, there has been a growth in multi-level, integrative analytical approaches. This has improved since 1991, when Gottfredson *et al.* (1991: 201) stated: 'we know of only three multi-level studies of the effect of area characteristics on individual criminal involvement.' Wikström (1998) argues that few studies measure all factors empirically, and most studies that do attempt this focus on limited aspects of the problem. Such studies have faced 'difficult problems of measurement and methodology that sometimes make it difficult to draw straightforward conclusions' (1998: 273).

A review of this literature shows that elements of community context, family and individual (usually social situational measures) characteristics have been found to have an influence on individual offending. However, it would appear that disentangling the relative weight of these effects and how they operate is still at an early stage. Martens (1993) argues that, in multivariate analysis, structural variables (i.e. neighbourhood context) have the weakest explanatory power, whereas individual variables tend to have the highest explanatory power. For instance, Gottfredson *et al.* (1991) reported that their measure of community context only explained 1 per cent of the variance regarding their delinquency measures. This is likely to be explained by the proximity of the measures employed to an individual's social action.

Individual characteristics are more proximate to social action whereas most community-level measures, for example, are relatively remote from an individual's social action. More refined measures of community are needed. Sophisticated measures of context that take account of the contextual impact on individual action would be beneficial in enhancing the explanation of crime. Few multi-level studies have, as yet, attempted to solve this problem of more complex measurement of community characteristics. Indeed, Earls and Buka (2000) comment that the study of community influences on human development is at an early stage of scientific refinement. More sophisticated measures of school environments, which can be replicated in other research, are needed for studies of school effects regarding pupil offending behaviour. An issue related to the relatively weak proportion of variance explained by community and other contextual variables in regression models when compared with individual-level variables is over-control in statistical models. Contextual variables are likely to have affected how individual-level characteristics develop, but statistical tools such as regression-based analyses cannot take this into account.

There are gaps in the approaches of these multi-level studies. For example, few take a measure of individual disposition (e.g. low self-control, pro-social values and sense of shame), which seem to be strong predictors of individual offending (see, for example, Pratt and Cullen 2000). These studies also tend to overlook the role of schools in their analysis. They tend to focus on the relative importance of community and individual explanations of offending. However, integrative approaches have shown that contextual factors are important in relation to individual characteristics regarding offending behaviour (see Wikström and Loeber 2000; Wikström 2002).

Summary

From the above discussion the following can be said:

- Studies of pupil offending in schools should recognise the fact that schools do not operate in isolation from the rest of society.

- General criminological theory regarding communities and individual and family factors can have great utility in helping to understand why some pupils offend in schools and others do not.

- Integrating analytical approaches is essential in gaining a better understanding of why some schools experience higher pupil offending rates than others and what factors cause and predict pupils' offending behaviour in schools.

The school: a systemic view

So far previous literature relating to crime in the school context has been reviewed and previous contextual, individual and integrative research has been discussed. Now the focus will move forward discussing the school and its role in the wider social system and how this system can affect the school and the school's pupils. Of central importance is young people's behaviour in the school context and the explanation of criminal or delinquent behaviour. The idea that different schools can have different impacts on individuals has been mooted in both educational and criminological research. Governments, policy-makers and researchers all seek to see if something about schools can influence individual attainment and behaviour. Can schools make a difference in terms of individuals' achieving the Aristotelian virtues of moral and intellectual excellence? Do similar school contexts affect different types of individuals differently? Do schools have differential influences on different types of individuals, who have developed in different community and family contexts? If the answer to the last question is 'yes', then straightforward one-size-fits-all solutions aimed at improving behaviour and achievement are less likely to be found. However, targeted solutions may be achievable which should make a difference for groups of pupils.

The school context has been studied in a variety of ways, using a variety of variables, theories, methodologies and models. Terms used to investigate school context include school ethos (e.g. Rutter *et al.* 1979), school climate (e.g. Welsh *et al.* 1999) and, indeed, school context (Lindström 1993). In this book school context is the preferred term for assessing the influence of schools on pupils; however, school climate is conceptualised as a part of the school context, as will be discussed in Chapter 7. Research into school context is complex and involves assessing and making order of a range of variables, on a range of levels, which also interact (see Anderson 1982). The school context is also part of a wider social system, which affects the composition of the school and its operation. Thus, studies that focus solely on school organisation and management factors may be limited as other factors may have a stronger influence on pupil behaviour in school. For example, differential rates in pupil offending between schools could possibly be caused simply by the fact that some schools have a higher proportion of high-risk pupils (in terms of offending) than others. School context may not, therefore, have a great influence. A conceptual issue concerns what is meant by the term context in relation to the individual. For instance, the composition of the pupils around the individual pupil in school may be considered to be part of the context, which influences the individual, and indeed this is how it is treated in Chapter 10.

Schools are part of a wide social system. A social system can be considered as 'a complex object whose parts or components are held together by bonds of some kind' (Bunge 2004: 7). Bunge (1999: 61) argues that 'a social system is analysable into its _composition_ or membership, _environment_ or context, _structure_ or relationships, and _mechanism_ or the processes that make it tick'. He refers to this systemic approach as the CESM view. It is useful to think of the school in this systemic way, and particularly the factors that may influence individual action and between-school differences in crime rates when one considers the school as a setting for action, but also as part of a wider social system. The following illustrates the ways in which the CESM view may instruct our understanding of important factors that should be considered when trying to explain individual differences in offending in the school context and also between-school differences. This is a simplification of reality, but it is analytically and theoretically helpful to outline just how complex the school is as a unit to study.

Composition

The composition of the school consists mainly of pupils (majority), teachers and administrators. These actors will be influenced by the wider social system in terms of their experiences, attitudes and perception. Other elements that make up the _composition_ of the school include the resources the school has and its physical design, building and grounds.

Environment

The environment of the school can be considered to be the collection of natural, social and artificial items linked to the members (actors) of the system (the school). Thus, one can consider that the neighbourhood pupils originate from and live in, the family backgrounds they come from and the social positions they occupy will all influence the school context. Also, previous educational experiences and schooling will influence how individuals act within their present setting. The environment is likely to be influenced by the characteristics of the actors of which the school is composed.

Structure

The structure of the school system consists of the relations that occur in the school – for example, between staff and management, pupils and staff, pupils and management, etc. This includes how the school is affected by relations with other socio-systems such as the political context in which it operates and, for instance, its relations with other schools and the local education authority. The main aim of the school structure is the education of pupils. The relations involved in achieving this aim occur within the school structure but are influenced by relations with outside systems. For instance, the school's relationships with parents and local powerbrokers (e.g. politicians, governors of the school and the LEA (local education authority)) will influence how it achieves its aims. The relations within the school context are dependent on individuals, and thus the composition of the school in terms of pupils and staff is vitally important.

Mechanisms
These are the collection of processes that determine (alter or maintain) the structure of the system. Mechanisms affect and are affected by the composition, environment and structure of the school. Examples of mechanisms that occur in the school context are teaching and learning, sanctioning and reward systems, the creation or absence of social trust and capital. Such mechanisms are crucial in the development of pupils and achieving the central Aristotelian goals of education.

This exploration of the school system in terms of the CESM model illustrates that factors other than the school will have an influence on individual behaviour, and should thus be included in an investigation of pupil offending in secondary schools. This discussion is furthered below.

Schools and individual development

In terms of gaining an understanding of how community, family and schools are related to pupils' action in the school context, Bronfenbrenner's (1979) ecology of human development model provides an interesting insight, especially following on from the CESM model discussed previously. Although Bronfenbrenner's model focused on individual development, which cannot be comprehensively addressed in a cross-sectional study of this nature, it provides a focus as to how contextual factors relate to individuals and also a view of how the school operates as part of a wider societal system in influencing individual development and how this may impact on behaviour.

Bronfenbrenner conceived the ecological environment of humans as a set of nested structures, 'each inside the next, like a set of Russian dolls' (1979: 3). At the innermost level is the individual within the immediate setting (the micro-system). Outside this is the mesosystem; according to Garbarino and Ganzel (2000), mesosystems are relationships between microsystems in which the individual experiences reality. These links themselves operate to form a system. One such example may be the school setting. How well are the school and the individual's family, for example, connected? This can be measured, and is later (Chapter 7), by measuring parental interest in pupils' schooling. The argument suggests that the greater the number and quality of connections between microsystems, the more positive effects will be felt for the development of the individual, and this may also be true regarding how the individual acts. Outside the mesosystem exists the exosystem. Exosystems are settings that have a bearing on children's development, but in which children do not play a direct role. Examples include parents' place of work, occupation, school boards, teachers' meetings and town planners that make decisions which affect individuals' day-to-day lives. Garbarino and Ganzel (2000: 79) argue: 'the concept of an exosystem illustrates the projective nature of the ecological perspective, for the same setting that is an exosystem for a child may be a microsystem for the parent and vice versa.' These systems exist and operate within the macrosystem. The macrosystem refers to 'the general organisation of the world as it is and as it might be' (Garbarino and Ganzel 2000). The macrosystem, thus, refers to societal factors, including ideological perspectives, demographics, institutions, governance and resources.

It is argued that this ecological perspective provides a structure and an explanation as to how community, family and school contextual characteristics can act, relate and influence individuals' social situational, dispositional and lifestyle characteristics. The relationships between the individual and the outer systems are dynamic; the individual both affects the environment and is affected by the environment in which he or she acts. This model is an important inspiration for the design of the empirical research that follows.

School as behaviour setting and context of action

The Bronfenbrenner perspective indicates that the school is part of a wider societal context and that individuals within the school setting will be influenced by wider societal factors, which will also influence how they perceive the school setting. Pupils encounter many different settings in the course of their everyday lives. Schools, neighbourhoods, streets, shops, stadiums and homes all provide distinct settings for human behaviour to occur. These settings may be thought of as distinct ecological units or behaviour settings (Barker and Gump 1964; Barker 1968; Schoggen 1989). Behaviour settings refer not to the behaviour of particular individuals but to groups of individuals behaving together. Behaviour settings are naturally occurring units, having physical, behavioural and temporal properties, and they reveal a variety of complex inter-relationships among their parts. The school setting can be seen as a behaviour setting. It can also be divided into various behaviour settings (for example, classes, assemblies, playground, dining hall and playing fields). During the course of a school day the behaviour settings that the spatial structure exerts may change as different behaviours occur in them. For instance, a school hall may be home to gym lessons in the morning, but may double as a canteen at lunchtime and then play home to an assembly after lunch. The spatial structure remains the same – i.e. the school hall – but the behaviours that occur in it change through the day. Wikström and Loeber (2000, 1114) state:

> It is plausible to argue that community structural characteristics and related social processes, through the features of the *behaviour settings* it supplies, affect the individual's choice to offend or not by influencing his or her perceptions of temptations (e.g. attractive commodities) and provocations (e.g. insults and threats) and his or her evaluation of the risk of punishment (formal and informal sanctions) associated with a particular temptation or provocation.

The same can be said of school contexts. Schools vary in the behaviour settings that they supply (Barker and Gump 1964). Some schools may provide more criminogenic behaviour settings than others and, indeed, within schools, some behaviour settings may be more criminogenic than others. The other point to bear in mind is that pupils may vary in their assessment of behaviour settings (for example, a criminogenic behaviour setting for one person may not be for another). Referring back to the school hall example, it may be the case that, during gym lessons, pupils will experience higher levels of control due to the teacher's presence. However, at lunch the level of control may be substantially weaker, meaning that more crime may occur during this period, especially as pupils from different years mix, which may cause further frictions. Wikström and Sampson (2003: 125) argue that 'individuals' encounters with behaviour settings create situations (perception of opportunities and prospects) in which the individuals may express their propensies by making judgements and choices

63

resulting in actions'. These actions will vary based on individuals' social situational, dispositional and lifestyle characteristics and on the basis to which they react to the behaviour setting in which they find themselves. Wikström and Loeber (2000) identified that different groups of adolescents (based on their individual characteristics) reacted in different ways to the neighbourhood contexts in which they were brought up.

Thus, when focusing on offending in schools and differences in rates of offending between schools, it is necessary to take into account how different individuals behave in different contexts; this is an issue that will be investigated in Chapter 10. The interaction between individual and context is of prime interest when focusing on why some individuals offend in certain behaviour settings and others choose not to. The ecology of human development model and the theory of behaviour settings both offer great utility in terms of a theoretical basis with which to investigate offending in schools both in terms of *individual* differences and *between-school* differences. Schools that suffer lower rates of pupil offending may well supply less criminogenic environments, meaning that pupils are less likely to offend due perhaps to their perceptions of high risk of punishment or getting caught, or the weaker temptations offered by the setting. The next section will explore Wikström's model concerning key factors that influence offending behaviour. This model brings together the ecological influence on individual development, the importance of behaviour settings, and the temptations and risks in terms of getting caught that, together, affect the pupil's decision or choice concerning whether or not to offend.

Model of individual offending behaviour

In the discussions above, we have explored the importance of contextual factors in providing contexts of action (for example, the discussion of behaviour settings) and in providing contexts of development (for example, the discussion of Bronfenbrenner's ecology of human development). The systemic approach and the ecology of human development model suggest all these factors are related and connected in complex and dynamic ways, and these connections are also important in determining how individuals act. Wikström and Sampson (2003: 139) argue that the nature and strength of contextual influences on an individual's propensity to offend are 'dependent on the individual's previous developmental history'. Wikström has developed a model which aims to explain individual differences in offending behaviour (see, for example, Wikström 1995, 1996, 1998, 2002; Wikström and Sampson 2003). This model looks specifically at how individuals act in the behaviour settings they encounter in everyday life and the factors that shape their actions. This model has relevance in helping to explain offending in schools. A modified version of this model is shown in Figure 3.1.

Wikström and Sampson (2003: 121) argue that:

> an act of crime may be seen as primarily caused by the individual's reason (motivation) to commit the particular act of crime, emerging from the interaction between the individual's propensity to engage in criminality and the criminogenic features of the behaviour setting in which the individual finds him- or herself.

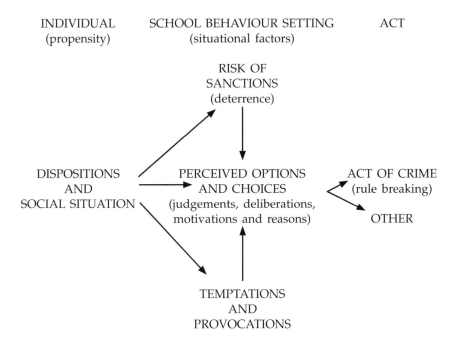

Source: After Wikström and Sampson (2003)

Figure 3.1 Wikström's model of key factors influencing individual behaviour

65

This suggests that, as explored in the previous section, some behaviour settings are more likely to be perceived by the individual as situations where crime is an option and therefore the individual may act upon this. For instance, the behaviour setting supplied by the school hall at lunchtime may be seen by the individual as more suitable for a particular act of crime than during the morning gym class, because in the gym class there may be a greater chance of getting caught due to the controlling influence of the teacher and the fewer number of pupils involved in the lesson. Lunchtime may also provide situations in the school hall where there are more provocations and temptations.

The model suggests that different pupils will have varying *propensities* or general likelihoods, within the same *behaviour setting*, to see crime as an option and then actually to act upon that. This suggests that in the school hall at lunchtime some individuals will see crime as an option and act upon this, but others, although experiencing the same behaviour setting, will decide crime is not an option.

This model is usually discussed in relation to the community context. However, it has great utility in enhancing understanding and explanation regarding the influence of school contexts. Schools, if operating effectively, may provide an ideal opportunity not experienced often in the community, to promote the development of pro-social lifestyles and encourage more law-abiding propensities in the pupils that pass through the system. Schools offer a more controlled environment than that which some pupils may have experienced up to that point in life. The days are rigidly organised and pupils are generally highly supervised, meaning that schools could be effective sites for promoting strategies that encourage pro-social development and lifestyles, thus helping to prevent crime.

In terms of this controlled environment, schools may influence the prevalence of criminogenic behaviour settings that pupils move through in their day-to-day lives and, thus, may influence their decisions to offend in school. To this extent, schools may vary in how effectively they exert controls over pupils. However, it must be stipulated that a cornerstone of this argument is the notion of individual propensity, which varies widely. Thus, although schools may well exert similar controls and display similar behaviour settings, it may be the case that some schools have a greater proportion of pupils who have greater propensities to engage in criminal behaviour and who may themselves have lower thresholds in identifying suitable behaviour settings in which to engage in criminal activities.

Empirical investigation

When seeking to explain why young people offend in school and why some schools experience higher rates of offending than others, there is a myriad of factors that can be taken into account. In what follows some of these key factors are explored empirically, taking into account elements of Bronfenbrenner's model, behaviour settings and the CESM model of Bunge, as well as theories relating to community, school, family and the individual. The framework employed in the following chapters is based on the theoretical, methodological and analytical discussions presented in this chapter.

Table 3.1 illustrates the key explanatory constructs explored in the following chapters. These constructs include community, school, family, individual social situational and dispositional, and lifestyle factors, and are examined in relation to pupil offending in school.

Summary

This chapter has shown that pupils' offending behaviour in schools is an under-researched topic in criminology and educational research, particularly in the UK. A research agenda for future investigations of the causes of offending in schools has been provided, as has a discussion of the strengths and weaknesses of research following either the contextual or individual tradition, or research that seeks to integrate perspectives. Future research should concentrate on developing integrative analytical approaches, and this is what is attempted in the following chapters. These chapters will investigate individual differences and between-school differences in offending in an integrative, analytical framework drawing on theory and research reviewed in this chapter. The following chapters will investigate how family background, community, school and individual characteristics are related to pupils' offending behaviour employing a strategy that will investigate which factors are the strongest predictors of pupil offending in schools and how contextual factors interact with individual factors in relation to pupils' offending behaviour.

Note

1 In 1996, the Department of Education and Employment stated that the cost of crime in England's schools, excluding unreported costs, such as uninsured losses and minor damage, amounted to £49 million in the period 1992–3 (Bissel 1996).

Table 3.1 Key explanatory constructs: descriptive statistics

Construct	Range	High score implies	Mean	SD	Alpha
Chapter 5					
*Area of residence structural risk**	−3–+3	Risk	0.09	2.11	
Chapter 6					
*Family social position**	−3–+3	Risk	−0.92	1.10	
Socioeconomic status*	0–3	Low	1.53	0.71	
Family structure (parental comp.)*	0–3	Care	0.49	0.76	
Family size*	0–4	Large	2.18	1.21	
Chapter 7					
*School context**	−5–+5	Poor	−1.34	1.53	
School climate*	−3–+3	Poor	−0.41	1.11	
Parental school interest*	0–18	Low	6.15	3.12	0.70
School ethos*	0–18	Poor	9.90	3.03	0.77
Respect for school authority*	0–15	Low	6.82	2.90	0.76
Pupil relations*	−2–+2	Poor	−1.00	0.87	
Social capital*	0–8	Low	2.72	1.68	0.65
School disorder*	0–12	High	3.63	1.97	0.54
Chapter 8					
*Individual risk-protective score**	−6–+6	Risk	−2.26	2.29	
Social situation					
Weak family bonds**	0–8	Weak	3.11	1.81	0.63
Weak school bonds*	0–18	Weak	8.07	3.17	0.78
Parental monitoring**	0–9	Poor	3.02	2.13	0.77
Disposition					
Low self-control***	0–37	Low	17.25	5.85	0.77
Pro-social values****	0–42	Strong	33.21	7.7	0.92
High shaming**	0–12	High	8.45	3.25	0.87
Chapter 9					
*Lifestyle**	−3–+3	Risk	−1.97	1.26	
General peer delinquency*	0–12	Risk	1.66	2.79	0.79
School peer delinquency*	0–10	Risk	3.26	2.57	0.82
Substance use*	0–15	High	2.45	2.99	0.75

Notes:

* Scale created by author.

** Based on scale employed by Wikström (see 2002: 78).

*** Modified version of the Grasmick *et al.* (1993) self-control scales; also used by Wikström (2002).

**** Based on scale used in the Pittsburgh Youth Study; also used by Wikström (2002).

Chapter 4

Offending in Cardiff's schools: individual and between-school differences

This chapter will give a detailed account of the level and nature of offending in school reported by the 3,103 Year 10 pupils in the Cardiff School Study. Later chapters will examine explanatory factors in relation to pupil offending in school but, first, it is essential to examine the outcome variables (dependent variables) and gain an understanding of the level and nature of offending reported by Year 10 pupils in Cardiff.

This is the first study in over 20 years in the UK that reports, in such detail, individual and between-school differences in pupil offending rates in schools (the last being *Fifteen Thousand hours*; Rutter *et al.* 1979). Prevalence of pupil offending in school refers to the percentage of pupils who have ever reported offending, while frequency of pupil offending is a measure of how often the pupil reports committing the said offences or offence over the time period, which, in this research, was over a period of approximately 12 months. When examining between-school differences the rates used will be the percentage of pupils in the school's Year 10 population who report offending in school. This chapter will also report regarding the prevalence of pupils' general offending by school (i.e. offending that does not necessarily occur in school), giving an indication of the level of general offending by each school's Year 10 population.

Offending

This section will focus on pupil offending in schools. Table 4.1 indicates the prevalence and frequency of pupil offending in schools for the whole Year 10 pupil population examined in this study. Several categories of offending in schools have been used which include personal crime and property crime. These include theft, assault, vandalism, robbery and breaking into the school. However, these categories are not exhaustive and do not include all crimes which may occur in schools. This may lead to an under-representation of how much offending occurs in schools in this study (for example, car theft and offences of a sexual nature were not included). In the study, pupils in the 20 schools in Cardiff reported 1,705 offences. Of these offences, 412 thefts, 764 assaults, 457 acts of vandalism and 72 serious offences (acts of robbery and school break-ins) were reported.

Table 4.1 indicates the following regarding the level of pupil offending in the Year 10 population in Cardiff's schools:

- One in five pupils reports committing an offence in school.
- Approximately one in eight pupils reports committing an assault in school.
- The majority of those who reported offending in school have offended more than once.

Sex differences

Table 4.1 shows the prevalence and frequency of offending among pupils by sex in the Year 10 population in Cardiff. This shows that generally, in schools, boys offend more prevalently than girls. The following can be said:

- Approximately one in four males reports offending in schools compared with approximately one in eight females.

- Only 0.2 per cent of females report robbery, and only 0.1 per cent reports breaking in to their schools. However, very few males or females have committed these offences.

- The average rates of offending (lambda) by pupils in schools are not that different for males and females, being 2.9 and 2.7 respectively.

- Of the high frequency offenders (those who have committed six or more crimes), males are represented more than twice as much as

Table 4.1 Offending in schools in the total population

School offending	Prevalence*	Prevalence by no. of offences**						Lambda***	n****
		1	2	3	4	5	6+		
Population									
Theft	6.0	2.7	1.5	0.4	0.2	0.4	0.9	2.5	2,874
Assault	13.2	7.3	2.5	0.8	0.6	0.3	1.4	1.6	2,871
Vandalism	6.7	3.0	1.5	0.6	0.3	0.2	1.1	2.4	2,863
Robbery	0.7	0.4	0.1	0.0	0.0	0.0	0.2	2.3	2,815
Break-in	0.7	0.5	0.1	0.0	0.0	0.1	0.1	1.3	2,821
All offences	20.3	9.2	4.1	1.7	0.9	0.9	3.5	3.0	2,889
Males									
Theft	7.7	3.3	2.1	0.5	0.3	0.3	1.2	2.8	1,452
Assault	18.6	9.8	3.6	1.2	0.9	0.5	2.4	2.4	1,449
Vandalism	8.3	3.8	1.6	0.7	0.1	0.3	1.2	2.7	1,446
Robbery	1.1	0.6	0.1	0.1	0.0	0.1	0.3	3.7	1,419
Break-in	0.8	0.3	0.2	0.0	0.0	0.1	0.1	2.6	1,421
All offences	26.9	12.1	5.3	2.2	1.2	1.1	5.0	2.9	1,462
Females									
Theft	4.2	2.2	0.8	0.3	0.0	0.3	0.6	2.6	1,422
Assault	7.7	5.2	1.3	0.4	0.3	0.0	0.5	1.8	1,422
Vandalism	5.2	1.9	1.4	0.5	0.5	0.1	0.9	2.9	1,417
Robbery	0.4	0.3	0.1	0.0	0.0	0.0	0.0	1.3	1,396
Break-in	0.1	0.1	0.0	0.0	0.0	0.0	0.0	0.0	1,400
All offences	13.6	6.4	2.9	1.1	0.5	0.7	2.0	2.7	1,427

Notes:

   * Percent of juveniles who have committed the crime.

  ** Percent of all juveniles who have committed the crime once, twice, etc.

 *** Average crimes per offender. Lambda is underestimated. The maximum count for separate categories of crime is 6 (i.e. reports of 6 or more crimes are all counted as 6). For 'All crimes' the maximum count of crime is 30 (i.e. 5 categories times maximum frequency of 6).

**** n is the number of pupils in the survey who responded to this question.

females. Some 5 per cent of the males report offending six or more times compared with 2 per cent of females.

Similarly to general offending behaviour (as shown in Chapter 2), males are more likely to report offending in school than females.

Between-school differences

Table 4.2 indicates the percentage of Year 10 pupils who report offending in each school. This table shows that schools clearly experience differences in the percentages of pupils that report having offended in school. Indeed, in terms of proportions some schools appear to have three times as many pupils who report offending than others do. In the school with the highest level of pupil offending, 31.7 per cent of pupils report offending in school. This means that almost one in three pupils has offended in the school during the last year. This is in comparison with just 10.5 per cent of pupils who reported offending in the school that experiences the lowest level of overall pupil offending. This equates to just over one in 10 pupils who has reported offending in school. The more serious categories of offending, which include school break-in and robbery, seem to cluster in the 11 schools which experience the highest level of overall pupil offending prevalence in school. The six schools which experience the lowest overall rates of pupil offending experience almost no pupils who report serious offences (robbery and school break-in) in schools. This table indicates that some schools have a higher percentage of pupils who report having offended than others do. This may mean that they will also experience a greater proportion of pupils who offend frequently, in schools, as well. Table 4.2 indicates the number of pupils who admit at least one offence in each offending category.

The following can be said from Table 4.2:

- Ten times as many pupils report they have committed theft in the school that experiences the highest rate of theft in comparison with the school that experiences the lowest rate of theft by pupils.

- There are four times as many pupils who report assault in the school with the highest rate of pupils reporting assault, compared with the school that experiences the lowest rate of assault.

- There are approximately 13 times as many offenders who report vandalism in the top school than in the bottom school.

Table 4.2 Percentage of pupils who report offending in schools by offence type: between-school differences

School	Theft	Assault	Vandalism	Robbery	Broken into school	Overall offending in schools	Rank (overall)
Thomas	10.0	22.4	13.8	0.0	0.0	31.7	(1)
Parker	8.1	18.0	12.6	1.8	0.9	30.6	(2)
Ruddock	12.9	14.3	7.9	1.5	0.0	27.1	(3)
Shanklin	8.1	17.8	10.3	1.1	2.2	26.5	(4)
Robinson	8.9	20.5	5.7	0.8	1.7	26.0	(5)
Morris	2.5	20.3	8.9	1.3	1.3	25.3	(6)
Henson	10.8	17.7	6.3	1.7	3.4	24.8	(7)
Bennett	7.2	13.5	7.2	0.0	0.0	23.2	(8)
Jenkins	5.4	17.6	6.1	0.8	0.8	22.7	(9)
Phillips	5.3	11.3	8.1	0.0	0.0	22.7	(9)
Owen	4.9	17.0	5.5	0.0	0.0	22.4	(11)
Charvis	9.1	16.2	6.6	3.1	1.5	21.8	(12)
Jones	4.9	8.6	8.2	0.4	0.0	18.4	(13)
Peel	4.8	10.8	3.2	0.6	1.0	15.9	(14)
Williams	1.0	9.6	8.0	0.0	0.0	15.7	(15)
Davies	5.0	9.9	7.8	0.0	0.0	15.7	(15)
Luscombe	4.2	10.3	4.3	0.0	0.0	15.1	(17)
Llewellyn	2.9	8.0	4.0	0.0	0.0	12.6	(18)
Sweeney	3.8	5.0	6.9	0.6	0.0	11.2	(19)
Cockbain	1.1	9.5	1.1	0.0	0.0	10.5	(20)
All*	5.1	11.6	5.5	0.5	0.4	20.3	

Note:
*All is the total population in the study.

- Schools in Cardiff clearly show a difference in the percentage of pupils who report having offended in school.

A comparison with past research in the UK is difficult, because of the sparse amount of research that exists. The last study to measure offending rates in terms of between-school differences was the Rutter *et al.* (1979) study. As stated in Chapter 3, the measure of school delinquency employed by Rutter and his colleagues is different in many ways from the measure of pupil offending used in this study. However, Rutter *et al.* (1979) reported that school rates for males varied between 16 per cent and 44 per cent and for females between 1 per cent and 11 per cent. This study replicates the Rutter *et al.* finding that some schools experience a greater prevalence of offenders than others. No other study in the UK, since the Rutter *et al.* study, has reported levels of pupil offending in schools, by school.

Pupils' offending in school compared to pupils' experiences of offending in general

Is there a relationship between pupil offending in general and offending in school at the school level? It is possible to assess this relationship here, because information concerning pupils' general offending was collected as part of the study. Analysis indicates that the range in terms of overall offending between schools is far greater when looking at general offending by pupils in comparison with looking specifically at pupil offending in schools. For example, the range is from 18 per cent of a Year 10 school population at the lowest end, to just over 62 per cent at the top end of the spectrum regarding pupils' general offending behaviour. This is a considerable range and does suggest that schools deal with quite different populations in terms of their general delinquency. It may be the case, then, that schools which serve a more criminally active population may also experience higher rates of pupil offending in school, although the relationship is not perfect.

Figure 4.1 displays a scatter-plot illustrating the relationship between the percentage of pupils who report general offending (i.e. shoplifting, vandalism, assault, car theft, residential and non-residential burglary) and the percentage of pupils who report offending in schools in a between-school comparison. This shows a positive relationship that suggests a school that has a greater percentage of pupils who offend in general is also likely to experience a greater percentage of pupils who report offending in school. This relationship shows a strong and statistically significant correlation ($r. = 0.735$, $p = 0.000$, $n = 20$).

Between-school differences in overall offending rates

Table 4.3 shows the prevalence of offending in schools, among pupils, by school, as well as illustrating the frequency of offending by Year 10 pupils in schools. The offending prevalence rate ranges from 10.5 to 31.7 per cent (those having committed at least one offence). In terms of chronic offenders in schools (those offenders who have committed six or more offences), the table illustrates that those schools that experience the highest prevalence of offenders also tend to contain the greatest percentage of chronic offenders (those who report offending in schools six or more times). The table illustrates that some schools do, indeed, experience greater percentages of pupils who report offending in schools and of pupils who report offending frequently in schools than others.

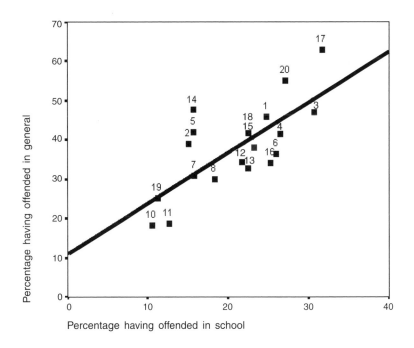

Figure 4.1 Scatterplot indicating the relationship between prevalence of general offending by school and prevalence of offending in school

Table 4.3 Overall pupil offending prevalence in school by school

School	Prevalence (%)	Frequency of offending (percent)						Lambda
		1	2	3	4	5	6+	
Thomas	31.7	10.3	8.6	1.4	1.4	1.4	8.5	4.1
Parker	30.6	9.8	6.7	5.0	1.7	0.0	7.4	3.6
Ruddock	27.1	14.1	3.2	2.6	0.6	1.3	5.0	3.3
Shanklin	26.5	6.4	7.4	2.1	1.6	2.6	6.3	3.9
Robinson	26.0	14.9	2.2	2.2	0.7	0.7	5.1	3.3
Morris	25.3	13.5	3.5	2.4	1.2	2.4	2.4	2.8
Henson	24.8	8.4	3.3	4.1	0.0	1.6	7.3	4.1
Bennett	23.2	6.7	7.8	1.7	0.0	0.9	6.1	3.2
Jenkins	22.7	14.3	2.6	1.9	0.6	0.0	3.7	3.0
Phillips	22.7	10.4	5.2	1.9	0.6	0.0	4.5	3.2
Owen	22.4	11.8	6.5	1.2	0.6	1.2	1.2	2.2
Charvis	21.8	5.6	7.1	1.0	1.0	0.5	6.5	5.2
Jones	18.4	9.1	4.0	1.2	1.6	0.8	1.6	2.5
Peel	15.9	7.2	3.1	1.9	0.6	0.9	2.1	2.6
Williams	15.7	10.3	2.1	0.5	1.1	0.0	1.6	2.6
Davies	15.7	8.0	1.9	1.0	1.0	1.0	2.9	2.7
Luscombe	15.1	10.3	1.6	0.8	0.0	1.6	0.8	2.1
Llewellyn	12.6	7.3	3.2	0.0	1.1	0.5	0.5	2.2
Sweeney	11.2	4.3	2.5	1.2	0.6	0.6	3.0	3.8
Cockbain	10.5	6.5	1.0	1.0	1.0	0.0	1.0	2.2

There is a positive, statistically significant and fairly strong correlation ($r = 0.52$, $p = 0.001$, $n = 20$) between offender prevalence in schools and the average number of offences each offender commits (lambda), indicating that schools that experience a greater prevalence of offenders in school are also most likely to experience a greater proportion of offenders who offend frequently in school. Schools that have more pupils who report having offended in them are more likely to contain offenders who offend at a high frequency.

The nature of offending in Cardiff's schools

Previous studies very rarely say much in detail regarding what types of offences occur in school. This section will provide information regarding the nature of offending in secondary schools. It will illustrate what is stolen in schools, how serious assaults are in schools, where offences take place and how often offenders are caught and reported in school. This section will thus present a clearer picture of the problem of offending in schools by Year 10 pupils.

Many offences occur in classrooms

Questions relating to where theft, vandalism, assault and robbery occurred were included in the survey. A breakdown of the results, from these questions, is shown in Table 4.4, which shows the following:

- The majority of offences regarding theft, vandalism and robbery occur in the classroom.
- Assaults commonly take place on the school playground or playing fields.
- School toilets appear to be a target for vandalism.

From this analysis it may be that crime prevention measures should be focused on the classroom, where it appears the majority of theft, vandalism and robberies occur. In terms of preventing assaults,

Table 4.4 Where did pupils offend last time (per cent)?

Place	Theft	Vandalism	Assault	Robbery
One of the entrances to the school	0.6	9.2	12.6	6.3
A hallway or stairs in the school	1.9	9.2	15.6	12.5
In the school cafeteria/hall	5.6	2.7	3.2	6.3
School toilets	2.5	21.1	3.0	12.5
School car park	0.6	8.6	2.2	6.3
School playing fields	3.1	6.5	20.4	0.0
School playground	3.1	11.4	26.3	25.0
Classroom	79.5	29.2	15.1	31.3
Gym/changing rooms	3.1	1.6	0.5	0.0
Other	0.0	0.5	1.1	0.0
Total	100	100	100	100
n	161	185	380	16
Missing*	11	8	8	5

Note:
*This is made up of pupils who have reported offending in school, but who failed to specify where.

it would appear that greater supervision during breaks of the playground and playing fields might help to prevent many assaults.

Few mobile phones were stolen

A follow-up question concerned what pupils, who reported theft in school, stole the last time (see Table 4.5). This showed, in conjunction with Table 4.4, that 79.5 per cent of thefts occurred in the classroom and the items most commonly stolen relate to school equipment. This category includes pens, pencils, rules, pencil cases, folders and schoolwork. One in nine reported stealing money, CDs, books, videos or tapes. An obvious way to cut down on such offending is to discourage strongly such items from being carried in schools. Few pupils reported stealing mobile phones in school.

Table 4.5 What did you steal last time?

Object	Percent
School equipment	55.2
CDs, tapes, books, videos, etc.	12.6
Money	11.2
Electronics (PC, TV, Walkman, etc.)	5.6
Mobile phone	3.5
Make-up	2.1
Food	2.1
Jewellery/watch	1.4
Bag/handbag	1.4
Wallet/purse	1.4
Weapon (knife, etc.)	0.7
Motor vehicle (car, moped, etc.)	0.7
Sport equipment	0.7
Cigarettes/lighter	0.7
Computer games/consoles	0.7
Total	100
n	143
Missing*	29

Note:
*This is made up of pupils who have reported theft in school, but did not say what.

Clearance rates in schools are relatively good

School authorities catch one in four violent offenders in school, and some are reported to the police (see Table 4.6). This is a much higher clearance rate than experienced in general society. For example, Wikström (2002) reported that, for general offending (i.e. not necessarily in school) in Peterborough, of those who had offended about 10 per cent were caught by the police. A possible explanation for higher clearance rates of pupil offenders in schools (by school authorities) may be that, in schools, there are restricted groups of subjects who may offend and the staff of the school may possess a greater knowledge of potential suspects.

Very few violent offenders reported using a weapon in their last offence. One in 50, who report assaulting used a knife in their last assault. This is a very small number who report using a knife, when considering the total population in the sample.

Table 4.6 Key characteristics of violent assaults: clearance rates and weapons used

Incident characteristics	Percent	Comment
Weapon use		
No weapon used	92.2	
Weapon used	6.8	
Knife	1.9	
Other sharp instrument*	0.8	
Blunt instrument**	4.0	
Other	1.1	
Total	100.0	$n = 372$, Missing cases*** = 8
Caught by school or police		
Yes, by school authorities, no police	21.7	
Yes, caught and reported to the police	4.6	
Not caught	73.6	
Total	100.0	$n = 368$, Missing cases*** = 12

Notes:

   * For example, razor or broken bottle.

  ** For example, a cricket bat or iron bar.

*** Pupils who have reported committing an offence but who failed to respond to these follow-up questions.

Frequent offenders in school commit many different types of offence

> In spite of years of tireless research motivated by a belief in specialisation, no creditable evidence of specialisation has been reported. In fact, the evidence of offender versatility is overwhelming (Gottfredson and Hirschi 1990: 91).

Pupils who report offending frequently in school also report committing a variety of different types of offence (see Figure 4.2), indicating that high-frequency offenders in schools are versatile rather than specialised. This is a finding that is consistent with much other criminological research (for example, Wolfgang *et al.* 1972; Klein 1984; Sampson and Laub 1993; Farrington 1997). Similarly, those pupils who report offending frequently are more likely to have committed serious offences (robbery and school break-in) in school. In terms of crime prevention in schools, it may be beneficial to target high-rate offenders. However, as mentioned above, there may be certain (situational) measures that can be taken which target certain types

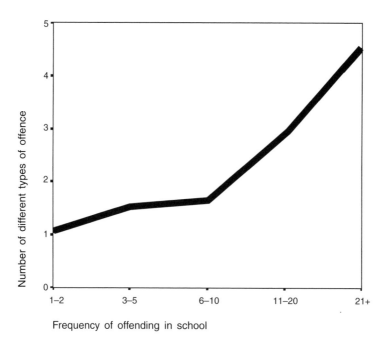

Figure 4.2 Mean number of different types of crime committed in school by frequency of offending

of offence in schools, which may reduce those types of offences (for example, mobile phone theft). Individuals are unlikely to pursue specialised paths in offending in schools.

The findings presented in Table 4.7 indicate that there are significant relationships between having committed one type of crime and having committed other types of crime in schools (i.e. versatility). A factor analysis was carried out (shown in Table 4.8) to illustrate the patterns in the relationships between offence types. This analysis identified two factors. The first can be labelled common offences in school (including theft, assault and vandalism). The second can be labelled offences of a more serious nature, which include robbery and breaking into the school. This categorisation of serious offences will be referred to in the chapters that follow. The two factors are correlated ($r. = -0.25$). This indicates that those who commit serious offences in schools are also most likely to commit common offences. The findings also indicate that those who commit common offences only are a far larger group than those who commit more serious offences. Cross-tabulating the two categories shows that 19.5 per cent of the total population have reported committing a common crime only (one or more of theft, vandalism or assault), while just 0.9 per cent of the total population have committed both (at least one) common offence and (at least one) offence of a more serious nature. Only 0.3 per cent of the population reported a more serious offence and not an offence of a common nature. However, not all crime types are included in this study. Thus, there is a possibility that pupils could have committed other (not included) types of crime (both common and serious).

Table 4.7 Zero-order correlations, frequencies of offending in schools categories

Offence	Theft	Assault	Vandalism	Robbery	Break-in
Theft	1.00				
Assault	0.18	1.00			
Vandalism	0.28	0.19	1.00		
Robbery	0.19	0.11	0.14	1.00	
Break-in	0.17	0.14	0.12	0.36	1.00

Note:
All correlations significant at 0.01 level or better; $n = 2,795$; Missing $= 308$ (9.9 per cent of sample).

Table 4.8 Factor analysis (oblique rotation), frequencies of offending categories

Offending categories	Factor 1 (common offences)	Factor 2 (crimes of a more serious nature)	h^2
School theft	<u>0.70</u>	−0.26	0.50
School assault	<u>0.62</u>	−0.14	0.38
School vandalism	<u>0.75</u>	−0.12	0.57
School robbery	0.21	<u>−0.82</u>	0.67
School break-in	0.20	<u>−0.82</u>	0.68
Eigenvalue	1.76	1.04	
Explained variance	35.10	20.80	

Inter-factor correlation: −0.25

Note:
Loadings of 0.4 and over are underlined.

Pupils who offend in school are more likely to be victimised in school

The risk of being a victim of crime in school is much higher for pupils who offend in school. This is consistent with previous criminological research, which has focused on the offending and victimisation link (see Sampson and Lauritsen 1990; Wittebrood and Nieuwbeerta 1999; Wikström 2002). Table 4.9 shows associations between all types of offending and victimisation. The association between assault and being a victim of violence is strongest.

The fact that those who offend in school are also most likely to be victimised in school may have important policy implications. Pupils who offend most frequently are also most likely to be repeatedly victimised and, as Wikström (2002) argues for this group, the role of offender and victim may well become hazy. This blurring may indicate that these pupils require programmes of social intervention. However, it should be stated that for this group it would be prudent to intervene prior to Year 10 (for a discussion of potential early intervention measures for crime prevention, see Wikström and Torstensson 1999), perhaps focusing on parenting, family factors and the early education system.

Table 4.9 Per cent of school offenders also victimised in school, by offence type and total (examining both prevalence (phi) and frequency (r))

Combinations	Per cent	Sig.	Phi	r
Victimised by theft				
Theft offenders	11.5			
Others	4.9	0.000	0.10	0.29**
Victimised by vandalism				
Vandalism offenders	18.1			
Others	5.2	0.000	0.14	0.33*
Victimised by violence				
Violent offenders	30.7			
Others	6.9	0.000	0.27	0.31***
All victimisations				
Offenders	46.2			
Non-offenders	21.5	0.000	0.23	0.16**

Notes:
  * Significant at 0.10 level.
  ** Significant at 0.05 level.
  *** Significant at 0.01 level.

Summary

This chapter has illustrated the level and nature of pupil offending among the Year 10 population in the 20 secondary schools in Cardiff. It has illustrated the extent to which the level of pupil offending varies between schools and between individuals. The following summarises some of the central findings regarding pupil offending in schools:

- One in five pupils reports having offended in school in the year time period.
- Boys have a greater prevalence of offending than girls (approximately twice as prevalent).
- There is a wide variation between schools regarding pupils' prevalence and frequency of offending.
- Pupils who offend frequently also tend to commit many types of offences. Pupils can therefore be considered versatile in their offending habits.

- Very few violent assaults in schools involved knives or other weapons.
- Classrooms seem to be a focus of a large amount of offending.
- Pupils who offend in school are more likely also to report being victimised in school.

Pupil offending is the dependent (or outcome) variable used in this book. This chapter has provided a thorough investigation of pupil offending in schools illustrating both between-school and between-individual differences. The results shown in this chapter will now be investigated with regards to a wide array of possible explanatory factors in the chapters that follow.

Chapter 5

Neighbourhood context

Neighbourhood contextual effects

The importance of neighbourhood contextual effects in relation to individual offending behaviour and risk of victimisation has been of critical interest to criminological researchers (Shaw and McKay 1969; Kornhauser 1978; Sampson and Groves 1989; Bottoms and Wiles 1997; Brooks-Gunn *et al.* 1997; Wikström 1998; Ingoldsby and Shaw 2002). Neighbourhoods, it is argued, can exert an influence on offending behaviour and victimisation risk through structural characteristics which, in turn, influence the effective operation of social processes such as social control and cohesion (Sampson and Groves 1989; Sampson *et al.* 1997; Wikström 2002). Structural characteristics refer to elements of the neighbourhood that include low socio-economic status, high population turnover and racial and ethnic heterogeneity (Shaw and McKay 1969). It is postulated that these characteristics have an effect on social processes such as control and social capital building, which may influence individuals' propensity to offend.

As stated in Chapter 3, the strength of neighbourhood influences on offending behaviour is a contentious issue (see also Martens 1993). Ingoldsby and Shaw (2002) state that, traditionally, the effects of neighbourhood have been thought to be indirect when considering the developmental pathways of individuals in early childhood and to become more direct in adolescence. In early childhood, when the individual may not come into regular and independent contact with the neighbourhood, the area of direct socialisation is the home. As the child moves towards and into adolescence, the more likely are they to become increasingly independent of the family and spend more time in the neighbourhood and, as such, to be exposed to high-risk, or criminogenic, behaviour settings that the neighbourhood may produce. Generally, this traditional argument fails to address the influence the neighbourhood has on parents and their parenting behaviour and in turn how these parenting behaviours affect child rearing. For example, do neighbourhoods influence the parenting that individuals receive, and is there possibly a recurring cycle where parenting styles are replicated through the generations, which could vary spatially and influence individual offending behaviour?

It is hypothesised that schools with a high average composition of pupils who come from disadvantaged neighbourhoods may experience a greater rate of pupil offending. One reason for this might be poorer social processes in the pupil community (possibly imported from the wider community), and the absence of, for example, high levels of control and social capital in the school, which may prevent offending. There could also be problems attracting good teachers to schools that deal with the most socially disadvantaged and challenging pupils. Pupils from disadvantaged neighbourhoods may experience poorer levels of control and monitoring generally in everyday life, which means that greater individual offending propensities due to this lack of community or family control may be imported into the school. It can be postulated that pupils from disadvantaged communities may be more likely to offend and, as a result, schools with a high proportion of pupils from disadvantaged communities may experience a higher rate of offending. This could become a self-fulfilling prophecy. In schools that have a high proportion of pupils from more disadvantaged neighbourhoods, rates of offending may be higher, which, in turn, may make the school context less conducive to learning and, thus, may affect pupils who may otherwise not offend (i.e. a spreading effect).

The index of multiple deprivation

The measure of pupils' neighbourhood (area of residence structural risk) used in this chapter is based on the index of multiple deprivation for Cardiff (Cardiff Research Centre 2002). This measure was devised by an Oxford University Index Team who produced an index of deprivation that could more accurately identify local areas of deprivation in Wales (National Assembly for Wales 2000). The index of multiple deprivation is based upon a weighted score including measures of income deprivation (25 per cent), employment deprivation (25 per cent), health deprivation and disability (15 per cent), education, skills and training deprivation (15 per cent), housing deprivation (10 per cent) and geographical access to services (10 per cent). This measure is arguably a more accurate and reliable measure of the situation in Cardiff in 2001–2, when the study took place, than the 1991 census data. There are several reasons why this is the case. First, there has been substantial redevelopment and gentrification in Cardiff since 1991; this is particularly true in central Cardiff. Secondly, the index of multiple deprivation is a much more up-to-date measure than 1991 census data.

The main disadvantage of using this index of multiple deprivation is that it is a measure at the enumeration division or ward level. This can be considered a disadvantage because ward boundaries are artificial and usually do not exist in space. Also, the measures do not account for the possibility of pockets or hotspots of deprivation or advantage that may exist inside these boundaries. This is a problem of many studies researching area influences and offending. Raudenbush and Sampson (1999) call for more refined measures of community and neighbourhood to be developed which they refer to as the field of 'ecometrics'.

Despite these measurement issues, there are distinct areas of advantage and disadvantage in Cardiff. The boundaries of areas shown in Figure 5.1 represent 'real' areas in the sense that people in Cardiff refer to deprived areas like Ely (the 'Ely riots' during the 1980s) and relatively advantaged areas such as Radyr and St Fagans – so, in a sense, these areas are part of everyday life in Cardiff. The measure of pupils' area of residence structural risk score is imperfect, but it should give us a guide as to how pupils' areas of residence differences are related to individual differences (and, later in the book, between-school differences) in offending behaviour.

The creation of the pupils' area of residence structural risk score

This section will describe how the pupils' area of residence structural risk score was created using the IMD2000 data. The construct is based on IMD scores for the 28 neighbourhoods in Cardiff. This was possible due to pupils assigning themselves a neighbourhood in the questionnaire and then also answering a question regarding their street name. This latter question was asked so that the researcher could more accurately assess and code which ward pupils lived in. While coding the data, it was noticeable that 144 pupils came from areas surrounding the city, from places like Penarth, Sully, Llantwit

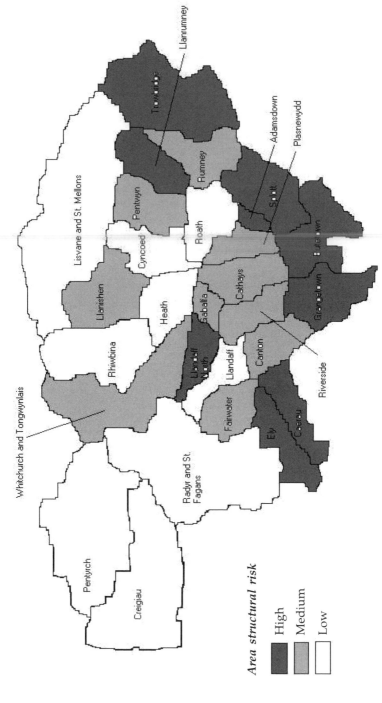

Area structural risk

High
Medium
Low

Figure 5.1 Cardiff electoral wards by distribution of area structural risk

Major, Barry and Caerphilly. This meant that deprivation scores were included for these areas using the Welsh index of multiple deprivation statistics (National Assembly for Wales 2000). In total, 35 neighbourhood scores were included. These neighbourhoods range in population from just over 2,000 to over 12,500 people in each electoral division. Grouping the IMD2000 scores into seven groups of five scores each created the construct. For example, the low-disadvantage group was based on the five lowest ward-disadvantage scores and the high-disadvantage group was based on the five highest ward-disadvantage scores. The distribution and number of pupils in each grouping are shown in Table 5.1.

Table 5.1 indicates that approximately 30 per cent of pupils live in areas of highest structural risk and approximately 30 per cent of pupils live in areas of structural advantage in terms of neighbourhood of residence. Figure 5.1 indicates where these areas are. Those living in areas that score −3 to −2 are considered areas of relative advantage (white shaded areas) those in areas −1 to +1 are considered areas of balance or medium scores (mid-shaded areas), and areas +2 to +3 are considered areas of structural risk (dark shaded areas). It should be noted that areas outside Cardiff that are included in the following analysis, are not included in this map. This is a relatively

Table 5.1 Number of boys and girls by area of residence structural risk groups

Area of residence structural risk	Boys (n)	Girls (n)	Total (n)	%
−3 (lowest)	279	239	518	16.9
−2	291	203	494	16.1
−1	79	99	178	5.8
0	154	156	310	10.1
+1	317	340	657	21.4
+2	205	197	402	13.1
+3 (highest)	257	252	509	16.6
Total	1,582	1,486	3,068	100.00
Missing data: 35*				

Note:

* Pupils living outside the Cardiff area and also those whose handwriting was illegible.

small population (*n* = 144; 4.6 per cent) in comparison with the total sample.

Figure 5.1 indicates that there are clusters of disadvantaged areas around the Cardiff Bay area, which is South Cardiff. These areas include Grangetown, Splott, Butetown and Adamsdown. Areas of North Cardiff tend to be more advantaged relatively. Areas such as Pentyrch, Radyr and St Fagans, Rhiwbina and Lisvane are all relatively advantaged. Generally, as one moves north from the bay area levels of disadvantage tend to diminish. However, areas like Ely, Caerau, Llanrumney and Trowbridge are also areas of relative disadvantage. This map gives an idea of the distribution of the areas of disadvantage (structural risk) in Cardiff under investigation.

Pupils' area of residence structural risk in relation to offending behaviour in schools

Table 5.2 indicates that there are very few statistically significant relationships between a pupil's area of residence structural risk and their offending prevalence in school. Only vandalism and overall offending in school have significant relationships (and these are weak, as illustrated by the gamma association measures). Boys appear to be more affected than girls regarding the relationship between area of residence structural risk and offending behaviour in school. There are statistically significant relationships regarding boys' theft, vandalism and overall offending prevalence in schools and their area of residence structural risk. Area of residence structural risk appears to be significantly related to the prevalence of females who assault in schools.

Table 5.3 shows that pupils' area of residence structural risk is related to the frequency of overall offending and assault in schools (for the total population). For males, area of residence structural risk is related to frequency of overall offending, theft and assault, and for females there are no discernible relationships between their area of residence structural risk scores and offending behaviour in schools. This suggests that, in terms of frequency of offending behaviour in schools, males appear to be more sensitive to their neighbourhood than females. However, where the relationships in Table 5.3 are statistically significant, the amount of variance explained by pupils' area of residence structural risk score is small, being always under 1 per cent (as indicated by eta^2).

Table 5.2 Pupils' area of residence structural risk by offending in school

| School offending | Area of residence structural risk** | | | | |
	Low (%)	Medium (%)	High (%)	Sig.	Gamma
Population					
Theft	5.5	5.3	7.6	n.s.	–
Assault	11.5	13.5	15.0	n.s.	–
Vandalism	5.5	6.3	8.7	0.020	0.16
Serious offences*	1.0	1.1	1.6	n.s.	–
Overall offending	18.3	19.9	23.5	0.021	0.10
Males					
Theft	7.6	5.6	10.7	0.019	0.12
Assault	15.9	20.7	20.0	n.s.	–
Vandalism	6.1	7.7	12.0	0.004	0.24
Serious offences*	1.5	1.6	3.0	n.s.	–
Overall offending	23.9	27.1	31.1	0.051	0.12
Females					
Theft	2.9	4.9	4.7	n.s.	–
Assault	5.9	7.2	10.4	0.045	0.20
Vandalism	4.8	5.1	5.7	n.s.	–
Serious offences*	0.2	0.5	0.2	n.s.	–
Overall offending	11.3	13.5	16.3	n.s.	–

Notes:
* Serious offences is a composite measure of school break-in and robbery.
** Area of residence structural risk divided into low (scores –3 to –2), medium (scores –1 to +1) and high (scores +2 to +3) risk groups.

Multiple regression analysis

Regression analyses indicate the relationships between sex and area of residence structural risk and pupils offending prevalence and frequency in school. Table 5.4 reports a logistic regression model, which indicates that both area of residence structural risk and sex are significant predictors of Year 10 pupil offending prevalence in schools in Cardiff. However, the amount of variance the model explains in total is weak, ranging from 1 to 6 per cent depending on the offence type under scrutiny and which method of estimating explained variance is used (i.e. either using the Cox and Snell R^2 or the Nagelkerke R^2).

Table 5.3 Frequency of offending in school by pupils' area of residence structural risk score, means, significance and eta^2

Pupils' area of residence structural risk score	Overall offending	Theft	Assault	Vandalism
Population				
Low	0.50	0.12	0.22	0.14
Medium	0.53	0.12	0.24	0.14
High	0.73	0.18	0.32	0.18
Sig.	0.013	n.s.	0.032	n.s.
Eta^2	0.003	–	0.002	–
Males				
Low	0.64	0.17	0.30	0.13
Medium	0.71	0.13	0.39	0.15
High	1.04	0.25	0.47	0.24
Sig.	0.008	0.050	0.047	n.s.
Eta^2	0.006	0.004	0.004	–
Females				
Low	0.31	0.05	0.11	0.14
Medium	0.36	0.12	0.11	0.13
High	0.40	0.10	0.17	0.13
Sig.	n.s.	n.s.	n.s.	n.s.
Eta^2	–	–	–	–

Table 5.5 shows ordinary least squares (OLS) multiple regressions for frequency of offending in school in relation to sex and area of residence structural risk. This indicates that pupils' area of residence structural risk is a significant predictor of frequency of overall offending and assault. In these two models the explained variance is low at just 2 per cent, for the other models concerning theft and vandalism, only a very marginal amount of variance is explained (being closer to 0 than 1).

Summary

The analyses reported in this chapter suggest that pupils' area of residence structural risk is a weak predictor of pupil offending in school. However, it is likely that pupils' area of residence is indirectly

Table 5.4 Logistic regression: sex and area of residence structural risk, offending prevalence in schools, odds ratios (exp (B)) and significance levels

	Overall		Theft		Assault		Vandalism	
	Exp. (B)	Sig.	Exp. (B)	Sig.	Exp. (B)	Sig.	Exp. (B)	Sig.
Sex	0.42	0.000	0.52	0.000	0.36	0.000	0.59	0.001
Area risk	1.19	0.000	1.18	0.043	1.20	0.001	1.27	0.002
Chi-square (prob.)	92 (0.000)		20 (0.000)		86 (0.000)		21 (0.000)	
−2 log	2,798		1,272		2,137		1,378	
Cox and Snell R^2	0.03		0.01		0.03		0.01	
Nagelkerke R^2	0.05		0.02		0.06		0.02	

Table 5.5 OLS regression: sex and area of residence structural risk, overall frequency of offending in schools, standardised beta coefficients and significance levels

	Overall		Theft		Assault		Vandalism	
	Beta	Prob.	Beta	Prob.	Beta	Prob.	Beta	Prob.
Sex	−0.119	0.000	−0.060	0.001	−0.141	0.000	−0.027	n.s.
Area risk	0.050	0.005	0.028	n.s.	0.045	0.013	0.027	n.s.
Multiple $R^2 \times 100$	2		0		2		0	

associated with pupil offending in school. Mediating mechanisms are likely to exist on which neighbourhood exerts a greater effect, which in turn will be more directly related to pupil offending in school. It is likely that as one measures factors closely related to individual social action, one will produce models with greater predictive power (i.e. indicating a greater explained variance).

In a cross-sectional study such as this, it is difficult to measure the extent the pupils' area of residence plays in the individual's social development. More refined measures of area of residence structural risk, which measures the influence of area of residence on individual development and behaviour, would provide stronger predictive power. The fact that an aggregate measure of pupils' area of residence based on official data employing artificial ward boundaries relating to thousands of people still explains a small amount of variance is a finding which suggests investigations of ecology and individual offending are certainly warranted. As science continues to advance more sophisticated analysis will doubtless further unravel the exact effects of ecological factors on human development and behaviour. In this book, this measure of area of residence structural risk will be shown as it impacts on other factors which are more strongly associated with pupil offending behaviour.

Chapter 6

Family social position

This chapter will examine the relationship between pupils' family social position and their offending behaviour in school. The family an individual grows up in will impact greatly on their life and their own personal position in society. Family characteristics will greatly influence young people's position in society, as the family is the primary arena of socialisation. Measures of family social position include 1) the pupils' family socioeconomic status; 2) family composition (parental composition and family size); and 3) ethnic background. It is argued that all these factors influence an individuals' socialisation, which may in turn influence individual offending. The central investigative aims for this chapter are as follows:

1 Does pupils' family social position predict offending behaviour in school?
2 Are schools with a high proportion of pupils in disadvantaged family social positions likely to have higher levels of pupil offending behaviour?

The chapter will be split in to five main sections. The first will examine family socioeconomic status (based on parental occupational status), the second will investigate family composition (based on parents' marital status), the third will look at family size (number of siblings), the fourth will focus on ethnicity/immigrant status and the fifth will look at the creation of a family social position risk score that will be examined in relation to offending in schools.

Family socioeconomic status and offending in schools

> A judge may have before him a succession of five or six juvenile offenders in a single day whose families are in dire poverty. He may therefore conclude that poverty is the sole or at any rate the chief cause of their anti-social behaviour. But for each delinquent who comes from economically underprivileged homes a law-abiding youngster can be produced whose family also is handicapped by inadequate income (Glueck and Glueck 1952: 9).

The issue of whether there is a relationship between socioeconomic status and individual offending has caused much debate in criminology. Tittle *et al.* (1978: 643), after an analysis of 35 separate studies, concluded: 'the overall results show only a slight negative relationship between class and criminality, with self-report studies reflecting lower associations than official statistics studies.' This conclusion suggests that there is not a strong link between social class and offending and leads Tittle *et al.* (1978) to entitle their famous paper 'The myth of social class and criminality'. Contrary to this, Braithwaite (1981) argued that there is a relationship between social class and offending. Perhaps most notably for this study, he argued: 'Of the 53 studies of class and juvenile crime which have been reviewed here, 44 showed lower class juveniles to have substantially higher offence rates than middle class juveniles' (1981: 38). Thornberry and Farnworth (1982) contended on the basis of empirical research (*n* = 567, response rate = 58 per cent) using the Philadelphia birth cohort of 1945 (see Wolfgang *et al.* 1972) that juveniles' social class is indeed weakly related to offending, but that the relationship between social status (class) and adult criminality is strong and inverse. More recently, Dunaway *et al.* (2000) found that, regardless of how crime or class was measured, social class exerted little direct influence on adult criminality in the general population. This debate continues today in the realms of criminology and the media, where the relationship is often assumed but is not often proven. This may be due to the preconceived popularity of assuming that social class is a major cause of offending. Such preconceptions are rarely based in evidence, as Tittle *et al.* (1982: 437) comment: 'The myth to which the title of our paper referred is precisely the tendency of sociologists, criminologists, and laymen to begin with the preconceived notion – the prejudice – that lower-class people are characterised by pejorative traits such as immorality, inferiority, and criminality.'

This section will investigate the relevance of family social class on offending in schools for the Year 10 pupils surveyed. As argued in Chapter 3, such individual background factors may have relevance for pupil offending in schools, because they have been suggested previously in criminology to be important predictors of offending behaviour in general.

The measure of pupils' family socioeconomic status

A measure of social class was derived by asking questions about both the individual's parents' (or step-parents') occupational status. The pupils were asked to give specific information regarding what their father's/step-father's job was, and what their mother's/stepmother's job was. From this information, the parent with the highest occupational status was used as an indication of family socioeconomic status. The family socioeconomic status score was divided into four main categories. These were 1) unemployed; 2) lower working-class and working-class workers (including unskilled workers, skilled manual workers and low-rank white-collar employees); 3) middle class, including officials, public servants (such as teachers) and small-scale entrepreneurs; and 4) upper middle class, including large-scale entrepreneurs, high-rank officials, private sector professionals (lawyers and accountants) and other high-rank white-collar workers. The classification by socioeconomic status can be seen in Figure 6.1.

There may be some issues regarding reliability and validity of the measure of pupils' family socioeconomic status. For instance, some parents who have no jobs and who are classified as unemployed could be relatively wealthy if they are, for example, pensioners or have inherited wealth. However, an attempt has been made to validate the family socioeconomic status measure by exploring its relationship with reported car ownership. Figure 6.2 shows that, the higher the socioeconomic status, the more often the subject's family has two or more cars. This finding gives an indication that the socioeconomic status scale may identify some of the key differences in the subjects' family socioeconomic status.

Family socioeconomic status is not related directly to pupils' offending in schools

Table 6.1 indicates that pupils' family socioeconomic status is not significantly related to prevalence of pupils' offending behaviour in school. ANOVA tests regarding the relationship between the frequency of offending in schools (for all types) and pupils' family socioeconomic

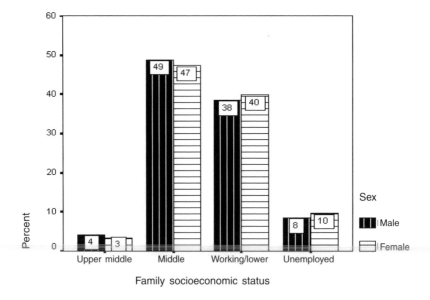

Figure 6.1 Family socioeconomic status, distribution (n = 3,087)

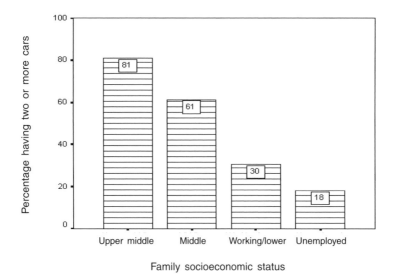

Figure 6.2 Per cent families with two or more cars by family socioeconomic status

Table 6.1 Self-reported offending prevalence in schools by family socioeconomic status

Offence type	Unemployed	Working/ lower working	Middle	Upper middle	Sig.
	(%)	(%)	(%)	(%)	
Theft	5.6	6.2	5.9	6.2	n.s.
Assault	16.2	14.5	11.9	12.4	n.s.
Vandalism	6.4	7.6	6.6	1.8	n.s.
Serious offences*	2.2	1.2	1.0	0.9	n.s.
Overall offending**	23.1	21.7	19.2	16.8	n.s.

Notes:
 * Serious offences is a composite measure of pupils who have broken into school and who have committed robbery at school. This is based on the factor analysis reported in Chapter 4.
** Overall offending in school is a composite measure of all offences measured in school (i.e. theft, vandalism, assault, robbery and school break-in).

status indicated no statistically significant relationships. A possible explanation for this is that the school context may even outclass differences among pupils, due to greater levels of control in school (i.e. schools are a relatively well supervised environment for adolescents) than that which may be found in the pupils' neighbourhoods or home contexts. However, such a finding is consistent with a breadth of criminological research which is succinctly summarised by Entner Wright *et al.* (1999), who state: 'empirical studies have consistently found weak or nonexistent correlations between individuals' SES and their self-reported delinquent behaviour.'

The analysis in this section adds to this breadth of criminological research by indicating that, for self-reported pupil offending in school, there are no significant relationships with pupils' family socioeconomic status regarding both prevalence and frequency of offending. Those who believe social class differences to be a direct cause of offending have to answer this question: why is it that there are so many people from low socioeconomic status backgrounds who do not offend? Social class may, of course, be associated with mediating factors that may explain offending behaviour in school. This is a point made eloquently by Glueck and Glueck (1952: 4):

Since poverty operates differently on different types of persons, it should be obvious that something more than poverty (or unemployment, or the fluctuations in the price of some standard commodity, or the vicissitudes of the business cycle) must be examined before the role of poverty in the genesis of delinquency and crime can be understood.

Such relationships between socioeconomic status and other factors are examined later in this book.

Pupils' family structure and offending in schools

The question as to whether family composition influences youth involvement in crime is a contentious question in criminology, in the media and in politics. With reference to Cardiff, this is particularly interesting, when considering politics on a national scale. In 1994 the Secretary of State for Wales, based on the Cardiff suburb of Saint Mellons, suggested that local single mothers were responsible for social decline, scrounging, rising levels of anti-social behaviour and crime levels (see BBC, September 2002 at http://news.bbc.co.uk/1/hi/wales/2264473.stm). The solution, according to John Redwood (the then Secretary of State for Wales), was a two-parent family unit. This speech became keynote in the Conservative government's 'Back to basics' campaign of 1994. Good 'old-fashioned' family values were seen as key in restoring morals among the nation's youth and thus reducing crime and disorder.

In this study, the measure of family structure is based on whom the pupil lives with. This can be said to be a measure of family disruption and within this category falls the area of parental absence, as opposed to a measure of parental relations. Loeber and Stouthamer-Loeber (1986: 78) in their meta-analysis of 'families and delinquency', argue: 'taking all the evidence together, marital discord has a stronger relationship with delinquency and aggression than parental absence.' However, their review of the literature does suggest that family disruption in terms of parental absence may be a potential risk factor for delinquency. In this study there is no measure regarding marital discord, but the family unit, in terms of composition, can be investigated. Wikström (2002) found that family disruption was linked to an increased general offending risk for girls but not for boys. However, no previous research in the UK has investigated this in relation to pupil offending behaviour in schools. A hypothesis can be made (based on previous criminological research – see above) that those pupils from complete families will offend less in the school environment. A proposed mechanism as to why this may be the case is that pupils from complete families experience better nurturing, including stronger family bonds and a more stable and secure background.

Pupils' family structure (parental composition)

In order to gain a measure of pupils' family structure, in terms of parental composition, a question was asked regarding whom the individual usually lives with. The responses were 1) both mother and father; 2) only my father; 3) only my mother; 4) my father and step-mother (or father's girlfriend); 5) my mother and step-father (or mother's boyfriend); and 6) my foster parents. A seventh option was provided, where the young people could indicate whom they lived with if it was none of these options. Figure 6.3 indicates that, in Cardiff, approximately two in three juveniles live with both their mother and father. In Peterborough, Wikström (2002) found that 62.7 per cent of juveniles lived with their biological parents. Such a finding may further confirm the reliability of the self-report tool employed in this investigation.

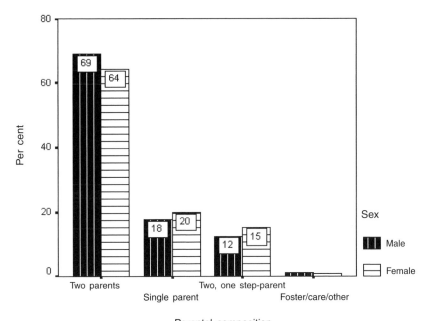

Figure 6.3 Pupils' parental composition, distribution ($n = 3,087$)

Males and females from split families offend more in schools

In this section the effect of living with both parents (complete) will be assessed in comparison with those pupils who live in split families (this includes all categories other than the two biological parents' category). Figure 6.4 indicates that males and females who live in a complete family are less likely to offend in schools than those who live in split families.

This relationship, shown in Figure 6.4, is statistically significant for both males and females. Regarding male offending in school, there is a statistically significant association with parental composition ($p = 0.030$, phi = 0.057). However, this relationship between pupils' family structure and overall offending in schools is stronger for females ($p = 0.001$, phi = 0.089). Thus, there is an association between whether pupils live in split or complete families and overall offending in schools. This association is true for both sexes.

Pupils from disrupted families are more likely to have offended in school

Pupils' parental composition is associated with some types of offending (particularly assault and overall offending) in school. These relationships are illustrated in Table 6.2. For the whole population there are statistically significant relationships between pupils' family structure and prevalence of school assault, and overall offending in

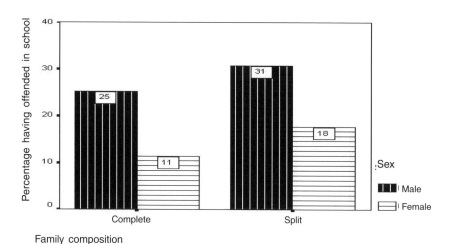

Figure 6.4 Percentage having offended in school by family composition and sex

schools. However, when looking at male offending, overall offending in school is not statistically significantly associated with pupils' family structure (it is, however, significant at the 0.10 level). For assault in schools, living with two biological parents would appear to limit a pupil's risk of offending. For females, there is a statistically significant relationship between parental composition and school assault and overall offending. Thus, certain types of offending in school are associated with pupils' parental composition. Living with two biological parents may reduce the likelihood of pupils' offending prevalence in schools. ANOVA tests regarding the relationship between the frequency of offending in schools (for all types) and pupils' parental composition indicated no statistically significant relationships.

When considering the attack on single parents, it may be interesting to compare family composition in terms of single parents and two parents, where one is a step-parent. Table 6.2 indicates that pupils living with two parents, where one is a step-parent, report a slightly higher prevalence of offending for most types of offending behaviour in schools. It may be that two-parent families, where one is a step-parent, may have higher levels of marital discord or family discord. Such a conclusion would be in keeping with Loeber and Stouthamer-Loeber's (1986) assessment of extant criminological research which, they suggest, generally minimises the importance of the relationship between broken homes and individual offending behaviour and stresses that marital discord is a stronger risk factor.

Pupils' family size and offending in schools

The relationship between family size and individual offending behaviour has long been noted in criminological research. Hirschi (1991) argues that family size has proven to be a powerful predictor of delinquency but despite this, it has been largely ignored in modern criminology. Sampson and Laub (2003) suggest this neglect is a mistake, since a range of research relating family size to occupational achievement and investment in education has shown it to be a significant predictor. Rutter *et al.* (1998) argue that being reared in a family with at least four children has long been noted as a significant risk factor for delinquency. West and Farrington (1973) found that the percentage of delinquents among boys, with four or more siblings, was significantly higher than among the remainder of the sample. Their investigation also suggests: 'it was the actual size

Table 6.2 Family structure (parental composition) by prevalence of offending in school (by total population and sex)

Offence type	Two parents (%)	Single parent (%)	Two, one step-parent (%)	Foster/ care/ relatives (%)	Sig.	Gamma
Population						
Theft	5.5	6.7	7.3	4.0	n.s.	–
Assault	11.5	14.7	19.2	20.0	0.000	0.21
Vandalism	6.4	6.9	7.6	8.0	n.s.	–
Serious offences	1.1	0.8	1.9	0.0	n.s.	–
Overall offending	18.7	22.3	25.7	23.1	0.010	0.14
Male						
Theft	7.4	7.4	11.2	0.0	n.s	–
Assault	16.5	22.0	25.9	16.7	0.000	0.20
Vandalism	8.0	7.0	11.2	8.3	n.s.	–
Serious offences	1.9	1.3	3.7	0.0	n.s.	–
Overall offending	25.2	28.9	34.1	23.1	0.089	0.13
Female						
Theft	3.5	6.2	4.3	7.7	n.s.	–
Assault	5.9	8.3	13.7	23.1	0.000	0.32
Vandalism	4.6	6.9	4.7	7.7	n.s.	–
Serious offences	0.2	0.4	0.5	0.0	n.s.	–
Overall offending	11.3	16.5	18.9	23.1	0.007	0.23

of the sibship rather than its composition by age or sex which was associated with future delinquency' (1973: 32). However, Blumstein et al. (1986) comment on the fact that family size appears related to delinquency, but that explanation as to why this may be the case is not yet established. This section will investigate the relationship of family size with pupil offending in schools. The criminological literature would suggest the following hypothesis: pupils from larger families will be more likely to offend in schools than pupils from small families. Possible reasons for this, from a control theory perspective, may relate to higher levels of parental monitoring which may be achievable in smaller family units. Family bonds may also be stronger in small families because parents may be able to focus more attention on their children. If young people feel well monitored by and bonded to their family this may reduce their risk of offending in school.

The measure of family size is based on how many siblings the individual has. This was gained by asking how many brothers and sisters each pupil had; step and half-brothers and sisters were included. Figure 6.5 illustrates how many brothers and sisters pupils have in Cardiff. The mean number of siblings per pupil in Cardiff in this Year 10 population is 2.2. The chart indicates that one in 20 is an only child and that one in five has four or more siblings. This latter figure may appear quite high, but this is probably due to the number of step and half-brothers and sisters these young people may have. The following section will investigate the relationship between pupils' family size and their offending behaviour in schools.

Pupils' family size is related to offending in schools

Table 6.3 illustrates that, for the overall population, it seems that family size is associated with pupils' offending prevalence in school for all types of offending with the exception of serious offences (this may be due to the small number of pupils who report having committed robbery in school and who have broken into school). However, looking at males and females, it can be seen that this relationship between family size and offending in schools appears

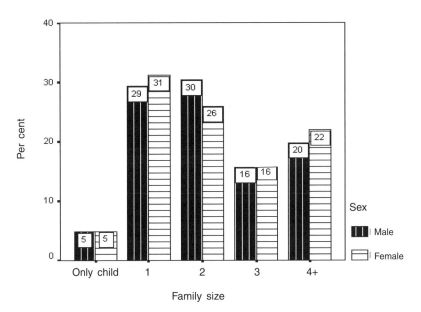

Figure 6.5 Family size (number of siblings), per cent ($n = 3,098$)

to weaken. For males, family size is only related to overall offending prevalence in school. For females, the relationship holds for school assault, vandalism and overall offending. This indicates that family size may exert a slightly stronger association with female offending prevalence in school, in comparison with males. ANOVA tests revealed no statistically significant relationship between family size and frequency of offending for both boys and girls and when taken together.

Table 6.3 Prevalence of pupils' offending in schools by family size (number of siblings), total population and by sex

Offence type	Only child	1	2	3	4+	Sig.	Gamma
	(%)	(%)	(%)	(%)	(%)		
Population							
Theft	1.5	5.8	4.9	7.0	8.1	0.020	0.15
Assault	8.3	10.5	13.1	15.4	17.0	0.001	0.17
Vandalism	4.5	5.6	5.2	8.9	9.5	0.003	0.19
Serious offences	0.0	1.0	1.0	1.6	1.6	n.s.	–
Overall offending	11.9	17.1	18.7	24.3	26.5	0.000	0.18
Male							
Theft	3.0	8.0	6.1	9.1	9.9	n.s.	–
Assault	13.6	16.7	17.4	21.2	22.7	n.s.	–
Vandalism	7.6	8.0	6.2	9.5	11.3	n.s.	–
Serious offences	0.0	1.9	1.6	3.2	2.2	n.s.	–
Overall offending	19.4	25.5	24.0	28.8	33.8	0.021	0.12
Female							
Theft	0.0	3.7	3.5	4.9	6.3	n.s.	–
Assault	3.0	4.6	8.0	9.7	11.7	0.003	0.29
Vandalism	1.5	3.3	4.1	8.4	7.7	0.005	0.31
Serious offences	0.0	0.2	0.3	0.0	1.0	n.s.	–
Overall offending	4.5	9.0	12.3	19.8	19.6	0.000	0.30

Pupils' family ethnicity/immigrant status

There is a wide literature on the possible influence of individual ethnic status in relation to crime. There are certainly variations, on ethnic grounds, regarding prison populations in the UK. For example, in England and Wales young black males are some five to six times as likely as whites to be imprisoned (Rutter *et al.* 1998). However, this is not a measure that necessarily reflects an association between ethnicity or race and offending. Previous self-report surveys that investigate ethnicity/race in relation to offending behaviour indicate little variation in offending rates between groups. Graham and Bowling (1995) show small variations between white and black populations in the UK. However, they do show that people in the UK from South Asia (India, Pakistan and Bangladesh) report lower rates of offending. Flood-Page *et al.* (2000) found no statistically significant relationships overall between different ethnic groups and offending behaviour. This finding was true for both males and females. However, they did find lower rates of offending among Indian, Pakistani and Bangladeshi females. This sample was very small (i.e. just 20 female Bangladeshi respondents). Wikström (2002) found that females of Asian origin reported less offending in the Peterborough Youth Study. There is a debate regarding whether minority groups under-report offending behaviour (see discussion by Hindelang *et al.* 1981).

Wilson and Herrnstein (1985: 459) argue that, in one sense, such group differences on ethnic and race grounds are not particularly interesting. They state that for almost any behaviour there is more variation among individuals within a given ethnic group than there is between the members of two groups. They argue that individual differences 'are far greater in magnitude than the differences between the average traits of any two groups'. However, as Wilson and Herrnstein go on to state, group differences may be of great significance. It is of interest to see whether certain ethnic groups are more prone to offend than others and then to investigate possible mechanisms that may cause these differences. This may not be due to their ethnicity directly, but it could be to do with other factors (for example, the group's situation in society). This section will investigate offending by two measures of ethnicity. The first regards the pupils' family immigrant status and the second regards family ethnic background.

Immigrant status and pupils' offending behaviour

The measure of immigrant status was gained by asking the pupils about where they were born and where their respective parents were born. The logic behind such a course of investigation stems from a field of knowledge which suggests that first- and second-generation immigrants may live in areas of the city that are socially disorganised and which, as a result, may experience higher rates of offending (see, for example, Park *et al*. 1925; Shaw and McKay 1969). The constructs used in this study regarding immigrant status are as follows: 1) UK (both parents and the subject are born in the UK); 2) first generation (the subject is born abroad); and 3) second generation (at least one of the parents born abroad, while the subject was born in the UK). Figure 6.6 shows the percentage by immigrant status of the pupils in Year 10 in Cardiff.

There are no significant relationships between immigrant status and pupils' offending behaviour

An investigation of the relationship between pupils' immigrant status and offending prevalence in schools revealed no statistically significant differences between groups. Figure 6.7 illustrates this finding. There is, however, a noticeable trend which suggests males from first-generation immigrant families may be more likely to offend in schools (this relationship was, however, statistically insignificant). This finding of insignificance regarding immigrant status group differences concurs with Wikström's (2002) findings regarding pupils' immigrant status in relation to general offending behaviour.

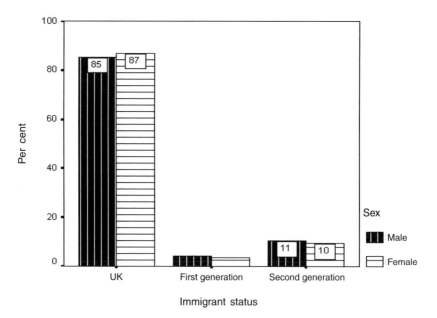

Figure 6.6 Pupils' immigrant status, per cent (*n* = 3,101)

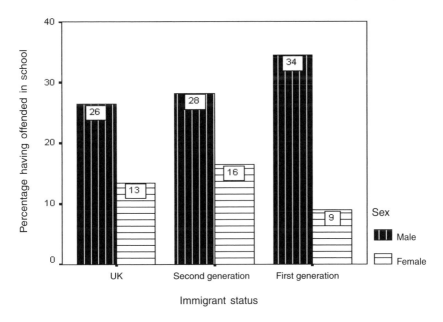

Figure 6.7 Overall offending prevalence in school by immigrant status and sex

An investigation regarding pupils' immigrant status and offending frequency, in school, for all offence types and overall, also showed no statistically significant immigrant status group differences concerning offending behaviour.

Pupils' ethnic background

Classifying the individuals into UK, Asians and foreign non-Asians created the construct of ethnic background. This classification was based on questions which asked where (which country) each of the pupils' parents was born. There are several reasons for using this particular classification: 1) the Asian group is the largest ethnic background in Cardiff among the pupils with an immigrant background (a fact confirmed in Chapter 2 looking at census data); and 2) it is of interest to test the hypothesis that Asians (particularly females) do not offend as much as other ethnic groupings (see Graham and Bowling 1995; Wikström 2002). Although these findings were not related to offending in schools, it is of interest to see whether they hold for offending behaviour in schools. The other immigrant groups in Cardiff account for a relatively small proportion of the population.

Thus it was judged inappropriate (and statistically unreliable) to present findings in more detail for the non-Asian group. In the non-Asian group the great majority come from (in rank order): continental Europe, Africa, the Middle East and North America. This group is quite diverse and cannot really be classifiable as an ethnic group because they may only share a foreign background.

When looking at Figures 6.6 and 6.8, it can be seen that the proportion of UK-origin pupils is higher by ethnic background (only slightly) in comparison with immigrant status. The reason for this is that there is a small group of subjects who were born to two UK parents during a temporary period abroad. For instance, being an armed forces child is a typical example of this. The family ethnic background measure includes both first and second-generation immigrants. The latter provide the largest group, meaning that the subjects have been born and brought up in the UK. However, as stated above, immigrant status influences on offending prevalence and frequency in schools were found to be statistically non-significant.

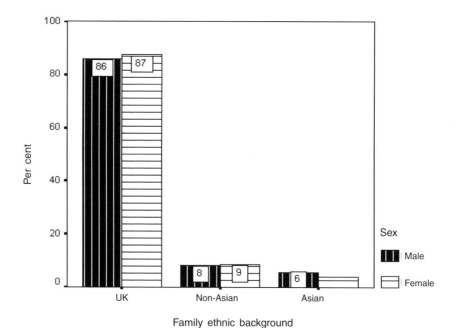

Figure 6.8 Pupils' family ethnic background, percent (n = 3,099)

Pupils' family ethnic background and offending in schools

An analysis of pupils' family ethnic background and its relationship with offending prevalence in school revealed only small and non-significant variations between the compared groups. This is illustrated in Figure 6.9.

Table 6.4 shows no statistically significant relationships between pupils' ethnic background and offending behaviours in schools. Asian females do not appear to offend significantly less in schools than females from the UK or who are classified as foreign non-Asian.

ANOVA tests concerning the relationship between the frequencies of pupil offending in schools (for all types) and pupils' family ethnic backgrounds indicated no statistically significant relationships. The analysis in this section indicates no statistically significant direct relationships between immigrant and ethnic status in relation to all types of offending prevalence and frequency in school. This may suggest notions of ethnically/racially based criminal subcultures are flawed. There is no evidence in this study that there are offending differences between different ethnic or immigrant status groups.

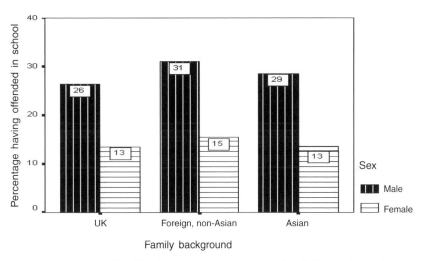

Figure 6.9 Overall offending prevalence in school by subjects' ethnic background and sex

Table 6.4 Prevalence of offending in school by pupils' family ethnic background, total population and sex

Offence type	UK (%)	Foreign, non-Asian (%)	Asian (%)	Sig.	Gamma
Population					
Theft	5.7	8.8	5.8	n.s.	–
Assault	12.7	16.7	16.5	n.s.	–
Vandalism	6.7	8.4	4.3	n.s.	–
Serious offences	1.0	2.3	2.2	n.s.	–
Overall offending	20.0	23.0	22.3	n.s.	–
Male					
Theft	7.3	12.6	6.0	n.s.	–
Assault	18.0	23.6	21.4	n.s.	–
Vandalism	8.2	10.9	6.0	n.s.	–
Serious offences	1.6	4.6	2.4	n.s.	–
Overall offending	26.4	31.0	28.6	n.s.	–
Female					
Theft	4.1	5.2	5.5	n.s.	–
Assault	7.5	10.3	9.1	n.s.	–
Vandalism	5.2	6.0	1.8	n.s.	–
Serious offences	0.3	0.0	1.8	n.s.	–
Overall offending	13.5	15.4	12.7	n.s.	–

Family social position risk score

Creation of the family social position risk score

Three constructs are used in the creation of the family social position risk score. They were all shown to have varying degrees of association with pupil offending in schools. The constructs to be included are family composition, family size and family socioeconomic status. Family ethnicity is not included in this score. Family socioeconomic status was split up in the following manner: 1) those pupils who have parents who are unemployed were scored as +1; 2) those pupils who have working-class or lower working-class parents were scored as 0; and 3) those pupils who have middle-class/upper middle-class backgrounds were scored as –1. On this scale it is argued that –1 is a low-risk score, and +1 is a high-risk score, with 0 being a medium-risk score.

Family composition was also treated along similar lines: 1) subjects living in a complete (biological) family were scored as –1; 2) those living with single parents or in split families with a step-parent or with a parent's boyfriend or girlfriend were scored as 0; and 3) those living with foster parents or relatives were scored as +1. The argument was that those living in the last group are more at risk than those living in the two first categories, and those in split families are more at risk. Those 1) with no siblings were scored –1 on the family size risk scale; 2) individuals with 1–3 siblings were scored as 0; and 3) those with four or more were scored as +1. Summing these three variables then created an index of structural risk. This index varies between –3 and +3, with +3 indicating high risk (living with foster parents/relatives, from low social class and with four or more brothers and sisters. (*Note:* in this study half and step-siblings count.) In the +3 category there were only four individuals. The distribution of the risk score is shown in Figure 6.10. This shows that the majority of individuals come from low or medium-risk family backgrounds. For the purposes of later analysis, the scale was reduced into three categories. Those scoring –3 and –2 were scored as –1 (being from low-risk backgrounds). Those scoring –1 and 0 were scored as 0, indicating that they came from medium-risk backgrounds, and those scoring +1 to +3 were scored as +1, indicating that they came from relatively higher-risk backgrounds (overall in this latter category $n = 367$).

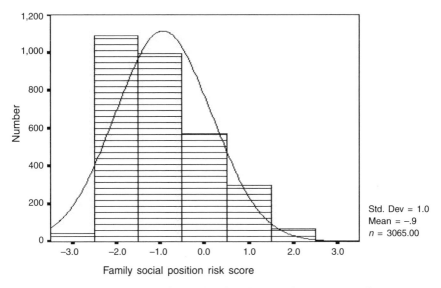

Figure 6.10 Distribution of pupils' family social position risk-protective scores (–3 = protective, +3 = risk)

Family social position is related to pupils' offending behaviour in school

Table 6.5 shows the relationship between pupils' family social position risk score and offending in school, for the whole population and by sex. This indicates significant associations for all types of offending in school with the exception of theft when considering the total population.

For males, there are significant associations between pupils' family social position and assault, vandalism and overall offending. For females there is a significant association between family social position and theft. Indeed, the only non-significant relationship is with vandalism in school. Measures of association between family social position and overall offending in schools are generally stronger for females, suggesting the possibility that females are more affected by their family social position than males. Table 6.5 indicates that there are relationships between pupils' family social position and pupils' prevalence of offending behaviour in schools although, as

Table 6.5 Family social position risk-protective score by offending prevalence in schools for the whole population and by sex

School offending	Low (%)	Medium (%)	High (%)	Sig.	Gamma
Population					
Theft	5.0	6.4	7.9	n.s.	–
Assault	10.0	13.9	20.7	0.000	0.23
Vandalism	5.1	7.9	6.9	0.020	0.15
Serious offences	1.2	0.9	2.4	0.054	0.11
Overall offending	16.7	21.4	28.3	0.000	0.19
Male					
Theft	6.4	8.9	8.2	n.s.	–
Assault	14.4	20.3	26.7	0.001	0.22
Vandalism	6.1	10.3	6.7	0.020	0.16
Serious offences	2.1	1.7	2.9	n.s.	–
Overall offending	22.5	28.7	36.3	0.002	0.19
Female					
Theft	3.5	3.8	7.6	0.044	0.20
Assault	5.2	7.4	16.3	0.000	0.34
Vandalism	4.0	5.4	7.1	n.s.	–
Serious offences	0.2	0.0	2.1	n.s.	–
Overall offending	10.2	13.8	22.6	0.000	0.26

will be shown later, the measures of association are fairly weak in comparison with other measures employed in this study.

Table 6.6 shows the relationship between the pupils' family social position risk-protective score and *frequency* of offending behaviour in schools. It can be seen that, for the total population (both boys and girls), family social position is significantly related to frequency of overall offending, assault and vandalism. However, for males the only statistically significant relationship is between family social position and frequency of assault. For females, statistically significant relationships are apparent between family social position and frequency of overall offending, theft and assault. Where significant relationships exist between frequency of offending in schools and pupils' family social position, they are fairly weak, with family social position explaining 1 per cent of the variance or less in terms of frequency of offending behaviour.

This section has shown that family social position of pupils does explain some differences in both the prevalence and frequency of

Table 6.6 Pupils' family social position risk score by offending frequency (per capita) in schools by population and sex, means, significance and eta^2

	Overall offending	Theft	Assault	Vandalism
Total population				
Protected	0.45	0.11	0.20	0.11
Balanced	0.62	0.14	0.27	0.18
Risk	0.75	0.21	0.38	0.15
Sig.	0.009	n.s.	0.005	0.049
Eta^2	0.00	–	0.00	0.00
Males				
Protected	0.63	0.15	0.29	0.12
Balanced	0.87	0.19	0.41	0.22
Risk	0.87	0.19	0.54	0.12
Sig.	n.s.	n.s.	0.013	n.s.
Eta^2	–	–	0.01	–
Females				
Protected	0.25	0.05	0.10	0.09
Balanced	0.34	0.09	0.11	0.15
Risk	0.65	0.22	0.25	0.17
Sig.	0.001	0.003	0.007	n.s.
Eta^2	0.01	0.01	0.01	–

pupils' offending behaviour in schools. Those from backgrounds of greater risk (i.e. large family size, disrupted family backgrounds and from low socioeconomic status backgrounds) report having offended in schools at a greater rate, as well as offending at a greater frequency than those from protected family backgrounds. These relationships are statistically significant for most types of offending behaviour in school but are also fairly weak, as indicated by the gamma measures of association and the eta^2 measures that explain variance between family social position and offending behaviour in schools.

The relationship between area of residence structural risk and pupils' family social position score

Table 6.7 shows the relationship between aspects of pupils' family social position and area of residence structural risk. It indicates that pupils from higher-risk family social positions more often live in areas of high structural risk. This relationship, whereby pupils from less advantaged family social positions live in less advantaged residential areas, is to be expected generally. However, the relationship is imperfect, as the analyses in Tables 6.7 and 6.8 illustrate.

The strongest relationship in Table 6.7 is between pupils' family socioeconomic status and area of residence structural risk. The table also shows that there are tendencies for pupils who live in split families and in bigger families to live in more disadvantaged areas. There appears to be a significant relationship suggesting that those from non-UK backgrounds tend to live in marginally more advantaged neighbourhoods than those from a UK background.

When measures are taken together as the overall family social position risk score it can be seen that those from high-risk family backgrounds are more likely to be located in deprived areas of residence.

These findings are confirmed in Table 6.8. This OLS multiple regression analysis of the influence of family social position factors on area of residence structural risk score shows that by far the strongest predictor of pupils' area of residence structural risk score is family socioeconomic status, followed by Asian family background, split family and large family size. Another analysis was run to include sex, but this proved to be non-significant (with a T-value of 1.6) when controlling for the variables in the model shown in Table 6.6. This confirmed the unsurprising finding that the sex of a child has no influence on where families live.

Table 6.7 Pupils' area of residence structural risk score by family social position variables, means, significance and eta^2

Family social position	Area of residence mean structural risk score
Family social class	
Upper middle class	−1.6
Middle class	−0.7
Working class/lower working class	0.9
Unemployed	1.2
Sig.	0.000
Eta^2	0.17
Family structure	
Two parents (biol.)	−0.2
Two parents (one step-parent)	0.6
Single parent	0.6
Care/relatives/foster	0.8
Sig.	0.000
Eta^2	0.03
Family size	
Only child	0.3
One	−0.3
Two	−0.0
Three	0.2
Four plus	0.6
Sig.	0.000
Eta^2	0.03
Family ethnicity	
Native	0.1
Foreign, non-Asian	−0.2
Asian	−0.2
Sig.	0.025
Eta^2	0.002
Family social position risk score	
Protected	−0.4
Balanced	0.1
Risk	0.4
Sig.	0.000
Eta^2	0.10

Table 6.8 OLS multiple linear regression: pupils' area of residence structural risk score by family compositional characteristics (family structural risk)

Variable	Standardised beta	T-value	Sig.
Asian family background	–0.08	–4.5	0.000
Large family size	0.05	4.82	0.000
Split family	0.08	2.70	0.007
Low family social class	0.38	22.16	0.000
Multiple $R^2 \times 100 = 17$			

Aggregate-level analysis

This section will investigate the relationship between offending behaviours in school and family social position risk at the aggregate level. In order to do this a mean school structural risk score was derived for each school. The score was derived by transforming the individuals' family social position risk-protective score (the creation of this was described above) and then aggregating the score for each school, thus gaining a mean of pupils' family social position risk-protective score for each school. Thus, each school has a mean pupils' family social position risk score, which may also be referred to as a mean family social position risk score for each school. These school scores were then compared with the rates of pupil offending in schools. The results are shown below.

The relationship between mean school family social position risk and offending in school

Figure 6.11 indicates a relationship between the school's mean pupils' family social position score with overall offending prevalence in schools. Schools that are composed on average of pupils from more risky family backgrounds are shown to have a higher proportion of pupils who report having offended overall in schools. Schools with pupils from a structurally disadvantaged family background (on average) experience higher rates of pupils who report having offended in schools. This finding indicates that pupil composition in terms of pupils' family background can have an effect on offence rates in the school. One factor that may help to explain differences in offending rates between schools may be the composition of the pupils who attend the schools and their family social positions. The present analysis indicates that the family backgrounds of pupils who attend schools may be influential in explaining why some schools experience more pupil offending behaviour than others.

When considering the percentage of pupils who report assault in school and the mean family social position scores of the pupils who attend the school, a similar relationship ($p = 0.008$, $r. = 0.57$) is found as for overall offending in schools. However, the relationships were found to be weaker for vandalism in school and school theft. Family social position appears to be not so important in explaining differences between schools in these cases. This can be shown by the correlations which, for vandalism and theft in schools, are statistically insignificant.

From this analysis overall offending and assault rates can be said to be related to the mean family social positions of the pupils in the school. Schools with pupils who on average come from disadvantaged family backgrounds (larger family size, disrupted parental composition and lower socioeconomic status) generally experience higher overall offending and assault rates. This is not to say that all pupils from structurally disadvantageous backgrounds will offend in school, and nor is it to say that this is a causal mechanism. It is to say, however, that an association can be seen at the aggregate level.

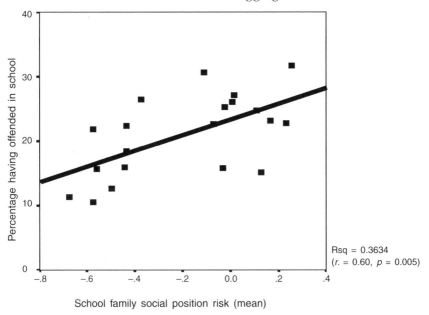

Figure 6.11 Mean school structural risk score by percentage having offended (overall) in school

Multiple regression analysis

It has been shown that, when taken together, the factors that make up a pupil's family social position have an association with the *prevalence* of most types of offending in schools (overall, assault, vandalism and serious offences). For males, family social position is related to *prevalence* of vandalism, assault and overall offending prevalence in schools and, for females, family social position is related to *prevalence* of theft, assault and overall offending.

Pupils' family social position is significantly related to *frequency* of overall offending, assault and vandalism in schools for the total population. For males, there is only a relationship between pupils' family social position and frequency of assault in schools. For females relationships exist between *frequency* of assault, theft and overall offending in schools and family social position. This may indicate that females in terms of *frequency* of offending are more sensitive to their family backgrounds. This chapter has indicated, so far, that, separately, family background factors do not exert a strong influence on pupils' offending in schools, but when taken together they explain pupil differences a little more strongly. This is possibly because the family social position risk score created actually takes greater account of where each individual is positioned in society. It provides a more detailed portrayal of reality by taking account of several family social position factors and incorporating them into one scale. However, this section will examine multiple regression analyses to see which aspects of pupils' family social position most strongly predict offending in schools.

Table 6.9 illustrates a multiple logistic regression analysis, which investigates the explanatory variables used in this chapter in relation to *prevalence* of overall offending, theft, assault and vandalism in schools. The analysis indicates that for all offending in school categories, being female lowers the risk of being involved in offending. For all types of offending in schools, pupils coming from large families are at an increased risk of offending. For overall offending and assault in schools, coming from a split or incomplete family (i.e. not living with two biological parents) also increases the risk of pupil offending in schools. The analysis indicates that pupils' family socioeconomic status and family ethnic background have no statistically significant effect on pupil offending in schools.

Table 6.10 shows an ordinary least squares (OLS) regression with frequency of overall offending, assault, theft and vandalism in schools as the dependent variables. The analysis shows that being female

Table 6.9 Logistic regression: sex and key structural variables, school offending measures, prevalence, odds ratios (exp. (B)) and significance levels

Variable	Overall		Theft		Assault		Vandalism	
	Exp. (B)	Sig.	Exp. (B)	Sig.	Exp. (B)	Sig.	Exp. (B)	Sig.
Female	0.65	0.000	0.72	0.000	0.60	0.000	0.77	0.001
Asian	1.01	n.s.	1.04	n.s.	1.08	n.s.	0.92	n.s.
Split family	1.11	0.029	1.07	n.s.	1.23	0.000	0.99	n.s.
Large family	1.26	0.000	1.24	0.015	1.16	0.017	1.34	0.000
*Family social class**								
Middle	0.79	n.s.	1.40	n.s.	0.87	n.s.	0.32	n.s.
Working/lower working class	0.96	n.s.	1.36	n.s.	0.87	n.s.	1.26	n.s.
Unemployed	1.06	n.s.	1.38	n.s.	1.03	n.s.	1.39	n.s.
Chi-square (prob.)	116.5 (0.000)		26.0 (0.001)		108 (0.000)		33 (0.000)	
−2 log	2764		1261		2099		1360	
Cox and Snell R^2	0.04		0.01		0.04		0.01	
Nagelkerke R^2	0.06		0.03		0.07		0.03	

Note:
*Upper middle class is the reference category.

significantly reduces the risk of overall offending, theft and assault in schools. However, for vandalism, being female has no statistically significant effect for female frequency of offending; rather, being of Asian origin may reduce the risk of vandalism in schools. As shown in the previous logistic regression, Table 6.10 indicates that coming from a large family increases the risk of pupils' offending at a high frequency in schools, for all categories of offending in schools. Coming from a split family, or from a family of low socioeconomic status, has no significant predictive power concerning frequency of offending in schools, when these other family social position factors are controlled for. Thus, when examining these family social position variables, it seems that, when controlling for the other variables, the two most significant predictors of offending in schools that may explain individual differences are sex and family size. However, the total variance explained by sex and the other family social positional characteristics in relation to offending in school by the OLS regression models is modest, ranging between 1 and 2 per cent.

Summary

This chapter has shown how pupils' sex and family social positional characteristics are related to offending in schools. Analyses have shown the relative importance of sex and family social positional characteristics in explaining pupils' individual differences in offending in the school context. Between-school differences have been examined in relation to pupils' family social positional characteristics. Pupil composition in school in terms of pupils' family social positions is

Table **6.10** OLS regression: sex and key structural variables, overall frequency of offending in schools, standardised beta coefficients and significance levels

Variable	Overall		Theft		Assault		Vandalism	
	Beta	Sig.	Beta	Sig.	Beta	Sig.	Beta	Sig.
Female	−0.12	0.000	−0.06	0.001	−0.14	0.000	−0.03	n.s.
Asian	0.00	n.s.	0.03	n.s.	0.01	n.s.	−0.04	0.026
Split family	0.02	n.s.	0.02	n.s.	0.03	n.s.	−0.01	n.s.
Large family	0.08	0.000	0.05	0.011	0.04	0.050	0.08	0.000
Low SES	0.01	n.s.	0.00	n.s.	0.01	n.s.	0.01	n.s.
Multiple $R^2 \times 100$	2		1		2		1	

particularly related to overall offending in schools and for assault in schools.

It has been shown that sex and some family social positional characteristics are significant predictors of pupil offending in schools. However, the regression analyses presented in the last section show that, when all pupils' family social positional characteristics are included in the models, they do not explain a great deal of variation between pupils in their offending. This is a similar finding to Wikström's (2002) finding regarding individuals' family social position and general offending in the Peterborough Youth Study. He argues that: 'There is no obvious reason why social position in society should have a direct impact on adolescent offending' (2002: 76). It seems much more likely that pupils' family social position has an indirect effect on offending, being mediated possibly by its influence on pupils' immediate social situation (e.g. school bonds, family bonds and parental monitoring) and their development of dispositions (e.g. self-control, pro-social values and sense of shame). However, this chapter has illustrated that pupils' family social position and sex are significant, albeit weak, predictors of individual variation in pupil offending behaviour in schools, and also that schools which on average serve pupils who are from more risky family backgrounds tend to experience higher rates of pupils offending overall and reporting assault in school.

Chapter 7

The school context

Criminological inquiry has paid some, but insufficient, attention to the role that schools play in young people's socialisation and offending behaviour (see Rutter *et al.* 1998; and Chapter 3). Gottfredson and Hirschi (1990) recognised the importance of the school as an arena for socialisation in society. They argued that most people are sufficiently socialised in the family context to avoid involvement in crime. They suggest, however, that those not sufficiently socialised by the family may eventually learn self-control and be socialised through the operation of other institutions or systems. In modern society schools are principally given this responsibility. The prime reasons for this, Gottfredson and Hirschi (1990: 105) argue, are:

> As compared to the family the school has several advantages as a socialising institution. First, it can more effectively monitor behaviour than the family, with one teacher overseeing many children at a time. Second, as compared to most parents, teachers generally have no difficulty recognising deviant or disruptive behaviour. Third, as compared to the family, the school has such a clear interest in maintaining order and discipline that it can be expected to do what it can to control disruptive behaviour. Finally, like the family, the school in theory has the authority and the means to punish lapses in self-control.

Schools have an important role to play in the socialisation of pupils and on curbing offending behaviour, but how successful they are may vary (see Rutter *et al.* 1979). Scherer (1978) argues that a high community profile and strong legitimisation combine to make schools the most powerful formal institutions of socialisation in the community, second in influence only to the family. This all suggests that schools are an important context of pupils' development.

Schools may also influence pupils' offending behaviour risk through what Wikström (2002: 122) calls 'contexts of action'. Schools provide a focus for youths to meet and offend or be victimised. For most children, school is a central part of the routine activities of everyday life. School structures the day for five days a week: from the journey to and from school to attending lessons, the day is mapped out and organised. Schools by their very nature bring together potential offenders and victims at the same place and at the same time – sometimes in the absence of capable guardians (for example, breaks, etc.).

Schools also provide the *behaviour settings* (Barker and Gump 1964; Barker 1968) in which these youths mix and act. Schools play an important role in the development of adolescents and also in the contexts in which pupils act. It should be the case that schools with favourable contexts will affect pupils' behaviour in a positive way. A wide array of research has investigated how school context influences pupils' intellectual outcomes (MacBeath and Mortimore 2001; Bryk and Schneider 2002). However, very few studies have focused on the influence of schools on pupils' behaviour (Rutter *et al.* 1998). Hargreaves (2001: 490) argues that this is a weakness in a great deal of school effects research. He argues, based on Aristotle's ideas, that school research should concentrate on both intellectual and moral excellences: 'The purpose of education is to initiate the young into these excellences, through which they acquire the disposition to make sound intellectual and moral judgements and choices.'

Chapter 3 showed that, since 1979, very little research has been done on the influence of schools on pupils' behavioural development in the UK. Rutter and Maughan (2002) contend that the role of schooling in relation to behavioural development and outcomes remains much less fully explored in comparison with measures of educational attainment. This chapter will, thus, aim to explore the relationship between elements of school context with pupils' offending behaviour in schools. As this is a cross-sectional study the focus will be more on schools in terms of pupils' contexts of action. However, it is argued that the findings may inform how schools operate in terms of contexts of development and what factors are important in influencing pupil development.

A particularly difficult problem with researching the influence of schools, or indeed neighbourhoods, regarding their influences on individuals' behaviour is that of disentangling which effects are due to school or neighbourhood characteristics and which are due to individual characteristics (as investigated in Chapters 6 and 7) (see Kornhauser 1978; Wikström and Loeber 2000; Wikström 2002). A central question is to what degree contextual factors influence individual characteristics and vice versa. Schools are, for instance, likely to vary in terms of pupil composition (pupil composition is in itself a contextual factor in which the individual is located). Thus, some schools may attract a great many pupils who display high-risk individual characteristics in relation to others. Interactions between contexts and individual characteristics (i.e. social situational and dispositional characteristics) will be explored later in the book.

School context

In this chapter, five measures relating to school context are examined (see Table 7.1). These measures are based on the pupils' view of their school context. Two particular dimensions of school context are examined in detail. The first is labelled *school climate* and relates to pupils' respect for school authority, view of ethos and a measure examining the pupils' views of their parents' interest in their schooling. These all relate to the general running, organisation and atmosphere of the school. The second dimension examines *pupil relations* and includes measures of pupils' social capital and views of

Table 7.1 Pupils' views of school context, key constructs

Scales	No. items	Alpha
School climate		
Parental interest in schooling*	6	0.70
School ethos*	6	0.77
School authority*	5	0.76
Pupil relations		
Social capital*	4	0.65
School disorder*	4	0.54

Note:
*Scale created by author.

school disorder. These two dimensions are part of what is referred to as school context in the rest of this book.

Parental school interest

Gottfredson and Hirschi (1990) argue that a major reason for the limited success of modern schooling in terms of behavioural outcomes stems from the lack of support and co-operation it receives from families that have already failed in the socialisation process. Pupils whose parents pay little attention to their schooling and do not support the work of schools have been shown to offend more in general in previous research (see Graham and Utting 1996). Heath and Clifford (1980) argue that a measure of parental interest in schooling should be included in school studies, given the positive association with offending found in prior research. Furthermore, Bryk and Schneider (2002) have shown that high levels of parent–teacher trust can improve the educational climate of schools and result in better academic results. This section investigates the relationship between parental school interest and pupils' offending behaviour in schools. The hypothesis is as follows. Pupils whose parents show little or no interest in their schooling will offend more in school. Pupils whose parents show little interest in their education and schooling may think that their parents will never find out what happens in school and, even if their parents do find out, the parents may not care. This absence of parental interest and possible sanction may result in pupils having a greater propensity to offend in school. Therefore, it is likely that schools where parents show little interest will suffer higher rates of pupil offending.

The creation of the parental school interest construct

The parental school interest scale is based on six questions which relate to 1) discussing work with parents; 2) parents helping with homework; 3) parents caring about how well their child does in school; 4) discussing problems at school with parents; 5) parents ability to help with homework; and 6) parents knowing who their child's friends are at school. The scale has a range between 0 and 18, with 18 indicating parents who have little or no interest in their child's education or schooling. A high score on the scale represents parents who hardly ever discuss school work with their children; who never help their children with homework; who have little interest in their child's progress at school; who never discuss school problems with their children; who have little ability to help their children with homework; and who do not know who their children's friends are at school.

The distribution of scores for the parental school interest measure is shown in Figure 7.1, which shows a skew towards strong parental school interest scores (represented by 0 on the scale). This indicates that most pupils perceive their parents to be interested in their schooling.

Pupils whose parents are interested in their schooling generally spend more time on homework everyday
One would expect that a scale testing parental school interest would show that those pupils with parents who have high interest in schooling would on average do more homework. Figure 7.2 confirms this, indicating that those pupils with parents who show great interest in their education and schooling have a greater likelihood of spending at least one hour a day on homework.

Offending in schools is associated with parental school interest
Pupils whose parents take an interest in their education and schooling offend in schools less prevalently than those pupils whose parents show little interest. Table 7.2 indicates that, for the whole Year 10 population, there are statistically significant associations between the

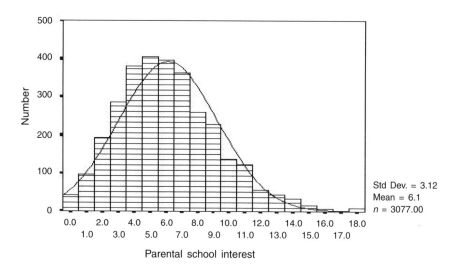

Figure 7.1 Distribution of parental school interest scores

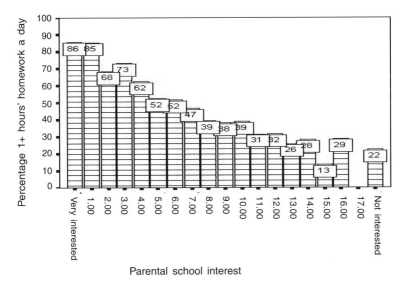

Figure 7.2 Parental school interest by percentage of adolescents who do at least one hours' homework a day

level of parental school interest and pupils' offending prevalence in schools. The grouping of levels of parental school interest scores was achieved by dividing the scale into thirds based on scoring attributed to individuals, thus gaining conceptually satisfactory groupings, as the scores reflect where individuals are on the scale in terms of the answers they give to the questions which make up the construct.

The relationship between parental school interest and offending in schools is similar for both boys and girls. The exception is for serious offences reported by females. It is also noticeable that boys offend at a greater prevalence across all levels of parental school interest scores when compared with girls.

School ethos

The term 'ethos' was coined by Aristotle and, according to the *Oxford English Dictionary*, refers to the characteristic spirit, prevalent tone of sentiment of a people or community. Some have taken ethos to refer to a kind of 'ideal excellence'. However, in this study school 'ethos' refers to a school's character as perceived by the community of pupils that attend it.

Rutter *et al.* (1979) investigated 'school ethos'. They argued that, in many cases, individual actions are less important in their own right

Table 7.2 School offending prevalence by parental school interest and sex

	High (%)	Medium (%)	Low (%)	Sig.	Gamma
		Parental school interest scale*			
Population					
School theft	4.4	6.8	14.6	0.000	0.28
School assault	9.1	15.8	31.4	0.000	0.34
School vandalism	5.3	7.2	19.0	0.000	0.25
Serious offences	1.0	0.9	6.3	0.000	0.23
Overall offending	15.4	23.4	41.0	0.000	0.29
Male					
School theft	6.0	8.3	16.7	0.008	0.23
School assault	13.2	21.8	37.3	0.000	0.33
School vandalism	6.7	8.6	20.7	0.001	0.22
Serious offences	1.7	1.6	8.9	0.000	0.24
Overall offending	20.6	30.7	45.2	0.000	0.29
Female					
School theft	3.0	4.9	11.6	0.008	0.31
School assault	5.6	8.8	23.3	0.000	0.31
School vandalism	4.1	5.6	16.7	0.001	0.25
Serious offences	0.4	0.2	2.5	n.s.	–
Overall offending	11.0	14.9	34.9	0.000	0.24

Note:
*Parental school interest scale grouped into high (scores 0–5), medium (scores 6–12) and low (scores 13–18).

than in the part they play in contributing to a wider school ethos or climate of expectations and modes of behaving. This suggests that pupils' actions taken together could form a general or wider pattern of behaviour or climate. However, in their research they also focused on particular happenings and behaviours as well. The reason for this, Rutter *et al.* (1979: 56) summarised, was:

> The impact for the pupil may derive from the overall ethos, but our concern was equally with the sorts of actions which teachers and pupils could take to contribute towards the establishment of an ethos which would enable all those in the school to function well. This concern necessitated a focus which is at least as much on the specific actions taken by teachers and children as on the more general attitudes which may lie behind them.

Thus, for Rutter *et al.* (1979), the conception of 'ethos' was essentially the climate of the school and everything to do with the operation of the school that contributed to this. This ranged from physical and administrative features of schools, school processes (for instance, group management in the classroom) to 'ecological influences'.

In this research the conception of school 'ethos' is somewhat narrower than in Rutter *et al.* (1979). The focus is on the 'characteristic spirit, prevalent tone of sentiment' of the pupils' perceptions, attitudes and experiences in their schools. This it is argued is one aspect of the school context and climate. However, it is likely that other constructs in this chapter are related to this construct in complex ways. For example, it is likely that, where social capital levels among pupils are high, the prevailing 'school ethos' will also be positive.

The creation of the school ethos construct

The school ethos construct is made up of six questions coded from 0 to 3. The scale ranges from 0 to 18, where 18 represents a negative school ethos. A score of 18 on this scale indicates that the pupil views the school as never being friendly or happy; teachers generally do not encourage them or support them with their work; their opinions are never welcomed in lessons; and there is never good order or behaviour in their classes. These pupils consider the characteristic spirit of the school to be relatively poor. The distribution of school ethos scores is shown in Figure 7.3.

Figure 7.3 indicates that pupils, generally, have a positive idea of their school ethos. Relatively few pupils score above 13 on the scale. Thus, there are relatively few pupils who consider their schools never to be friendly or happy; who never feel supported or encouraged in schools; who never feel their opinions are welcome; or who feel there is never good order or behaviour in their classes.

It can be argued that the school ethos measure employed here is also a measure of the pupils' stake in their school. If pupils feel they are supported, are happy, that people are friendly, that there is good behaviour and order, then the learning environment is likely to be positive and also one in which pupils are more likely to take responsibility and ownership, they are more likely to respect such an environment and therefore less likely to offend in it. It is hypothesised that pupils who perceive a positive school ethos will be less likely to offend in school.

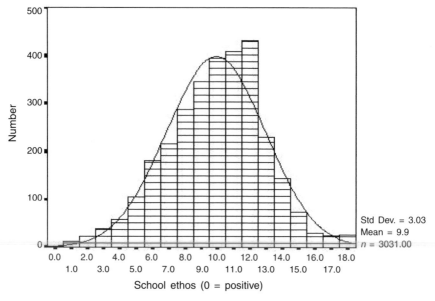

Figure 7.3   Distribution of school ethos scale

Those pupils who view the school ethos positively also think that the schools take the issue of bullying very seriously
A question relating to how seriously the pupils' school treats the issue of bullying was asked. Responses ranged from very seriously, quite seriously to not seriously enough. Those pupils who consider the ethos of the school to be positive should, it is hypothesised, also consider that schools take the issue of bullying very seriously. This is confirmed in Figure 7.4. Pupils who consider the school to have a positive ethos also consider that the school takes the issue of bullying very seriously.

Table 7.3 confirms that pupils who experience and perceive school ethos negatively tend to offend more in schools for all offences, and that this is true for boys and girls. The exception to this rule is serious offences reported by females. However, for all other offences and for overall offending in school, it can be seen that those who consider their school to have a poor ethos are much more likely to report having offended in school.

Pupils' respect for school authority

This section will investigate the relationship between pupils' respect for school authority and their offending behaviour in school. It is

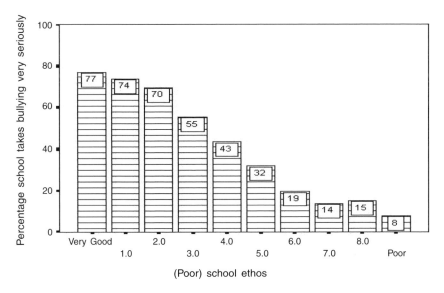

Figure 7.4 Percentage who think their school takes the issue of bullying very seriously, by school ethos

hypothesised that those pupils who understand and respect the school rules and feel that the authorities treat them fairly in school are less likely to offend in school because they believe in the authority that the school wields.

The creation of the construct

The responses for the five-item respect for school authority construct are coded 0 to 3, resulting in a scale ranging from 0 to 15. Those who score 0 on the scale understand the school rules clearly; agree with the school rules; believe that punishments and discipline at school are fair; think that everyone in school is treated the same no matter who they are; and believe that students are treated fairly by most teachers at school. Those who score 15 have little or no respect for school authority; disagree with the rules; do not understand the school rules; and believe that pupils are not fairly treated by the authorities and that some pupils get preferential treatment. The distribution of these scores is shown in Figure 7.5.

Pupils' respect for school authority is related to offending prevalence

Table 7.4 shows that pupils' levels of respect for school authority are statistically significantly related to the prevalence of offending

Table 7.3 (Poor) school ethos by offending prevalence in schools and by sex

	Good (%)	Balanced (%)	Poor (%)	Sig.	Gamma
		(Poor) school ethos scale*			
Population					
School theft	2.6	5.4	10.5	0.000	0.37
School assault	6.9	12.1	20.7	0.000	0.33
School vandalism	3.0	5.7	13.5	0.000	0.44
Serious offences	1.3	0.9	2.3	0.035	0.29
Overall offending	9.4	18.5	33.2	0.000	0.39
Male					
School theft	4.3	7.3	11.2	0.037	0.26
School assault	8.7	17.2	27.8	0.000	0.34
School vandalism	6.1	6.8	15.6	0.000	0.37
Serious offences	2.7	1.4	3.9	0.037	0.27
Overall offending	13.9	24.7	40.1	0.000	0.36
Female					
School theft	0.8	3.5	9.6	0.000	0.53
School assault	5.1	7.1	12.3	0.017	0.28
School vandalism	0.0	4.6	11.1	0.000	0.56
Serious offences	0.0	0.4	0.5	n.s.	–
Overall offending	5.1	12.4	24.7	0.000	0.43

Note:
*(Poor) school ethos scale is grouped into good (scores 0–5), balanced (scores 6–12) and poor (scores 13–18).

in school. This is the case for both males and females, for all offence types in schools, apart from serious offences for girls. The table indicates that, for overall offending prevalence in schools, the measure of association is slightly stronger for females than for males. Therefore, if schools seek to improve the behaviour of pupils, gaining their respect is likely to be a key factor.

Pupils' social capital in school

Coleman (1990) conceptualised social capital as a property of the relational ties among people within a social system (for example, a school). He argued that social capital evolved around sustained social interactions. Thus, it is possible to measure individuals' levels of social capital in terms of their relationships with others. In this

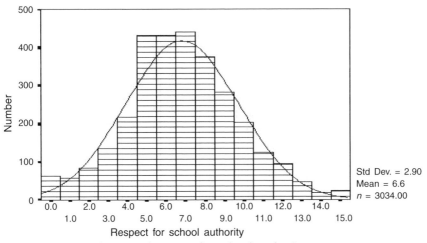

Figure 7.5 Distribution of respect for school authority scores

Table 7.4 Offending prevalence in school by level of respect for school authority

| School offending | Respect for school authority* | | | | |
	High (%)	Medium (%)	Low (%)	Sig.	Gamma
Population					
School theft	2.7	5.6	14.1	0.000	0.46
School assault	8.4	12.7	24.6	0.000	0.33
School vandalism	2.5	6.5	14.8	0.000	0.48
Serious offences	1.8	0.7	2.8	0.003	0.06
Overall affending	11.6	20.1	36.1	0.000	0.37
Male					
School theft	3.1	7.4	17.1	0.000	0.47
School assault	12.1	18.0	33.1	0.000	0.33
School vandalism	3.1	8.2	17.0	0.000	0.46
Serious offences	2.8	1.3	3.9	0.042	0.01
Overall offending	16.3	26.9	44.0	0.000	0.36
Female					
School theft	2.1	3.9	10.6	0.000	0.44
School assault	3.9	7.7	14.5	0.001	0.37
School vandalism	1.7	5.0	12.2	0.000	0.50
Serious offences	0.4	0.2	1.6	n.s.	–
Overall offending	5.9	13.6	26.5	0.000	0.44

Note:
*Respect for school authority scores grouped into high (scores 0–4), medium (scores 5–10) and low (scores 11–15).

study, the measure of social capital is based on the pupils' perception of how they relate to others, in terms of friendship and feeling supported by their classmates. The measure used in this section is closely related to Coleman's notion of social network closure. He argued that interconnectedness among individuals makes it easier for communication to occur. The measure also covers the density of relational ties between pupils, which makes it easier not only to communicate but also to make individual expectations clearer. If pupils have high levels of social capital and are well liked by their fellow pupils, they will be less likely to feel the need to offend. Pupils with high levels of social capital are more likely to feel involved in school, to have a stake in school and are more likely to act in a way where they make decisions based on how colleagues will perceive them. The measure in this section is one of pupils' social capital levels in schools. The scale measures how many close friends pupils have in school, how well they like their classmates and whether they feel they can ask their school friends for help if they find something difficult.

The social capital scale ranges from 0 to 8, with 8 representing pupils who do not like their classmates; who have very few close friends as school; who have very few close friends in their year; and who are unlikely ever to ask their classmates if they need help. This describes a pupil who has very low levels of social capital. The distribution of the pupils' social capital scale is shown in Figure 7.6. This indicates that most pupils perceive themselves to have adequate or better levels of social capital. Very few pupils dislike their classmates, have few friends in school or in their year at school and are unable to ask their school friends for help if needed.

Pupils who have low social capital report being bullied more
Figure 7.7 indicates that pupils who have poor levels of social capital more regularly report having been bullied in the last year. Pupils who do not like their classmates have few friends in school and are unable to ask peers for help, report a higher prevalence and frequency of having been bullied. This suggests that social capital levels among pupils may act as a protective factor in preventing bullying. It also suggests that the measure of social capital used in this study is reliable because it makes theoretical sense that pupils with high levels of social capital will suffer less bullying, as they could turn to friends for help, for example.

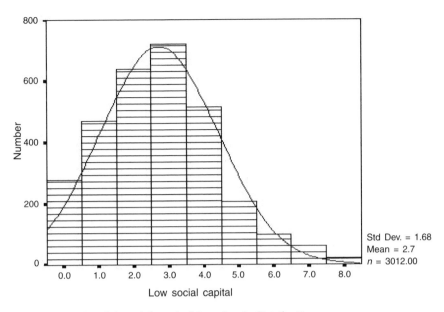

Figure 7.6   Pupils' social capital in school, distribution

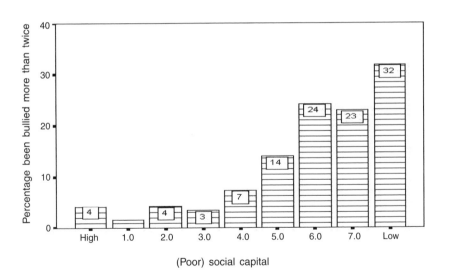

Figure 7.7   Percentage having been bullied more than twice in the last year by (poor) social capital

Social capital and offending prevalence in school

Table 7.5 indicates that poor social capital is related to an increased prevalence of offending in schools in terms of the total population for theft, assault and overall offending. Relative to other measures in this study the measures of association are fairly weak (i.e. in relation to respect for school authority, school ethos and parental school interest scales, and in later chapters' individual characteristic and lifestyle scales). Among males, social capital is very weakly related to overall offending, but more strongly associated with theft and serious offending. For all other offence types there are no significant associations between males and their levels of social capital. The associations between social capital and overall offending and theft in schools for females are statistically significant for their prevalence of

Table 7.5 Pupils' (low) social capital by offending prevalence in school, by population and sex

	Low social capital*				
	High (%)	Medium (%)	Low (%)	Sig.	Gamma
Population					
School theft	4.9	6.1	12.4	0.000	0.21
School assault	11.7	13.7	20.2	0.006	0.14
School vandalism	6.6	6.4	8.4	n.s.	–
Serious offences	1.0	1.1	3.0	n.s.	–
Overall offending	17.9	20.7	32.9	0.000	0.15
Male					
School theft	6.4	7.8	13.6	0.052	0.17
School assault	17.8	18.0	27.6	n.s.	–
School vandalism	9.2	7.0	9.3	n.s.	–
Serious offences	1.7	1.7	5.7	0.028	0.21
Overall offending	25.4	25.6	41.6	0.004	0.09
Female					
School theft	3.6	4.2	11.1	0.006	0.22
School assault	6.4	8.7	12.3	n.s.	–
School vandalism	4.3	5.8	7.5	n.s.	–
Serious offences	0.4	0.3	0.0	n.s.	–
Overall offending	11.3	14.9	23.5	0.005	0.20

Note:

*Low social capital scores grouped into high (scores 0–2), medium (scores 3–5) and low (scores 6–8).

offending in schools. For females, there are no significant associations for other offence types in school.

Pupils' perception of school disorder

This section will investigate the relationship between pupils' perception of the level of disorder in their school and their offending behaviour. It is argued that if pupils perceive that their schools are disorderly or unruly places they may be more likely to see offending as an alternative because, in disorderly schools, there may be more opportunities to offend and also, if there are high levels of social disorder, the chances of sanction may be perceived by the pupil to be relatively small.

The creation of the construct

The responses to the questions employed in the school disorder scale are coded 0 to 3. These responses are then summed, resulting in a scale ranging from 0 to 12, where 12 represents a pupil who reports staying away from school many times due to fear, who is afraid of many fellow pupils, who reports there is a lot of bullying at the school and who finds that their work is always disrupted by the behaviour of others. Zero represents a pupil who perceives the school to have a good level of order, which should be conducive to a good environment in which to learn. Figure 7.8 shows the distribution of

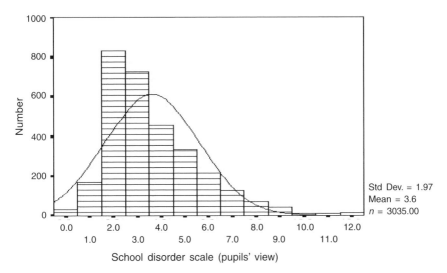

Figure 7.8 Distribution of pupils' view of school disorder

disorder scores among pupils in the Cardiff School Study. This figure shows that most pupils report that their schools have relatively good levels of order.

Pupils' view of school disorder and offending in schools
Table 7.6 indicates that pupils' perception of school disorder is significantly associated with offending prevalence in schools, for all types of offending, for the whole population. However, there appears to be no significant association between school disorder and males who report assaulting others in schools. There is also no significant association between school disorder and females who report serious offences. All other categories in Table 7.6 indicate significant relationships between pupils' view of school disorder and offending prevalence in schools. In terms of overall offending in schools, it

Table 7.6 Offending prevalence in school by pupils' perception of school disorder

| | School disorder* | | | | |
	Low (%)	Medium (%)	High (%)	Sig.	Gamma
Population					
School theft	4.9	7.2	12.1	0.004	0.23
School assault	11.8	14.7	22.2	0.008	0.15
School vandalism	5.2	9.0	11.1	0.000	0.29
Serious offences	0.7	1.6	6.8	0.000	0.50
Overall offending	17.6	23.6	30.3	0.000	0.19
Male					
School theft	6.3	9.8	13.8	0.028	0.24
School assault	16.8	20.7	29.6	n.s.	–
School vandalism	6.5	11.4	11.1	0.006	0.29
Serious offences	1.3	2.7	12.5	0.000	0.46
Overall offending	24.0	31.4	27.6	0.010	0.17
Female					
School theft	3.3	5.0	10.8	0.040	0.26
School assault	6.0	9.5	16.7	0.007	0.27
School vandalism	3.6	6.9	11.1	0.007	0.34
Serious offences	0.0	0.7	2.9	n.s.	–
Overall offending	10.3	16.9	32.4	0.000	0.31

Note:
*School disorder scores grouped into low (scores 0–3), medium (scores 4–8) and high (scores 9–12).

appears that females are more influenced by their perception of how disordered their schools are than males.

Two measures of school context

This section creates two measures of school context based on individual pupils' perceptions, attitudes and experiences of their schools, which employ the five constructs examined previously. The first construct is labelled school climate and concerns the pupils' view of how the school works and includes the following scales: 1) respect for authority; 2) school ethos; and 3) parental interest in school. The second construct is labelled pupil relations and includes 1) pupils' levels of social capital; and 2) how disordered they feel the school is.

In Table 7.7 the school bond measure, discussed later in this book, is shown to illustrate its relationship (zero-order correlations) to the school context measures discussed in this chapter. With the exception of school disorder, all measures are moderate to relatively strong correlates of school bonds. However, school disorder is correlated with pupils' level of social capital and school ethos. School disorder appears to be unrelated to school bonds, parental school interest and respect for school authority. The higher the pupil's perception of school disorder, the more likely they are to consider that their levels of social capital are poor and that they consider the ethos of the school to be poor. The table indicates that pupils with strong school

Table 7.7 Zero-order correlations between school context constructs and school bond scale

	School bond	Parental school interest	Respect for authority	Social capital	School ethos	School disorder
School bond	1.00					
Parental school interest	0.36	1.00				
Respect for authority	0.61	0.27	1.00			
Social capital	0.20	0.22	0.16	1.00		
School ethos	0.51	0.35	0.47	0.31	1.00	
School disorder	0.03	0.04	0.07	0.22	0.18	1.00

Note:
All correlations significant at the 0.05 level or better.

bonds tend to have higher respect for school authority and are more positive regarding the school ethos. Levels of social capital are not that strongly correlated to the school bond. This analysis indicates that the school climate measures of parental school interest, respect for authority and school ethos are more important in relation to the school bond than the pupil relations measure of pupils' social capital and school disorder. This suggests that how the school is run, organised and its ethos may be more important in determining individual's school bonds than how the individual perceives his or her relations with peers.

A factor analysis of the five constructs relating to school context (shown in Table 7.8), explaining 60.2 per cent of the variance, provides empirical support for the constructs of school climate and pupil relations – indicative of the fact that school context is not a one-dimensional construct. The first factor provides an empirical basis for the construct of school climate. This construct takes account of how the school is supported by the pupils' parents (in terms of the parents supporting their child's education), the respect shown by pupils to the school authorities and how positive the pupils perceive the ethos of the school to be. The second factor provides empirical evidence for the pupil relations construct which measures how well liked and supported by other pupils the pupil feels, and how much fear of other pupils the pupil feels, as well as how much bullying and disruption the pupil feels other pupils cause.

Table 7.8 Factor analysis: school context constructs, principal component

Constructs	Factor 1 (school climate) loadings	Factor 2 (pupil relations) loadings	Communalities
Social capital	0.31	0.63	0.49
School ethos	0.74	0.34	0.66
School authority	0.77	–	0.59
Parental school interest	0.71	–	0.50
School disorder	–	0.88	0.77
Eigenvalue	2.0	1.0	
Explained variance	39.6	20.5	
Total explained variance	60.2		

Note:
Factors with loadings above 0.4 are underlined.

The creation of the school climate and pupil relations measures

The measures of school climate and pupil relations are composite in nature. The former is composed of parental school interest, school ethos and pupils' respect for school authority constructs. The latter is composed of pupils' social capital and view of school disorder. The same formulation for the constructs was used in each case. Each of the constructs involved in the school climate measure was divided into the third of scores at the low-risk end of the distribution (given the score of −1), the third of scores in the middle (given the score of 0) and the third of scores at the high-risk end of the distribution (given the score of +1). These constructs were then summed, resulting in a scale ranging from −3 to +3. A score of +3 indicates that the pupil feels that their parents are unsupportive of the school and uninterested in their education, have no respect for school authority and view the ethos of the school poorly. The pupil relations measure was created in the same manner, with scores ranging from −2 to +2, where +2 represents pupils who feel they are not well liked and who feel there is a great deal of disorder in school.

Pupils' view of school climate

Figure 7.9 shows the distribution of pupils' perception of school climate in the Cardiff School Study by sex. This figure indicates that the majority of pupils perceive their schools to have good climates, based on school ethos, parental school interest and pupils' respect

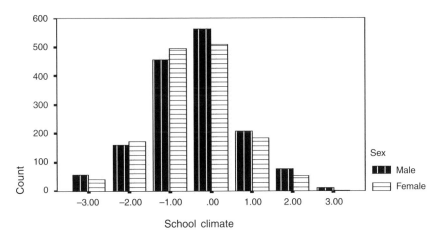

Figure 7.9 School climate scores, distribution by sex

for school authority. The figure indicates that there are no great sex differences regarding pupils' perception of school climate, although more males than females seem to view the school climate as poor (i.e. scores +1 to +3).

Pupils' view of school climate and offending in school

Table 7.9 illustrates the relationships between pupils' view of school climate and their offending behaviour in school. It indicates that statistically significant associations exist for all types of offending in schools in relation to levels of pupils' view of school climate. The exception is male and female serious offending, which is not statistically significantly associated with pupils' view of school climate.

Table 7.10 shows the relationship between pupils' frequency of offending in school and their view of school climate. This table

Table 7.9 Prevalence of pupil offending in schools by school climate

| | School climate* | | | | |
	Good (%)	Balanced (%)	Poor (%)	Sig.	Gamma
Population					
Theft	2.4	5.8	19.4	0.000	0.53
Assault	5.8	13.2	32.6	0.000	0.48
Vandalism	1.9	6.8	18.5	0.000	0.57
Serious offences	1.2	0.9	3.9	0.009	0.20
Overall offending	9.2	20.6	46.7	0.000	0.50
Males					
Theft	3.0	7.7	18.8	0.000	0.49
Assault	6.9	18.9	41.0	0.000	0.53
Vandalism	2.0	8.3	22.1	0.000	0.60
Serious offences	2.0	1.5	6.5	n.s.	–
Overall offending	11.3	27.4	54.3	0.000	0.53
Females					
Theft	1.9	3.9	20.4	0.000	0.57
Assault	4.8	7.6	20.4	0.001	0.36
Vandalism	1.9	5.4	13.2	0.003	0.49
Serious offences	0.5	0.4	0.0	n.s.	–
Overall offending	7.1	13.7	35.2	0.000	0.44

Note:
*School climate scores grouped into good (scores −3 to −2), balanced (scores −1 to +1) and poor (scores +2 to +3).

Table 7.10 Frequency of pupil offending in schools by pupils' view of school climate*, means, significance and eta²

	Overall offending	Theft	Assault	Vandalism
Population				
Good	0.16	0.05	0.07	0.02
Balanced	0.56	0.13	0.26	0.16
Poor	2.11	0.63	0.89	0.41
Sig.	0.000	0.000	0.000	0.000
Eta²	0.04	0.02	0.03	0.01
Males				
Good	0.21	0.05	0.10	0.03
Balanced	0.76	0.18	0.38	0.18
Poor	2.64	0.66	1.22	0.45
Sig.	0.000	0.000	0.000	0.000
Eta²	0.05	0.02	0.04	0.01
Females				
Good	0.10	0.04	0.05	0.01
Balanced	0.36	0.08	0.13	0.14
Poor	1.29	0.60	0.36	0.34
Sig.	0.000	0.000	0.002	0.004
Eta²	0.02	0.03	0.01	0.01

Note:
*School climate scores grouped into good (scores –3 to –2), balanced (scores –1 to +1) and poor (scores +2 to +3).

indicates that the poorer one views school climate the more likely one is to offend in schools frequently. The amount of variance explained by pupils' view of school climate, ranges from 1 to 5 per cent for offending behaviour in schools.

Pupil relations

Figure 7.10 shows the distribution of the pupil relations measures among pupils in the Cardiff School Study. This indicates that most pupils view pupil relations in their schools as being quite positive, meaning that they consider themselves to get on well with other pupils, are not afraid of other pupils, that bullying is not a big problem in their school and that their work is not often disrupted by the behaviour of other pupils. The figure also shows that there are no great sex differences concerning how they view pupil relations.

Figure 7.11 illustrates the relationship between the two measures of school context used in this study and the measure of school bonds used. This suggests that pupils who consider their school climates as being good are more likely to have strong school bonds (r = 0.58, p = 0.000). However, it appears that pupils' perception of pupil relations is not that strongly related to their school bonds. This could be because pupils can have many friends at school but still may not feel a great bond to school.

Pupil relations and offending behaviour in schools

Table 7.11 examines the relationship between pupil relations and pupil offending behaviour in schools in more detail. This shows that, for the whole population, there are statistically significant associations between pupils' view of pupil relations in school and self-reported offending behaviour in school. However, there are no significant associations for males who report assault and vandalism in schools and their view of pupil relations. Regarding offending prevalence,

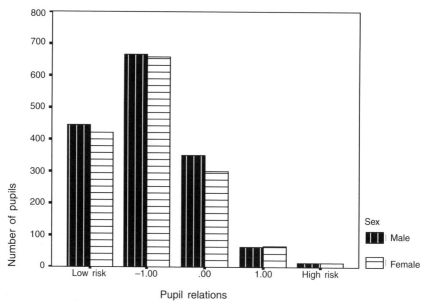

Figure 7.10 Pupil relations, distribution

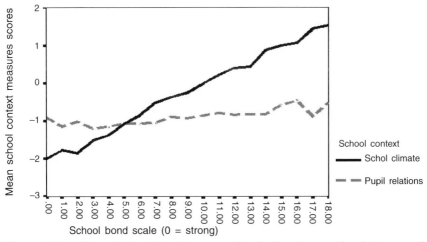

Figure 7.11 The relationship between school climate, pupil relations and school bonds

females are more affected by how they view pupil relations in schools. This is reflected by a stronger measure of association in all offending categories, with the exception of serious offending (the reason for this may be the small number of females who report serious offending, rather than anything more substantive).

Table 7.12 shows that pupil relations explain less than 1 per cent of the variance in pupil offending frequency in the cases where the associations are statistically significant.

This section has shown how these two new measures of school context are associated with pupil offending behaviour in school. Pupils' view of school climate seems to be more strongly associated with offending behaviour in schools, both for prevalence and frequency, in comparison with the measure of pupil relations. The next section will investigate the extent to which these factors predict offending in schools, using regression-based analysis.

Multiple regression analyses

Before exploring the efficacy of the two school context risk measures in predicting offending in schools, each independent school scale will be examined in regression-based analyses in relation to offending in schools. Table 7.13 illustrates how well each school scale predicts whether pupils offend or not in school (prevalence). This shows

Table 7.11 Pupils' prevalence of offending by pupil relations

	Good (%)	Balanced (%)	Poor (%)	Sig.	Gamma
		Pupil relations*			
Population					
Theft	4.9	7.6	14.5	0.000	0.32
Assault	12.2	14.0	21.8	0.003	0.15
Vandalism	6.0	7.8	10.7	0.044	0.17
Serious offences	0.8	1.5	5.0	0.000	0.49
Overall offending	18.4	22.0	36.3	0.000	0.20
Males					
Theft	6.2	10.3	15.7	0.001	0.31
Assault	17.5	18.9	27.9	n.s.	–
Vandalism	7.6	9.1	10.4	n.s.	–
Serious offences	1.3	2.6	8.8	0.000	0.51
Overall offending	24.7	28.5	40.8	0.007	0.16
Females					
Theft	3.6	4.5	13.3	0.000	0.32
Assault	6.9	8.7	16.2	0.013	0.22
Vandalism	4.4	6.3	11.0	0.032	0.26
Serious offences	0.3	0.4	1.4	n.s.	–
Overall offending	12.0	14.9	32.0	0.000	0.26

Note:
*Pupil relations scores grouped into good (scores –2 to –1), balanced (score 0) and poor (scores +1 to +2).

that sex, parental school interest, respect for authority and school disorder predict all types of offending in school. Pupils' social capital is not a significant predictor of overall offending, theft and assault. Interestingly, ethos is not a significant predictor of assault prevalence in schools.

Table 7.14 shows similar findings regarding the school context measures and pupils' offending frequency in schools. Parental school interest and respect for school authority are the strongest and most consistent predictors of offending, followed very closely by school disorder. The overall frequency of offending model shows that these school context measures, when taken together, explain 7 per cent of the variance in overall offending frequency.

Table 7.15 shows an OLS multiple regression analysis, which demonstrates how well the two school context risk constructs (pupil relations and school climate) created earlier in the chapter predict

Table 7.12 Pupils' frequency of offending by pupil relations*, means, significance and eta²

	Overall offending	Theft	Assault	Vandalism
Population				
Good	0.49	0.11	0.23	0.13
Balanced	0.76	0.20	0.32	0.21
Poor	1.09	0.35	0.40	0.19
Sig.	0.000	0.000	0.014	n.s.
Eta²	0.008	0.007	0.003	–
Males				
Good	0.68	0.15	0.35	0.15
Balanced	1.00	0.24	0.45	0.24
Poor	1.40	0.42	0.51	0.17
Sig.	0.002	0.006	n.s.	n.s.
Eta²	0.008	0.007	0.002	0.002
Females				
Good	0.29	0.07	0.11	0.11
Balanced	0.49	0.15	0.16	0.17
Poor	0.78	0.27	0.29	0.22
Sig.	0.001	0.005	0.013	n.s.
Eta²	0.009	0.007	0.006	0.002

Note:
*Pupil relations scores grouped into good (scores –2 to –1), balanced (score 0) and poor (scores +1 to +2).

offending behaviour in school. This indicates that pupils' view of school climate is the strongest predictor of offending in schools – significantly predicting all types of offending in schools. Pupil relations is not as strong a predictor as school climate and loses significance in relation to vandalism, theft (but only just) and assault in school. The overall model explains 6 per cent of the variance regarding overall offending, 2 per cent of variance regarding theft, 5 per cent regarding assault and 2 per cent concerning vandalism frequency in school. These measures will be used later on in the book when examining the predictive power of school context factors in relation to other individual-level data when explaining individual differences in offending. The explained variance is 1 per cent less in this model in comparison with Table 7.13 regarding overall offending, theft and

Table 7.13 Multiple logistic regression: prevalence of overall offending, theft, assault and vandalism in schools by sex and school context factors

	Overall		Theft		Assault		Vandalism	
	Exp. (B)	Sig.	Exp. (B)	Sig.	Exp. (B)	Sig.	Exp. (B)	Sig.
Sex	0.43	0.000	0.57	0.001	0.37	0.000	0.62	0.003
Parental school interest	1.24	0.000	1.20	0.023	1.31	0.000	1.28	0.002
Respect for authority	1.41	0.000	1.44	0.000	1.37	0.000	1.53	0.000
Ethos	1.19	0.005	1.28	0.017	1.10	n.s.	1.21	0.047
Social capital	0.95	n.s.	1.03	n.s.	0.96	n.s.	0.82	0.014
School disorder	1.23	0.000	1.16	0.045	1.20	0.002	1.28	0.001
Chi-square (prob.)	229 (0.000)		84 (0.000)		170 (0.000)		97 (0.000)	
–2 log	2,595		1,170		2,005		1,270	
Cox and Snell R^2	0.08		0.03		0.06		0.03	
Nagelkerke R^2	0.12		0.08		0.11		0.09	

Note:
Underline indicates significant finding at the 0.05 level or better.

Table 7.14 OLS multiple regression: frequencies of overall offending, theft, assault and vandalism in schools, by sex and school context factors

	Overall		Theft		Assault		Vandalism	
	Beta	Prob.	Beta	Prob.	Beta.	Prob.	Beta	Prob.
Sex	-0.11	0.000	-0.06	0.003	-0.14	0.000	-0.03	n.s.
Parental school interest	0.11	0.000	0.07	0.000	0.10	0.000	0.06	0.003
Respect for authority	0.13	0.000	0.08	0.000	0.12	0.000	0.10	0.000
Ethos	0.06	0.008	0.06	0.010	0.03	n.s.	0.03	n.s.
Social capital	-0.05	0.016	-0.03	n.s.	-0.03	n.s.	-0.05	0.020
School disorder	0.08	0.000	0.04	0.050	0.05	0.004	0.05	0.004
Multiple R^2	7		3		6		2	

Note:
Underline indicates significant finding at the 0.05 level or better.

Table 7.15 OLS multiple regression: frequencies of overall offending, theft, assault and vandalism in school by sex and key school context factors

Pupils' school context constructs	Overall		Theft		Assault		Vandalism	
	Beta	Prob.	Beta	Prob.	Beta.	Prob.	Beta	Prob.
Sex	−0.11	0.000	−0.05	0.003	−0.14	0.000	−0.02	n.s.
Pupil relations	0.04	0.036	0.04	0.051	0.02	n.s.	0.02	n.s.
School climate	0.19	0.000	0.12	0.000	0.17	0.000	0.12	0.000
Multiple R^2 × 100=	6		2		5		2	

assault, but it is argued that the two measures of school context are theoretically and empirically sound constructs (as discussed earlier in the chapter).

Summary

School context is a protean concept. In this chapter, five innovative scales have been created which all, to a varying degree, are associated with pupil offending prevalence and frequency in the school context. Empirical analysis has indicated that these five scales can be reduced into two theoretically sound constructs. These are 1) school climate, which concerns the school ethos, the respect pupils have for school authority and the level of parental school interest; and 2) pupil relations, which is a composite measure of the social capital and school disorder scales. The school climate scale is associated with how the school is run and organised, how it sits in the community and how it is experienced and valued by pupils and teachers alike. This construct out of the two is more strongly associated with pupil offending prevalence and frequency in the school context. Pupil relations are shown to be more weakly associated and predictive of pupil offending behaviour. This suggests that school climate is more important than pupil relations in determining levels of offending behaviour. However, both are likely to have an impact on offending levels in schools.

In comparison with previous chapters, the school context measures have generally stronger associations with pupil offending behaviour in the school than pupils' area of residence structural risk and family social position. In later chapters regression-based analyses will test this. However, it does seem to indicate that measures closer to individual decision-making are likely to be more predictive of the offending phenomenon. The findings presented in this chapter suggest that the school context may be an important arena for prevention strategies.

Chapter 8

Individual characteristics

So far we have investigated empirically, first, factors that are more distant influences on individual action (i.e. area of residence structural risk, family social position risk) and, secondly, factors that are more closely related to pupils' social action in school (i.e. the school climate and pupil relations measures). In this chapter, factors much more closely related to pupils' social action will be explored (i.e. pupils' individual social situational and dispositional characteristics). The relationship between pupils' individual characteristics and their offending behaviour in schools will be explored. It is contended that such individual characteristics are determined by developmental and socialisation processes (see Chapter 3; Hirschi 1969; Bronfenbrenner 1979; Gottfredson and Hirschi 1990). Indeed, contextual factors, such as family social position, school environment and neighbourhood, all influence individual characteristics and individual lifestyles. Where one lives, where one goes to school and one's family background will necessarily influence the places, spaces and people one encounters and the evolution of one's development in terms of integration into society and in terms of dispositions, such as self-control, and elements of morality, such as pro-social values and sense of shaming. Pupils' experiences and perceptions of contextual and background factors (such as neighbourhood, school and family) will influence pupils' social situational and dispositional characteristics as well as lifestyle. More will now be said regarding what is meant by individuals' social situation and dispositions.

Social situation refers to the pupil's integration into society, specifically focusing on relationships and bonds with others. Those who are poorly integrated into conventional society are more likely to offend than those who are well integrated (see, Hirschi 1969; Kornhauser 1978). This is consistent with control theory explanations of crime and deviance. These theories assume that delinquent or criminal acts occur when an individual's bond to society is weak or broken (Hirschi 1969). It can be hypothesised that those pupils with weak family and school bonds are at a greater risk of offending in school than those with strong family and school bonds, because they rely less on their relationships with others and have lower stakes in conformity as a result, which, it is argued, would otherwise keep them in check.

Another factor that concerns the level of integration of a child into the family unit is that of parental monitoring or supervision. If a pupil is well monitored by parents it is argued that he or she will be less likely to offend in school as the parents will take greater interest in what their child is doing, thus exerting a controlling influence. These elements may be referred to as socially situational. Bonding and monitoring processes directly affect pupils' socialisation and, in turn, their internalisation of conventional societal norms. It is hypothesised that those pupils who have weak bonds to family and school and who experience poor levels of parental monitoring are more likely to offend in schools. Previous empirical research has indicated that weak family bonds (e.g. Canter 1982; Cernkovich and Giordano 1987; Wikström 2002), weak school bonds (e.g. Jenkins 1997), and poor parental monitoring or supervision (e.g. Martens 1997) are predictive of juvenile offending behaviour in general. However, these aspects have rarely all been comprehensively examined in relation to pupil offending behaviour in the school context.

Individual dispositional characteristics refer to aspects of the pupil's morality (such as sense of shaming and pro-social values, although there are many others) and self-control. It is argued in criminological discussion (Gottfredson and Hirchi 1990; Hirschi and Gottfredson 1993) and shown in previous research (Grasmick *et al.* 1993; Pratt and Cullen 2000) that individuals with low self-control are more likely to offend than those with high levels of self-control. Self-control refers to whether an individual is impulsive and whether he or she is likely to act on the spur of the moment without thinking about it. Wikström and Sampson (2003: 124) state: 'Individual's self-control may be defined as their capability to inhibit or interrupt a response as an effect of the executive functions of their brain…, for example, their capability to resist acting upon a temptation or provocation that if carried out would constitute a breach of the law.'

Executive functions here refer to factors including self-regulation, flexibility, sequencing of behaviour, response inhibition, planning and organisation of behaviour (see Shonkoff and Phillips 2000). It is hypothesised that pupils who have low levels of self-control are more likely to offend in schools than pupils who have high levels of self-control.

Wikström and Sampson (2003: 124) defined individual morality:

> in terms of an evaluative function of events in the world. It includes what the individual cares about, how strongly they care about different things, how he or she thinks he or she should relate to other people, and what they consider as right and wrong (and associated feelings such as guilt or empathy).

Wikström and Sampson, in postulating a causal mechanism of individuals' choice and perception of alternatives in determining social action, argue how these dispositional factors relate to this mechanism. They argue that an individual's morality affects how he or she would see different options and what kind of options he or she would consider. Self-control would affect the individual's process of choice through his or her executive functions. It would affect the individual's degree of deliberation and reflection before he or she chose between options (i.e. weighing up the situation). The options, for pupils offending in the school context, would be a choice between committing an offence and acting in a law or norm-abiding way (see the model in Chapter 3). It is hypothesised that pupils who have anti-social values and a low sense of shaming will offend more in schools than pupils who have strong pro-social values and a high sense of shaming.

It seems reasonable, as individuals develop, to assume that bonds and integration in society are intrinsically linked to the development of the individual's morality and self-control. However, in a cross-sectional study such as this it is only possible to measure individuals' integration into society and morality and self-control at one moment in time. The question as to how individual dispositional and social situational characteristics relate and develop over time is, arguably, one of the most important questions facing social scientists today, especially in gaining an understanding of what factors are most influential in determining social action.

The constructs used in this chapter are summarised in Table 8.1. As can be seen, five out of the six constructs have been used in previous research. The Crohnbach's alphas are all above 0.60 (and usually much higher), suggesting a good level of internal consistency and scale reliability (i.e. the questions in the scale all seem to be tapping into the same underlying construct).

Social situation: bonds and monitoring

Although denied in some theories and ignored in others, the fact that delinquents are less likely than nondelinquents to be closely tied to their parents is one of the best documented findings of delinquency research (Hirschi 1969: 85).

In a response to the motivational theories of criminality that dominated the field before the 1960s, such as strain theories (Merton 1938) and differential association theories (Sutherland 1939; see also Sutherland and Cressey 1970), which sought to explain why some people do commit delinquent acts, Hirschi (1969) sought to explain why people obey the law. In his social control theory, there is an assumption that everyone has a predisposition to offend. However, most people do not offend in society because their bonds to conventional society are strong. When these bonds are weak it is hypothesised that people will break the law. The key elements in Hirschi's conception of

Table 8.1 Key individual pupil constructs

Domain	Scales	Number of items	Alpha
Social situation			
Social bonds	Weak family bonds*	4	0.63
	Weak school bonds**	6	0.78
Parental control	Parental monitoring*	3	0.77
Dispositions			
Self-control	Low self control***	13	0.77
Morality	Pro-social values****	14	0.92
	High shaming*	6	0.87

Notes:
 * Scales created by Wikström (see Wikström 2002: 78).
 ** Scale created by author.
 *** Modified version of the Grasmick *et al.* (1993) self-control scale, used by Wikström (2002).
 **** Based on a scale used in the Pittsburgh Youth Study; also used by Wikström (2002).

bonds to conventional society include attachment to other people, commitment to conventional society, involvement in conventional activities and belief in a common value system. In his study, Hirschi (1969) found that self-reported delinquency was associated with a lack of attachment to parents (i.e. the parental bond was weak, which was related to an increased likelihood of offending).

Another important bond that has been shown to be associated with delinquency in general is the school social bond (see Wikström 2002); however, it has rarely been tested in relation to offending in school (see Jenkins 1997). Jenkins tested the school social bond, using Hirschi's conception of bonds, in relation to school misbehaviour. Based on empirical evidence, she argued that the school social bond is an important intervening mechanism that helps to explain the effects of certain predictor variables on non-attendance, school misconduct and school crime in the middle school she examined in the USA. Jenkins' study was based on just one public middle school in the USA, thus caution should be attributed to the generalisability of her findings. This section will examine the relationship between pupils' school and family bonds and offending in school.

Weak family bonds construct

The four variables which create the weak family bonds construct have been coded from 0 to 2. The construct has a variation between 0 and 8, with 8 indicating a very weak family bond. Those with a score of 8 do not get on well with their parents, almost never have an evening meal with their parents, almost never talk to their parents if they have a problem and almost never do something fun with their parents. The distribution of weak family bonds scores among the pupils in this study is shown in Figure 8.1.

Weak school bonds construct

Six variables were used to create the weak school bonds construct. This construct is based on previous research, but it is original to this study. The individual variables are coded 0 to 3, with 3 indicating a weak score. There are six items in this construct, which gives a scale of 0 through 18, with 18 indicating a very weak school bond. The distribution of the scores for the weak school bond scale is shown in Figure 8.2. Those who score 18 on the scale do not like going to school, would not raise money for their school, do not care what their teachers think about them, think that their teachers do not like them, do not think their teachers are very good and do not like most

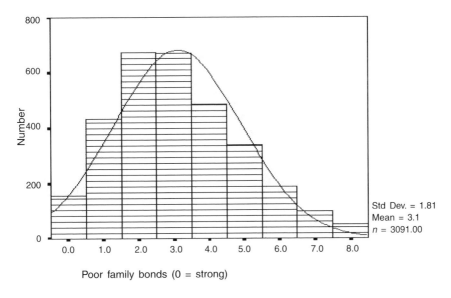

Figure 8.1 Distribution of weak family bonds scores

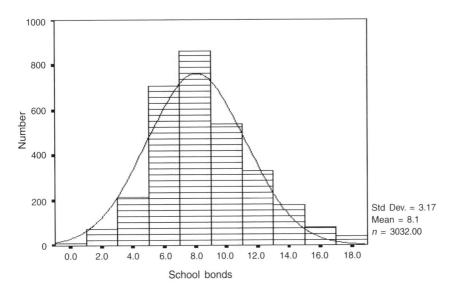

Figure 8.2 Distribution of weak school bonds

of their teachers. These factors, it is argued, are indicative of a very weak bond to school. Figure 8.2 indicates a fairly normal distribution in the population regarding the school bond. However, it can be seen that, in general, pupils tend to have strong school bonds (i.e. scores of 8 and lower) than weak bonds.

Youths with weak school bonds more often truant

The construct of school bonds was compared with levels of frequent truancy to assess how well the construct performed in picking up variations among the pupils in the study. This construct is new to this study, so it was deemed essential to see how well it worked. Theoretically it is reasonable to assume that pupils with weak school bonds would also be more likely to truant frequently. Figure 8.3 shows such a relationship clearly.

The weak family bonds construct was used in the Peterborough Youth Study and has been proven to pick up theoretically appropriate individual variation (see Wikström 2002). A similar scale was also used by Hirschi (1969).

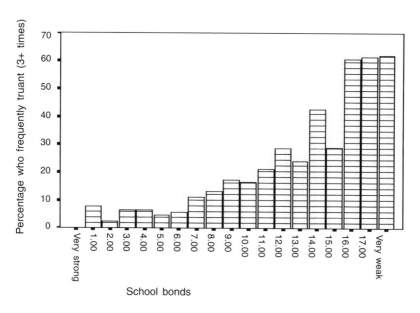

Figure 8.3 Percent frequently truant from school by level of (weak) school bonds

Parental monitoring

A host of criminological studies have indicated the efficacy of poor parental monitoring or supervision in relation to increased risk of offending (see, for example, Rutter and Giller 1983; Graham and Bowling 1995; Wikström 2002). These investigations have illustrated that those juveniles whose parents are less aware of what they are doing, where they are doing it and with whom they are doing it are more likely to offend than those individuals who are well monitored by parents.

In this study a tried and tested scale of parental monitoring was used (see, Wikström 2002). The combined scale has a range of 0–9, with 9 indicating very poor parental monitoring. Very poor parental monitoring consists of the pupils reporting that parents never know where they are, never know what they are doing and never know whom they are with. The distribution of this scale among pupils is shown in Figure 8.4. This indicates that there is a skew towards pupils generally being fairly well monitored by parents.

Parental monitoring is poor in families with weak family bonds

Parental monitoring is fairly closely related to family bonds. Pupils who have a poor bond to their family are also more likely to report that they experience lower levels of parental monitoring. Table 8.2 indicates that the zero-order correlation between the parental monitoring construct and the family bonds scale is a reasonably

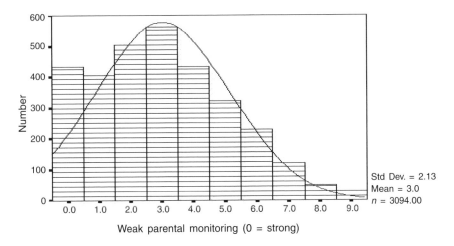

Figure 8.4 Distribution of poor parental monitoring

Table 8.2 Zero-order correlations between the key measures of individual social situation

Zero-order correlations	Weak family bonds	Weak school bonds	Weak parental monitoring
Weak family bonds	1.0		
Weak school bonds	0.34	1.0	
Weak parental monitoring	0.52	0.40	1.0

Note:
All correlation in this table are significant at the 0.05 level or better.

strong 0.52. As this study is cross-sectional, it is conjecture as to how pupils' family bonds and levels of parental monitoring are related. However, it is likely that parental monitoring and bonds to the family are intrinsically linked. The relationship between weak family bonds and poor parental monitoring is similar but slightly stronger for girls ($r = 0.56$, $p = 0.000$, $n = 1,490$) in comparison with boys ($r = 0.49$, $p = 0.000$, $n = 1,598$) in this Year 10 population in Cardiff.

Table 8.2 indicates that family bonds are associated with school bonds, and school bonds are associated with parental monitoring. The relationship between weak family bonds and weak school bonds is similar for boys ($r = 0.34$, $p = 0.000$, $n = 1,553$) and girls ($r = 0.37$, $p = 0.000$, $n = 1,468$) – pupils with weak family bonds are also likely to have weak school bonds. This makes theoretical sense when one considers that both the family and school are central to pupils' lives at the age of 14. If a pupil is not well integrated into the family it is likely to be the case that he or she has poor bonds to another major institution in society – the school.

Pupils who have weak bonds to schools and families can be considered to be less well integrated into conventional society than those with strong school and family bonds. The next section will look at how each of these constructs is associated with pupils' offending behaviour in school.

Pupils' social situation is related to offending in schools

Tables 8.3 show that a pupil's level of integration into conventional society (as measured by bonds and monitoring) is related to his or her likelihood of offending in schools. Previous research has shown that these factors are related to general offending prevalence (see Wikström 2002). Of critical interest is that these pupil social situational

Table 8.3 Offending prevalence in school by weak family bonds and sex

Social situation	Offence type	Strength of bonds or monitoring measure				
		Strong (%)	Medium (%)	Weak (%)	Sig.	Gamma
Weak family bonds*						
	Population					
	Theft	4.0	5.6	14.8	0.000	0.36
	Assault	9.1	14.3	23.9	0.000	0.31
	Vandalism	4.0	7.1	15.2	0.000	0.39
	Serious offences	0.9	0.9	3.1	0.004	0.26
	Overall offending	14.0	21.7	38.4	0.000	0.35
	Male					
	Theft	6.2	7.0	17.4	0.000	0.27
	Assault	13.5	19.6	35.1	0.000	0.32
	Vandalism	6.0	8.7	15.3	0.001	0.27
	Serious offences	1.5	1.8	5.0	0.026	0.29
	Overall offending	20.2	28.2	47.7	0.000	0.32
	Female					
	Theft	1.7	4.3	12.3	0.000	0.54
	Assault	4.5	9.1	13.0	0.000	0.35
	Vandalism	1.9	5.5	15.0	0.000	0.57
	Serious offences	0.4	0.0	1.3	n.s.	–
	Overall offending	7.3	15.3	29.0	0.000	0.45

Table 8.3 continues on page 164

Table 8.3 continued

Social situation	Offence type	Strength of bonds or monitoring measure					
		Strong (%)	Medium (%)	Weak (%)	Sig.	Gamma
Weak school bonds**							
	Population						
	Theft	2.7	5.5	14.9	0.000	0.47
	Assault	7.9	13.0	24.3	0.000	0.34
	Vandalism	4.2	6.1	15.6	0.000	0.37
	Serious offences	1.7	0.7	3.5	0.000	0.14
	Overall offending	11.8	19.7	38.4	0.000	0.39
	Male						
	Theft	3.3	7.1	15.6	0.000	0.43
	Assault	10.6	18.3	29.0	0.000	0.32
	Vandalism	5.6	7.1	17.0	0.000	0.35
	Serious offences	2.8	1.2	4.7	0.003	0.15
	Overall offending	16.2	25.8	43.2	0.000	0.36
	Female						
	Theft	2.3	4.0	13.6	0.000	0.46
	Assault	5.7	7.7	14.9	0.020	0.25
	Vandalism	3.0	5.0	12.6	0.002	0.37
	Serious offences	0.8	0.2	1.2	n.s.	–
	Overall offending	8.3	13.7	28.4	0.000	0.36

Weak parental monitoring***

Population					
Theft	3.7	8.5	15.8	0.000	0.46
Assault	8.7	18.9	29.0	0.000	0.44
Vandalism	3.5	10.5	19.7	0.000	0.55
Serious offences	0.6	1.6	3.9	0.000	0.51
Overall offending	13.5	28.6	45.9	0.000	0.48
Male					
Theft	5.1	10.4	15.3	0.000	0.38
Assault	12.2	24.8	38.2	0.000	0.44
Vandalism	4.2	12.6	19.1	0.000	0.52
Serious offences	1.2	2.2	6.7	0.001	0.44
Overall offending	18.0	35.5	52.7	0.000	0.47
Female					
Theft	2.5	5.9	16.4	0.000	0.52
Assault	5.7	11.1	15.1	0.000	0.36
Vandalism	2.8	7.8	20.5	0.000	0.57
Serious offences	0.1	0.8	0.0	n.s.	–
Overall offending	9.5	19.5	35.6	0.000	0.45

Notes:

* Weak family bond scale grouped into strong (scores 0–2), medium (scores 3–5) and weak (scores 6–8)
** Weak school bond scale grouped into strong (scores 0–5), medium (scores 6–12) and weak (scores 13–18)
*** Weak parental monitoring scale grouped into strong (scores 0–3), medium (scores 4–6) and weak (scores 7–9)

factors are associated with offending prevalence in schools (this has not been shown before in the UK context).

Weak family bonds
Table 8.3 shows that pupils with weak family bonds are statistically significantly more likely to have reported offending in schools. This is true for overall offending in schools and all other types of offending. In comparison to the measures of association (gammas) in Chapters 5 and 6, it can be seen that these social situational measures have, generally, a relatively stronger association with pupils' offending behaviour in schools. Table 8.3 shows that, in terms of overall offending in schools, weak family bonds may have a stronger influence on girls in comparison with boys (as indicated by the gamma measures of association).

Weak school bonds
Table 8.3 shows that having a weak school bond significantly increases the likelihood of offending in schools for both boys and girls. This is true for all the categories apart from girls who report committing serious offences in school (the reason that no statistically significant relationships exist in this category may be due to the very small number of girls who report committing robbery in school or breaking into the school). This finding is in keeping with Hirschi's (1969: 110) argument concerning the role of the school in conventional society:

> Between the conventional family and the conventional world of work and marriage lies the school, an eminently conventional institution. Insofar as this institution is able to command his attachment, involvement, and commitment, the adolescent is presumably able to move from childhood to adulthood with a minimum of delinquent acts.

Pupils with strong bonds to conventional institutions in society have been shown to be much less likely to offend in the school context. This is an empirical finding consistent with control theories. Pupils who are attached, involved, committed and have belief in the conventional institutions of school and family are great deal less likely to be involved in offending in the school context.

Poor parental monitoring
Pupils who are poorly monitored by their parents have an increased risk of offending in school. This is illustrated in Table 8.3 for all

offending types, for both boys and girls, apart from serious offending in school by females. The table indicates that at each level of bonding or monitoring (i.e. strong, medium and weak) boys are more at risk of offending than girls. This reflects the overall sex difference in prevalence of offending shown in Chapter 4 (see Table 4.1).

All these pupil social situational characteristics (bonds and monitoring) are more closely associated with pupil offending in schools in comparison with the family social position and area of residence structural risk characteristics considered in Chapters 5 and 6. A few possible hypotheses as to why this is the case can be postulated. Chapters 5 and 6 dealt with constructs, which may be deemed *structural*, whereas, in this chapter, pupils' social situational characteristics are under scrutiny, which may have a more direct influence on the pupils' social action in school (in a similar way as the school context factors in Chapter 7 are more closely related to individual action and decision-making in the school context) and may, therefore, more directly influence the pupils' decision or choice between offending or not. This does not mean an individual's position in society (in terms of community and family background) is unimportant when considering offending in schools. It is, in fact, likely that family background characteristics and area of residence will influence the development of an individual's integration into conventional society (see Bronfenbrenner 1979 and Chapter 3 for discussion). An attempt at exploring this relationship is made in the next section. However, as in Chapter 7, it can be seen that, as one begins measuring factors more closely related to individual social action, the relationships increase in strength (as shown by gamma).

Individual dispositions

The *Oxford English Dictionary* defines disposition as 'a person's temperament or attitude, especially as displayed in dealings with others (*a happy disposition*)'. In this study two main dispositions will be investigated in relation to offending in schools. These are self-control and morality. The latter is measured using pro-social values and shaming scales which, it is argued, measure aspects (but not all aspects) of an individual's morality (see, Wikström 2002; Wikström and Sampson 2003).

The constructs

Low self-control

The measure of self-control used in this research is based on that developed by Grasmick *et al.* (1993). They attempted to measure Gottfredson and Hirschi's (1990) concept of self-control by creating a scale of self-control that measured facets of the theory proposed in *A General Theory of Crime*. Gottfredson and Hirschi (1990) proposed that low self-control is developed in early childhood and is a product of poor family socialisation practices, including poor parental monitoring. Once developed, it remains stable over the life course and is relatively unaffected by the operation of other institutions. Individuals with low levels of self-control are more likely to commit crime, be unsuccessful in school, do poorly in relationships and struggle in the labour market. Items in the survey of pupils aimed to measure low-self control which, along with opportunity, Gottfredson and Hirschi (1990) argued, was essential for criminal acts to occur. Hirschi and Gottfredson (1993: 53) see some problems with measuring self-control in the way conducted in this research and by Grasmick *et al.* (1993), but they argue: 'Although we would not agree with Grasmick *et al.* that they have tested our theory under the most favourable circumstances, we are gratified that they made the effort and found the theory worthy of expansion, refinement and elaboration.' Numerous studies since Grasmick *et al.* have shown successfully that their scale measuring self-control is an important predictor of general offending (see the meta-analysis undertaken by Pratt and Cullen 2000). However, pupil measures of low self-control have not before been employed in a study examining offending in schools.

The self-control scale used in this research is based on a modified version of the Grasmick *et al.* (1993) scale, and is the same as that used by Wikström (2002). It uses 13 items based on pupils' responses, ranging from 'strongly disagree', 'mostly disagree', 'mostly agree' to 'strongly agree', which relate to a pupil's self-control. It includes items such as: 'I often act on the spur of the moment without stopping to think' and 'I lose my temper pretty easily'. Each statement was coded 0–3, where 3 indicates the lowest level of self-control. The scores for the 13 items are summed to form the overall measure of low self-control. Figure 8.5 shows the distribution of low self-control scores among the pupils in the survey. The scores can range from 0 to 39, with 39 representing an individual with extremely low self-control. Figure 8.5 shows a very close to normal distribution. This suggests that the majority of pupils in Cardiff have neither excessively high nor low levels of self-control.

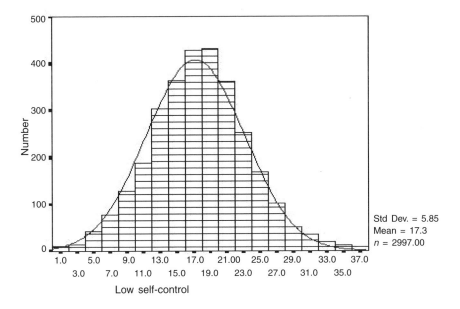

Figure 8.5 Distribution of low self-control scores

Morality (pro-social values and shaming)
The development of an individual's morality can be viewed as an integral part of the socialisation process. An individual's sense of shame and pro-social values can be considered to be part of the internalisation of norms, which is engendered by good socialisation experiences. In turn, good socialisation experiences are likely to be dependent on the individual's social situation (bonds to family, school, etc.) and his or her contextual experiences (family, school and community). Gottfredson and Hirschi (1990), when considering the causes of low self-control, submit that *low* self-control is not a product of training, tutelage or socialisation. They argue the causes of low self-control are negative rather than positive. Thus, individuals who have an absence of bonds to parents and conventional society are likely to have low self-control. Individuals who are well integrated into conventional society are likely to have higher levels of self-control. Similar arguments can be made for pro-social values and shaming. Socialisation is central in the development of these dispositional characteristics. An absence of positive socialisation experiences is likely to have negative consequences for the life chances of individuals.

Pro-social values

The pro-social values construct used in this study is based on that used in the Pittsburgh Youth Study (see Loeber *et al.* 2002 for an overview of the study). It asks young people to evaluate how wrong it is for someone of his or her age to commit a variety of acts including 'skip school without an excuse', 'steal something worth £5' and 'use hard drugs such as heroin'. It is a 14-item scale that requires individuals to respond with answers ranging from: 'very wrong', 'wrong', 'a little wrong' to 'not wrong at all'. The answers are coded 0–3, with 0 indicating high levels of anti-social values and 3 indicating highly pro-social values. The construct is based on the sum of the 14 items, thus ranging from 0 to 42, where 0 represents high levels of anti-social values. Figure 8.6 shows the distribution of pro-social values scores among pupils in the Cardiff School Study. It shows that most pupils have high levels of pro-social values, with few having very anti-social values.

Shaming

According to Svensson (2004a: 15), 'shame emerges when an individual feels that he or she has committed an act that violates internalised norms and has thus failed to live up to the norms of groups'. Possessing a sense of shame will prevent individuals from committing acts which they know others will disapprove of and

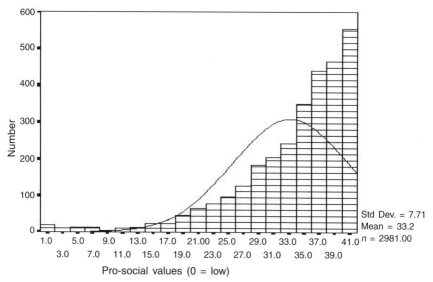

Figure 8.6 Distribution of pro-social values scores

which, if committed, will cause them to feel shame. Svensson (2004b: 479) postulates that an individual's sense of shame is intrinsically linked to the socialisation process and the internalisation of norms that the individual experiences as part of this. Effective socialisation will provide the individual with a well developed conscience or super-ego. Naturally, this socialisation process will be dependent upon the bonds the individual has with family, school and other institutions of conventional society and the contexts in which the individual develops.

The construct of shaming asks pupils to state the degree of shame they would feel if peers, teachers and parents found out that they had engaged in shoplifting or breaking into a car. This measure was devised and used by Wikström (2002). Summing the scores created the construct, where 0 indicates the lowest level of shame and 12 illustrates those with a high level of shame. Figure 8.7 shows the distribution of shaming scores among pupils in the Cardiff School Study. This shows a high skew, as with pro-social values, towards pupils' reporting high levels of shame if they were caught by parents, teachers or peers, having committed an offence.

There is a wide variation between levels of individual's sense of shame depending upon who catches them. For example, only 40.3 per cent would be very ashamed if their peers found out about them

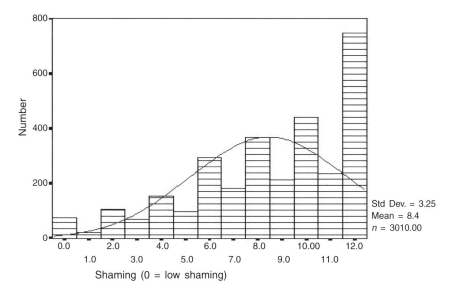

Figure 8.7 Distribution of shaming scores

breaking into a car, in comparison with 84.0 per cent reporting being very ashamed if their parents caught them. Pupils generally have a higher sense of shame concerning whether their parents catch them in comparison with teachers and peers. This suggests the importance of the family in terms of a pupil's socialisation.

Low self-control, pro-social values and (sense of) shaming are associated with offending in schools

Low self-control

Table 8.4 shows that pupils who have low levels of self-control are much more likely to have offended in schools. This is true for overall offending in schools and for all types of offending, apart from serious offending by females (this may be due, however, to the small number of females who report breaking into schools or committing robbery in schools). The measures of association (gammas) also indicate that offending is quite strongly associated with low self-control. This is true for both males and females. Males have higher prevalence rates for all types of offending in schools by levels of self-control in comparison with females.

Pupils who have low levels of self-control are more likely to offend at a higher frequency in schools than those who have high self-control. This is illustrated by Figure 8.8, which shows that the same trend is seen for both sexes.

Figure 8.9 shows those with low self-control are more likely to commit different offences and be more versatile in their offending behaviour. This confirms that frequent offenders tend to be versatile in their offending behaviour and also to display low levels of self-control. Pupils with low self-control are more likely to have offended in school, more likely to offend frequently in school and more likely to be versatile in their offending habits.

Pro-social values

Table 8.4 shows that there are statistically significant relationships between pro-social values and all types of pupil offending in school (with the exception of serious offences for females). It shows that boys offend more than girls at all levels of pro-social values and in relation to all offending types in schools. This reflects the trend identified in Chapter 4, which showed that males tend to offend more than females in school. Further analysis revealed similar patterns in relation to versatility of offending and frequency of offending as identified above for the low self-control construct.

Table 8.4 Percentage of pupils who offended in school in relation to level of self-control

Dispositional measure	Offence type	Strength of dispositional measure					
		High (%)	Medium (%)	Low (%)	Sig.	Gamma
Low self-control*						
	Population					
	Theft	1.4	6.0	14.6	0.000	0.58
	Assault	3.9	12.8	33.6	0.000	0.59
	Vandalism	1.4	6.1	21.7	0.000	0.67
	Serious offences	0.9	0.9	3.6	0.000	0.38
	Overall offending	5.8	20.6	46.7	0.000	0.62
	Male					
	Theft	1.3	7.4	17.6	0.000	0.58
	Assault	4.8	17.4	41.7	0.000	0.60
	Vandalism	2.2	6.6	25.6	0.000	0.65
	Serious offences	2.2	1.5	4.5	0.027	0.22
	Overall offending	7.9	25.9	55.1	0.000	0.61
	Female					
	Theft	1.4	4.5	9.5	0.001	0.51
	Assault	3.4	7.9	19.8	0.000	0.48
	Vandalism	0.8	5.6	15.1	0.000	0.67
	Serious offences	0.0	0.3	1.9	n.s.	–
	Overall offending	4.5	14.8	32.1	0.000	0.57

Table 8.4 continues on page 174

Table 8.4 continued

Dispositional measure	Offence type	Strength of dispositional measure			Sig.	Gamma
		High (%)	Medium (%)	Low (%)		
Pro-social values**						
	Population					
	Theft	3.9	11.2	27.9	0.000	0.59
	Assault	9.6	25.2	35.3	0.000	0.54
	Vandalism	4.2	14.0	30.1	0.000	0.62
	Serious offences	0.6	1.6	12.7	0.000	0.68
	Overall offending	14.7	38.9	54.0	0.000	0.59
	Male					
	Theft	5.3	11.8	29.2	0.000	0.52
	Assault	13.9	31.0	37.5	0.000	0.47
	Vandalism	5.5	13.8	30.6	0.000	0.54
	Serious offences	1.1	2.4	13.8	0.000	0.61
	Overall offending	20.2	44.3	56.1	0.000	0.53
	Female					
	Theft	2.6	10.4	23.8	0.000	0.65
	Assault	5.7	17.1	28.6	0.000	0.57
	Vandalism	3.1	14.3	28.6	0.000	0.70
	Serious offences	0.2	0.5	9.5	n.s.	–
	Overall offending	9.8	31.1	47.6	0.000	0.63

Shaming*

Population					
Theft	3.1	7.1	15.1	0.000	0.50
Assault	9.2	14.3	27.2	0.000	0.38
Vandalism	3.4	8.9	15.7	0.000	0.50
Serious offences	0.5	1.3	3.5	0.000	0.55
Overall offending	13.5	23.1	41.5	0.000	0.44
Male					
Theft	4.1	7.9	16.2	0.000	0.45
Assault	13.4	19.2	30.7	0.000	0.32
Vandalism	4.1	10.3	15.2	0.000	0.44
Serious offences	1.1	1.8	4.2	0.007	0.42
Overall offending	18.5	28.9	44.0	0.000	0.37
Female					
Theft	2.4	6.0	12.6	0.000	0.51
Assault	6.2	7.8	19.3	0.000	0.31
Vandalism	2.9	7.0	16.8	0.000	0.54
Serious offences	0.1	0.5	1.7	n.s.	–
Overall offending	9.9	15.5	35.8	0.000	0.41

Notes:

* Low self-control scale grouped into high (scores 0–12), medium (scores 13–24) and low (scores 25–39).

** Pro-social values scale grouped into high (scores 29–42), medium (scores 15–28) and low (scores 0–14).

*** Shaming scale grouped into high (scores 9–12), medium (scores 5–8) and low (scores 0–4).

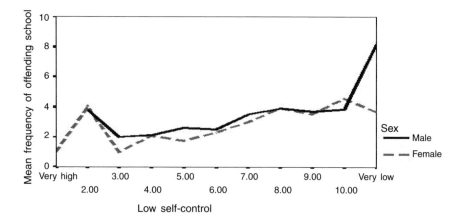

Figure 8.8 Average (mean) frequency of overall offending in school by (low) self-control

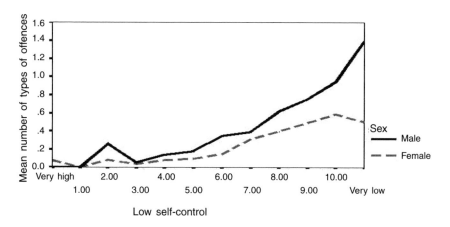

Figure 8.9 Pupils' mean number of different types of offence in school by (low) self-control

Shaming
Pupils who perceive that they would feel a great degree of shame if they were caught offending commit fewer offences than others. Table 8.4 shows that those with high levels of shaming offend much less prevalently in schools than others. The relationships are statistically significant for all offence types, apart from serious offending reported by females. As with pro-social values and low

self-control, the measures of association (gammas) are stronger in comparison with structural measures (i.e. area of residence structural risk and family social position), school context measures and, indeed, social situational measures reported earlier in this chapter. Pupils' dispositional and social situational measures may be deemed to be closer to their decision-making processes (particularly their dispositional characteristics), which may in turn guide their actions. Social situation and dispositional factors are more likely to influence directly the pupils' decision-making process than factors relating to their position in society, their school context and their area of residence which, as argued, may exert an indirect effect and be mediated by individual social situational and dispositional characteristics.

Family social position risk in relation to social situation and dispositions

Social situation
Table 8.5 shows how pupils' family social position characteristics are related to the pupils' bonds to society and their levels of parental monitoring. The table indicates that pupils' family social class has no significant influence on family bonds. However, family social class is related to pupils' levels of parental monitoring (however, this just misses statistical significance at the 0.05 level) and school bonds. Pupils from lower-class family backgrounds are more likely to be poorly supervised by their parents and have weaker bonds to the school. A possible explanation for the relationship between pupils' poorer school bonds and coming from lower socioeconomic status backgrounds is that it could be because of the lower value that is placed on education in lower socioeconomic status families. If parents are encouraged to value education and take an interest in their children's education this may lead to lower offending and victimisation in schools, as well as enabling higher academic performance to be achieved.

Family structure appears to be significantly (statistically) related to both school and family bonds and to parental monitoring. Those in care and those who do not live with both biological parents are more likely to report weaker levels of bonds and monitoring than others. Living with a single parent, however, is likely to give an individual a comparatively (in relation to living with a step-parent or in care, etc.) stronger bond to the family, and these pupils also report higher levels of parental monitoring, on average. Although the average difference is small, it has been shown that pupils from single-parent backgrounds offend marginally less than pupils from backgrounds where one

Table 8.5 Mean score of school and family bonds, by family social position variables, means, significance and eta^2

Family social position	Pro-social values	Self-control	Shaming	Weak family bonds	Weak parental monitoring	Weak school bonds
Family social class						
Upper middle	33.6	15.1	9.4	3.1	3.1	8.1
Middle	33.3	16.8	8.7	3.2	3.1	8.2
Working/lower working	33.1	17.9	8.1	3.1	2.9	8.0
Unemployed	33.0	18.0	8.1	2.9	2.8	7.2
Sig.	n.s.	0.000	0.000	n.s	0.054	0.017
Eta^2	–	0.015	0.013	–	0.002	0.003
Family structure						
Two parent (biol.)	33.5	16.9	8.6	3.0	2.9	7.9
Two parents (one step-parent)	32.5	18.1	8.0	3.2	3.2	8.4
Single parent	32.9	18.0	8.1	3.5	3.4	8.3
Care/relatives/foster	32.2	17.7	8.6	3.8	3.4	8.1
Sig.	0.026	0.000	0.000	0.000	0.000	0.017
Eta^2	0.003	0.009	0.007	0.014	0.009	0.003

Family size					
Only child	34.1	16.5	8.5	2.8	2.6	7.9
One	33.5	16.7	8.7	3.0	2.8	7.9
Two	33.5	16.8	8.6	3.1	3.0	8.2
Three	32.6	18.1	8.2	3.2	3.2	8.1
Four plus	32.6	18.2	8.0	3.4	3.4	8.1
Sig.	0.023	0.000	0.000	0.000	0.000	n.s.
Eta²	0.004	0.014	0.008	0.009	0.013	–
Family ethnicity					
Native	33.2	17.3	8.4	3.1	3.0	8.1
Foreign, non-Asian	32.7	17.3	8.4	3.0	3.1	8.2
Asian	34.6	16.2	9.2	2.9	2.8	7.3
Sig.	n.s.	n.s.	0.021	n.s.	n.s.	0.006
Eta²	–	–	0.003	–	–	0.003

parent is a step-parent. One reason for this may be that pupils from single-parent backgrounds may have stronger family bonds and are better supervised. It seems clear, though, that living with two biological parents is beneficial to pupils, both in terms of offending behaviour and in terms of their integration into conventional society. This integration into conventional society appears to be an important factor regarding pupils' propensity to offend in schools.

Family size seems to be related to both family bonds and parental monitoring, but not school bonds. Having lots of siblings seems to weaken family bonds and lower levels of monitoring. Theoretically this finding appears sound. Greater family size could mean that children will receive less attention in comparison with smaller families, possibly due to the attention of parents being more thinly spread. It is likely that monitoring levels will be lower for this reason too. It may be easier for parents to keep track of one child than four. Family bonds and levels of monitoring provide a theoretical explanation as to why individuals with large family size are consistently shown to be at a higher risk of offending in criminological research. Parental monitoring and family bonds may provide a mechanism that mediates large family size in influencing offending.

Family ethnic background has no relation to family bonds or parental monitoring; however, it is related to the school bond. Pupils from an Asian family background appear to have, on average, stronger school bonds. This replicates a similar finding by Wikström (2002).

Individual dispositional characteristics

Table 8.5 illustrates that pupils' family socioeconomic status and ethnic background are not statistically significantly related to their pro-social values. This suggests that notions regarding 'lower-class' subcultures of delinquency based on young people having different values from others in conventional society are flawed. These findings also suggest that youths from different ethnic backgrounds have similar values regarding right and wrong from the rest of conventional society, which suggests that the view that a reason for minority groups' involvement in crime is that they have different values regarding right and wrong is incorrect. This theme regarding subcultures will be discussed more thoroughly in Chapter 9. Table 8.5 indicates that there are significant differences between pupils' pro-social value levels in relation to their family parental composition and family size. Those from disrupted families or in care and who have larger family sizes tend to have weaker pro-social values.

Low self-control seems to be related to all the social background measures apart from ethnic background. Pupils from lower social classes, from disrupted families and from larger families tend to have lower self-control. This can also be said regarding pupils' sense of shaming levels. However, those from Asian backgrounds tend to have, on average, a higher sense of shaming.

Where there are relationships between dispositions and family social background, the amount of explained variance is low. Family socioeconomic status in relation to low self-control and shaming explains more than 1 per cent of the variance between pupils, as does family size in relation to low self-control. All the other significant relationships explain less than 1 per cent of the variance among pupils. This analysis gives credence to the idea that family social position may affect pupil delinquency rates in schools through influencing aspects of pupils' dispositions.

Like family social position in relation to social situation, the majority of significant associations with individual dispositional characteristics explain less than 1 per cent of the variance between groups of pupils, with only family structure in relation to family bonds, and family size in relation to parental monitoring explaining greater than 1 per cent of the variance, but these still explain less than 2 per cent of the variance between groups of pupils. It is possible that, in a study employing a longitudinal design, these relationships may be shown to be stronger, because it is likely that integration into conventional society is shaped over time, and family structural factors may impact on the studied social situational factors fairly strongly, especially if measured from an early stage in the child's development (i.e. from birth or pre-birth, even).

This chapter has shown that pupils' social situational and dispositional characteristics are related to pupil offending in schools. It has also indicated that family social position is related to pupils' social situational and dispositional characteristics.

Pupils with strong pro-social values, who have a high sense of shame and high levels of self-control, have stronger bonds, and are supervised more than others

This is a cross-sectional study which makes causality difficult to discern, as the data are based on a snapshot in time. Thus, causal assertions that can be made must be based on theoretical concepts and previous literature and research. It is difficult to say whether bonds to parents and bonds to school help increase an individual's level of self-control, shaming and pro-social values. It is likely that these aspects evolve together in a complex manner over the life course. Individuals with strong bonds to conventional society should also have higher levels of (sense of) shaming pro-social values and self-control than those individuals who are weakly integrated into society. Figures 8.10, 8.11 and 8.12 indicate that these factors do appear to be

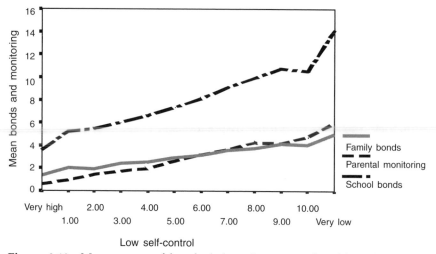

Figure 8.10 Mean scores of bonds (where 0 = strong bonds) and parental monitoring (where 0 = good monitoring) by level of self-control

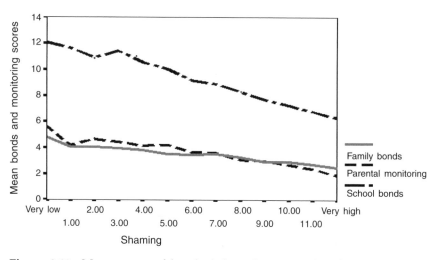

Figure 8.11 Mean scores of bonds (where 0 = strong bonds) and parental monitoring (where 0 = good monitoring) by level of shaming

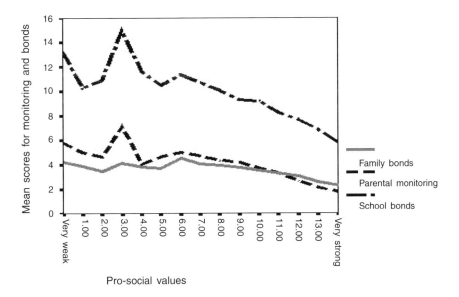

Figure 8.12 Mean scores of bonds (where 0 = strong bonds) and parental monitoring (where 0 = good monitoring) by level of pro-social values

related. Those with high levels of shaming, high levels of self-control and high levels of pro-social values appear to have stronger bonds and receive higher levels of parental monitoring.

Table 8.6 shows how social situational characteristics and individual dispositional characteristics are correlated. It can be seen that, generally, these factors are all fairly strongly correlated. More will be said about this later.

The creation of an individual risk-protective scale based on pupils' social situation and disposition

So far in this chapter it has been shown that pupils' individual social situational and dispositional characteristics that have been investigated are all associated with pupil offending in school. The analyses indicate that most pupils in Cardiff have adequate (i.e. medium strength) social bonds and levels of self-control, strong pro-social values and a high degree of (sense of) shaming. Most pupils also report that their parents monitor them adequately. It can be concluded from these analyses that pupils with weak social bonds, poor parental monitoring, low self-control, anti-social values and a

Table 8.6 Zero-order correlations between the six individual characteristic constructs

Individual characteristics	Weak family bonds	Weak parental monitoring	Weak school bonds	Low self-control	Strong pro-social values	Strong shaming
Weak family bonds	1.00					
Weak parental monitoring	0.52	1.00				
Weak school bonds	0.34	0.40	1.00			
Low self-control	0.33	0.46	0.50	1.00		
Strong pro-social values	-0.29	-0.44	-0.46	-0.51	1.00	
Strong shaming	-0.31	-0.43	-0.52	-0.52	0.55	1.00

Note:
All zero-order correlations are significant at the 0.05 level or better.

low degree of shaming are much more likely to offend in schools than pupils with these characteristics in the reverse. Offending in schools by pupils is closely related to these measured aspects of their individual social situation and dispositions.

This section will combine these elements of pupils' social situation and dispositional measures into an individual risk-protective scale. The rationale for doing this is that, by combining aspects of pupils' social situation and dispositions, it is possible to gain a measure of individuals that is more realistic and closer to how pupils act than by looking at different aspects of disposition or social situation. This is consistent with the analytical approach taken in this book which aims to take a person-oriented approach as opposed to a variable-oriented approach. By combining scores it is argued a more realistic view of each individual is achieved rather than by using a single variable approach. Analysis in this study is driven by theory and should therefore be theoretically consequent and rigorous. The idea is, thus, to obtain a score that takes into account all the measures that have been shown in this chapter to relate closely to pupils' offending in schools. Wikström (2002: 107) argues that such a composite measure of pupils 'may better (and more realistically) portray them as individuals'. This approach can be described as a more holistic approach, whereby the focus is on individuals rather than on different aspects of individuals. A study of different aspects of individuals has already been undertaken in this chapter. Wikström and Loeber (2000: 1118) argue that the rationale for this holistic approach is that 'individuals act as individuals'. The approach, thus, draws on a variety of individual characteristics that operate in complex and interacting ways. The individual risk-protective scale aims to measure individuals as individuals by combining these key aspects of pupils' social situation and disposition. Wikström and Loeber (2000: 1125) argue: 'we assume that single factors with different risk and protective characteristics operate jointly in complex ways and that classifying individuals by their set of risk and protective characteristics will capture some essentials regarding individual differences in decision making and perception of alternatives relevant to offending.' This is a goal of the present analysis concerning the individual risk-protective characteristics of pupils in Year 10 in the 20 Cardiff secondary schools being investigated.

Table 8.6, showed that all the constructs relating to pupils' individual social situation and disposition were fairly strongly correlated. Table 8.7 shows a factor analysis (principal component) of all the constructs used in this chapter, which shows that the constructs load on one factor displaying an eigenvalue above 1 and, together, explain 53 per cent of the variance. This factor analysis replicates the finding of Wikström (2002: 109) for a similarly aged sample of juveniles in the Peterborough Youth Study. It is argued that this factor can be regarded as an individual pupil's risk-protective dimension, which takes into account both their social situation and dispositions.

The pupils' individual risk-protective score

The risk-protective score is a composite measure of the three social situational constructs and the three dispositional constructs so far examined in this chapter. Each single construct was divided into three groups in the following manner: the third of the scores at the protective end of the distribution (given the value of −1); the third of scores in the middle (given the value of 0); and the third of scores at the risk end of the distribution (given the value of +1). For example, pupils having a score among the highest third of scores in terms of weak family bonds were given a score of +1, those belonging to the lowest third were assigned −1 and the third in the middle were assigned 0. The six constructs were then added, resulting in a scale varying from −6 to +6, where +6 signifies a pupil hypothesised to be at high risk of offending in school and −6 signifying a pupil who has protective individual characteristics, which is hypothesised to reduce the risk of the pupil offending in school.

Figure 8.13 shows the distribution of males and females on the individual risk-protective continuum. This figure illustrates that, generally, girls appear to be more likely to have more protective characteristics than boys. The mean risk-protective score for boys is −1.9 (SD = 2.4) and the mean risk-protective score for girls is −2.6

Table 8.7 Factor analysis: individual characteristics, principal components

Constructs	Factor loadings	Communalities
Weak family bonds	0.61	0.37
Weak school bonds	0.74	0.54
Poor parental monitoring	0.74	0.55
Low self-control	0.77	0.59
Strong pro-social values	−0.75	0.56
High shaming	−0.77	0.59
Eigenvalue	3.2	
Explained variance	53.4	

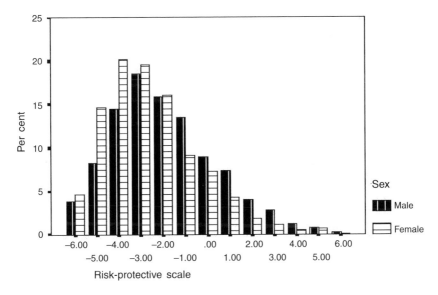

Figure 8.13 Pupils' individual risk-protective scores by sex: distribution

(SD = 2.1). This difference is statistically significant (p = 0.000, eta^2 = 0.03). Boys have a greater standard deviation from the mean than girls, suggesting that boys tend to vary to a greater degree at the extremes of the risk-protective continuum. Generally both males and females can be seen to display more protective characteristics than risk characteristics.

Table 8.8 indicates where the sex differences in the overall individual risk-protective scale lie. The table shows each construct, the means for males and females in relation to the construct, whether the difference is statistically significant and how much variance is explained by sex differences (eta^2). This table shows that the degree of shaming an individual pupil senses varies by sex the greatest, followed by self-control, weak school bonds and pro-social values. There is no statistically significant difference between the sexes for family bonds.

These findings indicate why females tend to have higher protective individual characteristics than males. Females on average have higher levels of shaming (in particular), self-control, pro-social values and also stronger school bonds. Females (at the age of 14/15) tend to have better adjusted dispositions on average, a finding that Wikström (2002) would concur with. However, this may be to do with developmental stage, something that longitudinal research may

Table 8.8 Sex differences in social situation and disposition constructs, means, significance and eta^2

Construct	Male	Female	Sig.	Eta^2
High shaming	7.7	9.2	0.000	0.05
Low self-control	18.1	16.3	0.000	0.02
Poor parental monitoring	3.3	2.8	0.000	0.01
Weak school bonds	8.5	7.6	0.000	0.02
Strong pro-social values	32.2	34.3	0.000	0.02
Weak family bonds	3.1	3.2	n.s.	–

shed more light on and which cannot lucidly be addressed in a cross-sectional study such as this. Females are also more likely to have stronger bonds to school and report that they are better monitored by parents. However, family bonds show no significant difference between males and females.

Wikström and Svensson (forthcoming) argue that these sex differences in individual social situation and dispositions go a long way in explaining sex differences in general offending rates. Their research was based on a sample of 2,283 subjects, aged 14 (a similar age group to the population under examination in this study), from two small cities and one medium-sized city in Sweden. Their argument suggests that it is not the fact that one is male or female that explains offending behaviour; rather, it is the differences in individual social situation and morality that account for juveniles' differential offending risk. Females were shown, as in this study, to have, on average, higher and more protective characteristics than males, thus offering an explanation as to why females have, on average, a lower propensity to offend. Furthermore, it could be argued that similar mechanisms are likely to explain differential rates of offending by males and females. If females generally have more protective mechanisms, this may help explain lower rates of offending.

Empirical findings such as these open debate regarding whether it is justified to have separate research paradigms investigating the aetiology of crime among females and crime among males, when the causes seem somewhat similar for both.

Asian girls in Cardiff have the highest average protective scores

In the Cardiff School Study, 4.9 per cent of pupils can be said to come from Asian backgrounds (as discussed in Chapter 6). Of this

4.9 per cent, 3 per cent are male and 1.9 per cent female. Thus there are 92 males of Asian background and 59 females of Asian background in the population. Wikström (2002) and Butterworth *et al.* (forthcoming) found that Asian girls on average display the most protective characteristics in the Peterborough Youth Study. The analysis in Table 8.9 confirms this view. In fact, Asian males and females on average display more protective characteristics than their non-Asian counterparts.

Asians (both males and females) on average have a higher sense of shaming, higher levels of self-control, better parental supervision, stronger school bonds, stronger pro-social values and (although statistically non-significant) stronger family bonds. Such findings may indicate why previous criminological research has found Asians to report offending less than other groups (see, for example, Wikström 2002; Butterworth *et al.* forthcoming). However, regarding offending in schools, this study has shown there to be no significant group differences, along ethnic lines, in terms of offending prevalence and frequency of offending behaviour.

Family social position is related to pupils' individual risk-protective characteristics

Figure 8.14 indicates that coming from a socially disadvantaged background influences the pupils' individual risk-protective scores.

Table 8.9 Mean scores of social situation and disposition constructs by Asian and non-Asian backgrounds and sex, mean, significance and eta^2

| | Mean score | | | | | |
| | Males | | Females | | | |
Construct	Non-Asian	Asian	Non-Asian	Asian	Sig.	Eta^2
High shaming	7.7	8.4	9.2	10.3	0.000	0.06
Low self-control	18.2	16.3	16.4	16.1	0.000	0.03
Poor parental monitoring	3.3	3.0	2.8	2.4	0.000	0.01
Weak school bonds	8.5	7.5	7.7	6.9	0.000	0.02
Strong pro-social values	32.1	33.5	34.2	36.3	0.000	0.02
Weak family bonds	3.1	2.9	3.2	2.7	n.s.	–
Risk-protective score*	–1.9	–2.4	–2.6	–3.2	0.000	0.03

Note:
*The higher the negative value, the higher the protective score.

The family social position risk score is the same as that developed in Chapter 6. It is based on family size, family SES and parental composition (all scores –1 to +1 and added to make a composite score ranging from +3 to –3; –3 indicates a protected background). The risk score was then divided into three groups on the following basis: –3 to –2 was scored –1 and indicates a protected family social position; –1 to 0 was scored 0 and indicates a balanced family social position; and +1 to +3 was scored +1 indicating a risky family social position.

Figure 8.14 shows that males and females from more protected family social positions tend to have more protective individual characteristics. Females have more protective characteristics at all levels than males. Males are more influenced by family social position than females. A comparison of means confirms this and shows that the relationship is significant for both males ($p = 0.000$, eta^2 = 0.03) and for females ($p = 0.001$, eta^2 = 0.01).

Family social position has a greater importance for non-Asian than for Asian pupils

Figure 8.15 illustrates the relationship between family social position and pupils' ethnic background and individual risk-protective characteristics. It indicates that non-Asian males seem to be most influenced by their social backgrounds in comparison with the other groups. However, the differences for males between Asian and non-

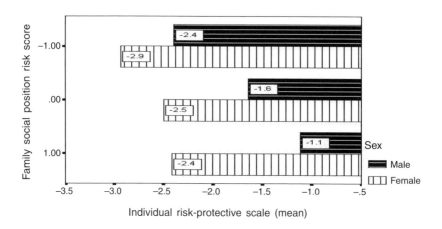

Figure 8.14 Pupils' risk-protective scores by family social position risk and sex

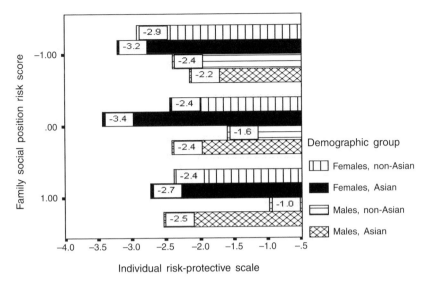

Figure 8.15 Family social position risk score by individual risk-protective score and demographic group

Asian are not significant (but are almost at $p = 0.065$) regarding family social position, they are however, for females ($p = 0.041$, eta^2 = 0.003).

Family social position is an important influence on pupils' individual risk-protective scores

Table 8.10 shows the results of a multiple regression that included pupils' family social position measures in predicting the outcome of pupils' individual risk-protective scores. The analysis shows that sex (being male or female) appears not to be a significant predictor of the individual risk-protective score. However, this is explained by the fact that the Asian female construct includes the male–female divide. The table indicates that being an Asian female is the best predictor of having protective characteristics (as indicated by the negative value). Thus, being female generally may be a good predictor of having protective characteristics. But being an Asian female is a particularly good predictor of having protective characteristics. The table also indicates that coming from advantaged socioeconomic backgrounds, from complete families and small families are all predictors of having protective characteristics. Low family SES, split family background and large family size are all positive predictors of individuals having more risk characteristics.

Table 8.10 OLS multiple regression: risk-protective score by sex and family social position

Construct	Individual risk-protective scale		
	Standardised beta	T-value	Prob.
Sex	0.12	1.36	n.s.
Asian female	−0.30	−3.32	0.001
Low family SES	0.06	3.36	0.001
Split family	0.06	3.34	0.001
Large family size	0.08	4.19	0.000
Multiple $R^2 \times 100 = 5$			

This model explains 5 per cent of the variance regarding pupils' individual risk-protective scores. Sex and family social position do exert an important influence on pupils' individual risk-protective scores and, as such, in relation to their social situation and dispositions.

Pupils' individual risk-protective scores are related to area of residence structural risk

The analyses that follow indicate that pupils' area of residence structural risk is significantly related to their individual risk-protective scores, but the relationship is not strong and one would be unable to predict a pupil's individual risk-protective score from knowledge of the subject's area of residence structural risk score.

Figure 8.16 shows that pupils' individual risk-protective scores do vary by area of residence structural risk score. There is a general trend that, the more disadvantaged the area of residence structural risk, the greater the percentage of pupils who have higher-risk individual risk-protective scores.

Table 8.11 indicates that the relationship between area of residence structural risk and the individual risk-protective score is statistically significant, but only approximately 1 per cent of the variance in the pupils' individual risk-protective scores can be attributed to their area of residence.

Table 8.11 provides a breakdown of the pupils' individual risk-protective score by area of residence structural risk scores. This shows that individuals' pro-social values and family bond scores are not statistically significantly related to area of residence structural risk but the other factors are. However, all the relationships are much

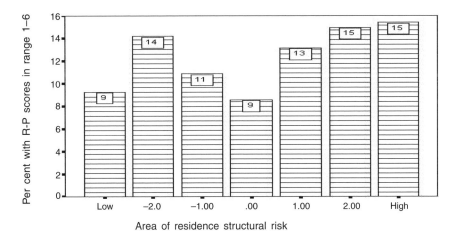

Figure 8.16 Per cent pupils with individual risk-protective scores in the range 1–6 (risk) by area of residence structural risk

Table 8.11 Mean social situation and disposition scores, and overall risk-protective score by area of residence structural risk group, ANOVA and zero-order correlations

Construct	ANOVA*		Zero-order correlations**	
	Eta²	Sig.	r	Sig.
Social situation				
Weak family bonds	–	n.s.	0.02	n.s.
Weak school bonds	0.01	0.002	0.04	0.026
Poor parental monitoring	0.01	0.008	0.04	0.009
Dispositions				
Low self-control	0.02	0.000	0.11	0.000
Pro-social values	–	n.s.	−0.03	n.s.
Shaming	0.02	0.000	−0.12	0.000
Overall risk-protective score	0.01	0.000	0.08	0.000

Notes:
 * ANOVA test of mean differences between the seven classes of area structural risk.
** Please note that *r* refers to correlations calculated on non-grouped data.

weaker than for the family social position factors. This replicates Wikström's (2002) finding, providing further evidence contrary to the theory that delinquent subcultures flourish among lower-class youths living in more disadvantaged areas. The fact is that most individuals can tell the difference between right and wrong concerning norm or law breaking, and those individuals who cannot appear to be spread across areas and across social positions.

The relationship between pupils' individual risk-protective scores and offending in schools

There is a strong relationship between the pupil's individual risk-protective score and offending behaviour in schools. Figure 8.17 illustrates a strong relationship between pupils' individual risk-protective scores with male and female offending prevalence in schools. The general pattern indicates the higher the individual risk-protective score, the more likely the pupil is to have reported offending in school. This indicates that pupils' individual characteristics, based on social situation and dispositions, are very important in relation to whether or not pupils have offended in school.

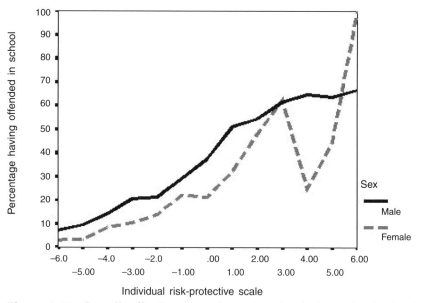

Figure 8.17 Overall offending prevalence in schools by individual risk-protective score and sex

Table 8.12 confirms this pattern illustrated in Figure 8.17, but with three groups of pupils divided into risk, balanced and protected groups. This was achieved by dividing the individual risk-protective score into three groups, based on grouping the scores into thirds. The first group (the protected group) includes those pupils with scores of −6 to −3, the middle group (balanced) includes those with scores −2 to +2 and the risk group was based on scores +3 to +6. It can be seen from this analysis that there are strong, statistically significant relationships between all types of offending in schools and whether pupils display risk, balanced or protective individual social situational and dispositional characteristics. This is true for both males and females (with the exception of serious offences reported by females – this is probably due to the small number involved).

Table 8.12 Pupils' individual risk-protective scores by offending in schools and sex

| | Individual risk-protective scale* | | | | |
	Protected (%)	Balanced (%)	Risk (%)	Sig.	Gamma
Population					
Theft	2.7	8.4	23.5	0.000	0.58
Assault	7.2	17.7	40.2	0.000	0.51
Vandalism	2.6	9.8	28.7	0.000	0.64
Serious offences	0.4	1.4	5.1	0.000	0.61
Overall offending	10.8	28.0	58.7	0.000	0.57
Male					
Theft	3.5	10.1	23.5	0.000	0.55
Assault	10.8	22.5	47.1	0.000	0.47
Vandalism	3.3	10.8	29.9	0.000	0.61
Serious offences	0.8	2.1	7.8	0.000	0.55
Overall offending	15.3	33.4	62.9	0.000	0.52
Female					
Theft	2.1	6.1	23.5	0.000	0.58
Assault	4.5	11.5	26.5	0.000	0.50
Vandalism	2.1	8.4	26.5	0.000	0.66
Serious offences	0.1	0.6	0.0	n.s.	
Overall offending	7.4	20.8	50.0	0.000	0.57

Note:

* Individual risk protective scale split into a protective group (score −6 to −3), a balanced group (scores −2 to +2) and a risk group (scores +3 to +6).

Pupils with high-risk individual characteristics are also versatile and offend frequently

As already shown, a pupil who has a high-risk individual risk-protective score is far more likely to offend in school than a pupil who has a protective score. Figure 8.18 illustrates a trend whereby, the higher risk the pupil's individual risk-protective score, the more frequent the offending by the offender. This general trend holds for offending in schools for both males and females.

As well as pupils with a high-risk individual risk-protective score tending to offend more frequently, they are also more likely to commit a greater variety of offences. Figure 8.19 displays that this is true for both males and females. This should be relatively unsurprising, as Chapter 4 indicates that those pupils who offend more frequently also tend to be more versatile in their offending habits.

Multiple regression analyses

In order to explore the relative importance of pupils' area of residence structural risk, family social position, school context (pupil relations and climate) and individual risk-protective characteristics in

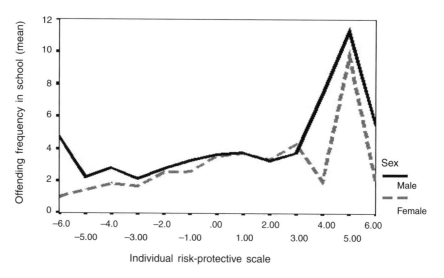

Figure 8.18 Offenders' frequency of offending in school by individual risk-protective score and sex

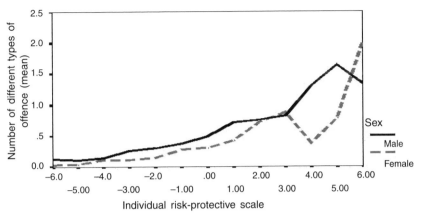

Figure 8.19 Versatility of offending in school by pupils' individual risk-protective score and sex

relation to offending frequency in schools, among Cardiff's Year 10 school pupils, a series of multiple regression analyses are presented in Tables 8.13 and 8.14. The first analysis (model 1) in Table 8.13, includes sex, area of residence structural risk, family social position risk, school climate risk, pupil relations risk and individual social situational measures (i.e. bonds and monitoring). This model indicates that parental monitoring and school bonds are statistically significant predictors of the frequency of offending by pupils in Cardiff's schools. However, the school climate as perceived by the pupils is also a significant predictor of frequency of pupil offending in school. Interestingly, family bonds are not a significant predictor of offending frequency in the school context. Theoretically, it may be the case that parental monitoring, school bonds and school climate are measures that more closely relate to pupils' social action in the school context, thus possibly explaining why family bonds, family social position and pupils' area of residence structural risk are not significant predictors of pupil offending in the school context. The school context, parental monitoring and school bonds are likely to have a closer influence on pupils' action in the behaviour setting provided by the school. However, it must be remembered that this analysis cannot account for the effects area of residence structural risk, family social position and school context have had on influencing the development of pupils' social situational characteristics. This is because the analysis is based on cross-sectional data and cannot take account of the individual development of pupils. For overall offending frequency, model 1 explains 8 per cent of the variance; for assault this falls to 6 per cent and for theft and vandalism only 3 per cent of the variance is explained.

Model 2 in Table 8.13 includes the three measures of pupils' dispositions included with those variables that were included in model 1. In this model, the two strongest predictors of pupil offending in schools appear to be pupils' pro-social values and self-control. For all offence categories, pro-social values are a significant predictor. For overall offending, assault and vandalism, low self-control is a significant predictor. Parental monitoring is a significant predictor of both overall offending and assault in schools when other factors are controlled for. Sex (being female) remains as a significant predictor of both overall offending and assault in schools. However, it is not as strong a predictor as pupils' dispositions, and it loses its statistical significance for theft and vandalism. The two strongest predictors of pupil offending in schools appear to be pupils' self-control and pro-social values. In this second model, family and school bonds lose their significance as predictors of all categories of pupils' frequency of offending in schools.

The fact that the majority of pupils' social situation constructs lose their significance as predictors of pupil offending in schools in model 2 reflects the possibility that pupils' dispositional characteristics are closer to how pupils make their decisions and act. Wikström (2002: 119) argues that: 'youths' dispositions are embedded in their social situation, which, in turn, is embedded in the youths' wider social position.'

These regression models demonstrate that, as one measures constructs more closely related to pupils' social action, the more distant factors (i.e. family social position factors) diminish in importance. This does not mean that such factors are unimportant, as it is highly likely that contextual factors and, in this example, family social position, area of residence structural risk and school contextual factors will be highly important in determining pupils' development of social situational and dispositional characteristics.

Model 2 in Table 8.13 indicates that, when area, family and school factors and pupils' individual social situation and dispositional measures are included as independent variables, the explained variance for pupils' overall offending in schools reaches 14 per cent (in contrast to only 2 per cent when just the family social positional characteristics were included in an OLS multiple regression model in Chapter 6).

Table 8.14 shows an OLS multiple regression model that replaces the individual social situation and disposition constructs with a

Table 8.13 Main types of offending (frequency) in schools, by family social position, social situation and dispositions, OLS multiple regression

Variable	Overall		Theft		Assault		Vandalism	
	Beta	Sig.	Beta	Sig.	Beta	Sig.	Beta	Sig.
Model 1								
Female	-0.10	0.000	-0.05	0.011	-0.13	0.000	-0.01	n.s.
Area risk	0.03	n.s.	0.02	n.s.	0.03	n.s.	0.01	n.s.
Family social position	0.03	n.s.	0.02	n.s.	0.03	n.s.	0.02	n.s.
Climate risk	0.07	0.002	0.06	0.012	0.07	0.002	0.02	n.s.
Pupil relations risk	0.04	0.029	0.03	n.s.	0.02	n.s.	0.03	n.s.
Weak family bonds	0.04	n.s.	0.01	n.s.	0.03	n.s.	0.04	n.s.
Poor parental monitoring	0.15	0.000	0.09	0.000	0.11	0.000	0.11	0.000
Weak school bonds	0.07	0.001	0.05	0.040	0.05	0.017	0.05	0.037
$R^2 \times 100 =$	8		3		6		3	
Model 2								
Female	-0.07	0.000	-0.03	n.s.	-0.11	0.000	0.01	n.s.
Area risk	0.03	n.s.	0.01	n.s.	0.03	n.s.	0.01	n.s.
Family social position	0.02	n.s.	0.02	n.s.	0.02	n.s.	0.01	n.s.
Climate risk	0.04	n.s.	0.04	n.s.	0.05	0.038	-0.00	n.s.
Pupil relations risk	0.04	0.025	0.03	n.s.	0.02	n.s.	0.03	n.s.
Weak family bonds	-0.04	n.s.	0.01	n.s.	0.02	n.s.	0.03	n.s.
Poor parental monitoring	0.06	0.005	0.04	n.s.	0.05	0.030	0.04	n.s.
Weak school bonds	-0.04	n.s.	-0.02	n.s.	-0.03	n.s.	-0.03	n.s.
Low self-control	0.09	0.000	0.04	n.s.	0.10	0.000	0.07	0.008
Pro-social values	-0.20	0.000	-0.12	0.000	-0.16	0.000	-0.14	0.000
Shaming	-0.05	0.039	-0.06	0.017	-0.01	n.s.	-0.05	n.s.
$R^2 \times 100 =$	14		5		10		5	

Table 8.14 Pupils' sex, family social position and individual risk-protective scores by main types of offending in schools (frequency), OLS multiple regression

Variable	Overall		Theft		Assault		Vandalism	
	Beta	Sig.	Beta	Sig.	Beta	Sig.	Beta	Sig.
Female	−0.08	0.000	−0.04	0.028	−0.11	0.000	0.00	n.s.
Area risk	0.03	n.s.	0.01	n.s.	0.03	n.s.	0.01	n.s.
Family social position	0.02	n.s.	0.01	n.s.	0.02	n.s.	0.02	n.s.
Climate risk	0.04	n.s.	0.04	n.s.	0.04	n.s.	−0.00	n.s.
Pupil relations risk	0.04	0.030	0.03	n.s.	0.02	n.s.	0.03	n.s.
Individual risk-protective score	0.28	0.000	0.16	0.000	0.23	0.000	0.20	0.000
Multiple $R^2 \times 100$ =	11		4		8		4	

single construct which measures pupils' individual risk-protective characteristics (a composite measure of all the individual social situation and disposition characteristics – its construction was described earlier in this chapter). This analysis indicates that this individual risk-protective score predicts offending as well as a model which includes each of the single constructs, although, for overall offending in schools, the model explains 3 per cent less of the variance and for each of the other offending categories 1 per cent (apart from assault which is 2 per cent) less of the variance. This illustrates that the individual risk-protective scale seems a sound measure of individuals and will, thus, be used in analyses later in the book.

Summary

This chapter has demonstrated that the strongest predictors of pupil offending in schools shown in this book so far are pupils' pro-social values and self-control. More importantly, perhaps, this chapter has demonstrated that, as one measures aspects more closely related to the individual action of pupils, these factors prove to be stronger predictors of both offending prevalence and frequency in schools. When pupils' dispositions are not controlled for in the analyses, school climate is a good, significant, predictor of pupil offending frequency in school. This suggests that pupils' view of school climate is important in determining pupils' offending in schools. Encouraging more positive views of school climate among pupils may prove a fruitful avenue in reducing offending in school. School bonds and parental monitoring were also shown to be important factors influencing offending frequency in schools when dispositions were not included in the equation.

Females, on average, display more protective social situational and dispositional characteristics than males. It is likely that such a finding can help explain a common finding in empirical research that females offend less than males. More importantly, though, the chapter indicates that similar factors are associated with both male and female offending, suggesting that future research should continue to examine sex differences in offending by examining both males and females – as their offending behaviour seems to share common causes. Separate research paradigms regarding male and female offending are likely to diminish the quality of findings and may lead to flawed perspectives.

Chapter 9

Lifestyle

This chapter will focus on the relationship between pupils' lifestyles and offending behaviour in schools. It is based on previous literature regarding routine activities and offending behaviour (Cohen and Felson 1979; Miethe and Meier 1994) and lifestyle research in relation to victimisation (Hindelang *et al.* 1978; Garofalo 1986; Lauritsen *et al.* 1991; Wittebrood and Neiuwbeerta 1999). It will contribute to knowledge through empirically testing the role of pupils' lifestyles in relation to pupils' offending behaviour in schools.

The concept of lifestyle

Lifestyles can be considered to be patterns of social action that differentiate people. Chaney (1996) argues that those who live in modern societies will use a notion of lifestyle to describe their own and others' actions. He states that distinctive patterns of social life are invariably summarised by the term 'culture'. However, explaining patterns of social life using purely cultural explanations may diminish the quality of explanation of what causes individuals to act because, as Chaney (1996: 5) argues, 'while lifestyles are dependent on cultural forms, each is a style, a manner, a way of using certain goods, places and times that is characteristic of a group but is not the totality of their social experience'. Garofalo (1986: 40) recognises that social forces, such as role expectations and structural constraints, shape lifestyles. An understanding of individuals' lifestyles may have great utility for strategies aimed at crime prevention. For instance, tax policies may be employed to prevent alcohol consumption in society, which may discourage individuals from attending public houses, thus changing individual routines and lifestyles, which may cut down on violent assaults. Lifestyle explanations recognise the fact that individuals are unlikely to lead their lives constrained by the so-called 'values' or 'identities' of a specific social grouping identified by an observer. The utility of the concept of lifestyle is that it helps to make sense of and aids explanation of what individuals do, why they act and what their actions mean to them and to others (see, Chaney 1996).

Criminological theory has often centred on the notion of culture and subcultures in attempting to explain juvenile offending (see, for example, Yinger 1960). Sykes and Matza (1957: 666) argue: 'the theoretical viewpoint that sees juvenile delinquency as a form of behaviour based on the values and norms of a deviant sub-culture in precisely the same way as law-abiding behaviour is based on the values and norms of the larger society is open to serious doubt.' Kornhauser (1978: 244) uncompromisingly argued that 'cultural deviance' perspectives have little utility in the explanation of offending: 'delinquent norms, delinquent values, and delinquent subcultures have for too long dominated the thinking of criminologists; there is no evidence of their existence.' More comprehensively, in her conclusion, Kornhauser (1978: 253) contends: 'So abused have been the concepts of culture and subculture in explanation of delinquency that if these terms were struck from the lexicon of criminologists, the study of delinquency would benefit from their absence … Cultural deviance models are without foundation in fact.'

Criminology may benefit from utilising the concept of lifestyle in the explanation of between-individual differences and between-group differences in offending. A lifestyle approach can focus on individual differences as well as focusing on between-group differences. Individuals can lead a variety of lifestyles which may involve them in many of types of contexts, at varying times and with different people. This conceptualisation, thus, allows the individual to be part of many groups or what traditional subcultural theorists term 'subcultures'. Individuals can be working class, football fans, surfers and rock fans simultaneously, which may affect their offending behaviour, as opposed to being categorised as belonging to a particular subculture (i.e. surfer subculture, rock subculture, etc.), the values of which are supposed to explain the individual's offending behaviour. A lifestyle approach allows for individuals to grasp aspects of many different cultures. It allows individuals the choice to take of culture what they want and does not assume that individuals are bound by the culture of certain groups. Critically, the concept allows people to belong to varying 'cultural groups' but does not suggest that their values will be influenced by these groups to the extent that they will have drastically different values from others in society, which will lead them to offend, as some traditional 'subcultural' theorists may have us believe.

The concept of lifestyle, thus, may address one of Kornhauser's (1978: 4) fundamental problems with subcultural explanations of crime:

> As fast as culture and subcultures disappear, they are planted anew by sociologists eager to supply what modern society finds it so difficult to maintain. There is scarcely any aggregate of individuals – no matter how tenuous, intermittent, or even non-existent their collective identity – that has not been endowed with a subculture, if its 'members' exhibit some similarity of outlook or behaviour.

Kornhauser further argues that members of such subcultures may exhibit differences greater than their similarities. Individuals who have 'subcultural' explanations thrust upon them may be antipathetic to them and feel ambiguity towards their new imagined shared identity (imagined by the social scientist studying them). Indeed, Kornhauser puts it succinctly: 'social analysts are so enchanted with culture as an explanatory concept that the people they study are sometimes compelled to bear witness to cultures they neither have nor want' (1978: 4).

The concept of lifestyle has predominantly been used in criminological discussion concerning issues of victimisation. Hindelang *et al.* (1978) state: 'briefly, lifestyle refers to routine daily activities, both vocational activities (work, school, keeping house, etc.) and leisure activities.' In their theory they outlined the antecedents of lifestyle and the mechanisms that linked lifestyle with victimisation. The antecedents of lifestyle employed by Hindelang *et al.* were based on structural factors including, for example, race, family income and marital status. These structural factors were used to argue that different people from different age groups, with varying family incomes, etc., would lead differential lifestyles and this would, as a result, affect the individual's risk of personal victimisation by influencing his or her exposure to situations in which individuals may be more susceptible to victimisation.

Almost concurrently with Hindelang *et al.*'s (1978) conception of lifestyle, Cohen and Felson (1979) postulated a theory of routine activities. They argued that individuals' changing routine activities were responsible for increasing crime rates in postwar US society. Routine activities were defined as: 'any recurrent and prevalent activities which provide for basic and population needs, whatever their biological or cultural origins. Thus routine activities would include formalised work, as well as the provision of standard food, shelter, sexual outlet, leisure, social interaction, learning and child rearing' (Cohen and Felson 1979: 593). They argued that, for an offence to occur, there must be a convergence in space and time of likely offenders, suitable targets and the absence of capable guardians. This conception allows routine activity theory to have utility both in explaining aggregate changes in offence rates and for explaining individual offending patterns. In much criminological literature the conceptions of lifestyle and routine activity are often used interchangeably (see, for example; Riley 1987; Sampson and Wooldredge 1987; Lauritsen *et al.* 1991). However, Osgood *et al.* (1996) argue that relatively little research has focused on the routine activity or lifestyle approach in relation to offending. This is relatively surprising, since much research has documented the link between offending and victimisation. Indeed, in this study data have indicated that those who offend are significantly more likely to be victimised.

It is, therefore, hypothesised that individuals who pursue high-risk lifestyles will be more likely to enter high-risk situations and may thus be more prone to commit offences (see Brantingham and Brantingham 1989 for a discussion of how people's routines bring them into risk situations). Some will be more protected (in terms of individual characteristics – i.e. their social situations and dispositions) than others and will not necessarily offend in these high-risk settings, whereas others will. This will also be affected by the frequency with which an individual comes into contact with risk. For example, pupils from disadvantaged neighbourhoods may come into contact with more risk situations than pupils from advantaged areas. Pupils' lifestyles are likely to be influenced by their social situation and psychological dispositions and their family, school and community contexts. Two possible mechanisms regarding pupil offending in schools and lifestyles are submitted. First, pupils who lead more risky lifestyles in general may be more prone to offending, and these offending habits may spill over into the school environment. Secondly, pupils with high-risk lifestyles may also find themselves in more high-risk situations in the school. For example, those who smoke and hang about with delinquent peers may enter more high-risk criminogenic situations, which may lead to a higher likelihood of offending. Pupils whose lifestyles bring them into behaviour settings where there is an absence of capable guardianship and a suitable target may produce a situation where an offence may occur. Those youths who hang around with numerous delinquent peers and who use substances are more likely to come into contact with high-risk behaviour settings (see Wikström 2002).

Previously, very few empirical studies measuring lifestyle and individual offending have been achieved (none involving offending in schools). However, measures of lifestyle employed include structural characteristics (e.g. Hindelang *et al.* 1978), leisure activities and hanging around with delinquent peers (see, for example, Osgood *et al.* 1996). In this study, the focus will be on a measure of lifestyle involving pupils' substance use both in school and in general, and whether or not pupils hang around with delinquent peers both in school and in general. This is a first attempt at measuring pupils' lifestyle and its possible relationship with offending in the school context, and the author recognises that this measure of lifestyle could be improved in future research. For example, a space-time budget could be employed to measure pupils' everyday routines both in school and in general (see Osgood *et al.* 1996; Wikström 2002).

The measure employed in this study is an adequate proxy measure of pupils' lifestyle – particularly how high risk that lifestyle is. It is argued that pupils who mix with delinquent peers and use substances are more likely to lead high-risk lifestyles, which will mean that they will more frequently encounter settings with greater temptations and frictions for offending, while levels of possible deterrence may be diminished. Table 9.1 shows the scales used to create the lifestyle construct.

Table 9.1 Scales used to create the lifestyle construct

Domain	Scale	Items	Alpha
Lifestyle	General peer delinquency*	7	0.79
	School peer delinquency**	10	0.82
	Substance use**	5	0.75

Notes:
 * Scale used by Wikström (2002).
 ** Scale created by author.

Peer delinquency

There has been a great deal of discussion concerning the role of delinquent peers in relation to individual offending behaviour (for example, Elliot *et al.* 1985; Sarnecki 1986; Reiss 1988; Gottfredson and Hirschi 1990; Rutter *et al.* 1998). Much less is known about the influence of delinquent peers on females as most research has focused on males (see Wikström 2002). In the UK, there has been very little research on the role of delinquent peers in relation to pupil offending behaviour in schools.

The fact that there is a very strong relationship between the delinquency of an individual and the delinquency of peers is one of the strongest correlations in the field of criminology (Gottfredson and Hirschi 1990). There is wide discussion regarding the causality of this relationship. For instance, the Gluecks (1950) suggested that peer delinquency was not a causal mechanism influencing the individual to offend at all, but rather a case of 'birds of a feather flocking together'. This suggests that delinquent individuals make friends with other similarly delinquent individuals. At the other end of the spectrum, there is a view that individuals learn delinquency through peer group interactions (Sutherland and Cressey 1970; Elliot *et al.* 1985). Neither of these perspectives has been conclusively proven. However, it may be the case that both explanations have merits. What is certain is that young people who mix with delinquent peers also report offending to a greater extent than those who do not. It is also true that those who mix with delinquent peers make a lifestyle decision – individuals decide through a process of choice (which is also likely to be contingent on a variety of factors such as development and context) with whom they associate. Those with delinquent peers are more likely to find themselves in high-risk public environments (see Wikström 2002) and are more likely to come into contact with more risk situations. This chapter contains two measures of delinquent peers: 1) a general delinquent peer measure (not necessarily in school); and 2) a measure of peer delinquency focusing on friends at schools. The reason for this is to see the different types of peer relationships young people build and how these are related to offending in school. Pupils' friendships outside school may vary considerably in relation to friendships within school. It is argued, though, that both types of peers may affect the actions of pupils inside the school. This is because friendships outside the school will influence individuals' socialisation and behaviour – elements of which the individual will take into the school. Peers within the school context may have a more proximal influence on pupils' behaviour, and may well be more directly related to individual offending in school. School peers are likely to be part of the behaviour setting in which the act of offending occurs.

Creation of the general peer delinquency construct

The general peer delinquency construct was based on seven variables included in the questionnaire. Six of these relate to the extent to which the pupils' peers had engaged in general offending. The types of offending referred to in these questions include shoplifting, vandalism, assault, car theft, and residential and non-residential burglary. These are dichotomous variables, which were coded 1 for having friends who had committed the offence and 0 for having friends who had not. The seventh variable included in the scale related to whether the subject had friends who had been caught by the police. The answers to this question were coded in the following manner: those who had no friends who were caught by the police scored 0; those with one or two friends caught by the police scored 1; and those with three or more friends caught by the police scored 2. The scale was created in the following way: the six scores relating to types of offences peers had committed were summed (note: it is possible for a subject to have one friend who has committed all six acts). Some 73.6 per cent of the subjects had friends who had committed at least one of these offences. To add an element of seriousness to the scale, this score was weighted using the score for the number of friends caught by the police. This resulted in a score varying between 0 and 12. Those subjects who had no friends caught by the police received a score of zero. Wikström (2002) found that, for general delinquency, the detection rate by the police for youths offending was 10 per cent. In this study, 4.6 per cent of pupils who reported assaulting somebody in school stated they had been reported to the police. However, 51.2 per cent of pupils report knowing a friend who has been caught by the police at least once. Some 14.5 per cent of this 51.2 per cent know a friend who has been caught by the police three or more times. The scale takes into account the seriousness of peer delinquency as opposed to just offending prevalence among friends in general (the latter is a focus of the school peer delinquency measure). The distribution of the general peer delinquency construct is shown in Figure 9.1. This shows that the majority of individuals surveyed have no peers who offend frequently or seriously.

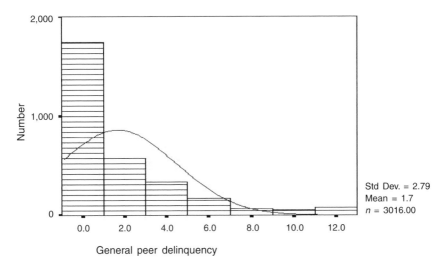

Figure 9.1 Distribution of (high) peer delinquency scores

General peer delinquency in relation to pupil offending in schools

Table 9.2 indicates that general peer delinquency is related to pupils' offending behaviour in schools. The measures of association (gamma) are stronger for all types of offending in school for females in comparison with males. This is similar to Wikström's (2002) finding concerning general offending in the Peterborough Youth Study, where the associations were stronger for females than males in terms of the relationship between general peer delinquency and general offending behaviour. Females are also more influenced by hanging around with delinquent peers generally (indicative of a high-risk lifestyle) in terms of their offending behaviour in school than boys.

General peer delinquency is clearly associated with both male and female prevalence of offending in schools. Table 9.3 explores this relationship for frequency of offending by males and females in Cardiff's schools. General peer delinquency is a significant and fairly strong predictor of frequency of overall offending in schools for both males and females, although the amount of variance explained by general peer delinquency in terms of overall offending is slightly stronger for males than females. General peer delinquency also shows a significant relationship with the frequency of male assaults (but not with female assault) in schools. No other significant relationships have been determined in relation to general peer delinquency and offending in schools.

Table 9.2 General peer delinquency and offending in school by population and sex

| School offending | General peer delinquency* | | | | |
	Low (%)	Medium (%)	High (%)	Sig.	Gamma
Population					
Theft	3.5	17.1	21.0	0.000	0.68
Assault	10.4	23.8	37.6	0.000	0.52
Vandalism	4.4	16.9	24.1	0.000	0.65
Serious offences	0.6	2.3	8.3	–	–
Overall offending	15.1	42.3	55.0	0.000	0.63
Male					
Theft	4.5	19.0	20.0	0.000	0.63
Assault	14.4	30.1	43.2	0.000	0.49
Vandalism	5.5	17.9	21.8	0.000	0.57
Serious offences	1.1	3.3	8.8	–	–
Overall offending	20.4	47.8	54.9	0.000	0.57
Female					
Theft	2.7	14.1	24.1	0.000	0.73
Assault	6.7	14.1	20.7	0.000	0.42
Vandalism	3.3	15.5	31.0	0.000	0.72
Serious offences	0.2	0.7	6.9	–	–
Overall offending	10.2	33.8	55.2	0.000	0.67

Note:

* General peer delinquency scores grouped into low (scores 0–3), medium (scores 4–8) and high (scores 9–12).

A possible interpretation of why no significant relationships were found between general peer delinquency and theft and vandalism in schools may be that general peers are different from the peer group individuals mix with in schools. School peers may be of more importance regarding pupils' offending behaviour in schools, because they will more immediately influence the situations individuals find themselves in. However, it may also be the case that general peers who are delinquent are influential in determining the attitudes and behaviours that an individual displays in schools.

School peer delinquency

This construct was based on ten variables relating to the pupils' peers' delinquent activities that had taken place at school in the last year.

Table 9.3 Mean frequency of offending in school by general peer delinquency and sex, means, significance and eta²

General peer delinquency risk*	All offences	Assault	Theft	Vandalism
Males				
Low	2.7	1.9	2.5	2.5
Medium	3.9	2.9	2.7	2.6
High	5.9	3.6	3.7	3.4
Sig.	0.000	0.000	n.s.	n.s.
Eta²	0.10	0.13	–	–
Females				
Low	2.4	1.6	2.3	2.6
Medium	3.7	2.4	2.9	3.2
High	4.4	2.3	2.9	3.7
Sig.	0.001	n.s.	n.s.	n.s.
Eta²	0.08	–	–	–

Note:

* General peer delinquency risk scores grouped into low (scores 0–3), medium (scores 4–8) and high (scores 9–12).

These variables are dichotomous in nature and range from knowing a fellow pupil who has been absent from school without an excuse, carrying a weapon in school, to taking drugs and drinking at school. The responses were coded as 1 for 'yes' and 0 for 'no', resulting in a scale which relates to the prevalence of pupils' delinquent peers at school. These scores were summed, resulting in a scale ranging from 0 to 10, where 10 indicates a high-risk school peer delinquency score (although this score may mean that the pupil knows one fellow pupil who has done all the said activities in school). The distribution of this measure is shown in Figure 9.2.

Table 9.4 shows the correlations between the scales that will make up the lifestyle risk measure. This shows a correlation of 0.54 between the general peer delinquency scale and the school peer delinquency scale. This suggests that there is a relationship between the two measures, but by no means a perfect one, indicative of the fact that pupils may have different school peers and general peers. Also, the school delinquent peer measure does not take into account seriousness in the same manner as the general peer delinquency measure, focusing rather on whether the subject has friends who

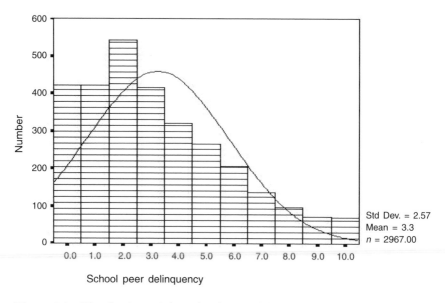

Figure 9.2 Distribution of the school peer delinquency scale

Table 9.4 Zero-order correlations between the three lifestyle scales

	General peer delinquency	School peer delinquency	Substance use
General peer delinquency	1.00		
School peer delinquency	0.54	1.00	
Substance use	0.52	0.49	1.00

Note:
All zero-order correlations are significant at the 0.05 level or better.

have committed various acts in school in the last year. Technically it is possible in this measure to have one friend who has committed all the acts mentioned. However, both constructs measure aspects of how risky a pupil's lifestyle is. Pupils who mix with delinquent peers in and outside school are highly likely to have riskier lifestyles than pupils who mix with well behaved peers.

Figure 9.2 suggests the majority of pupils have peers who have committed some type of school delinquency. It is hypothesised that those pupils who have peers who have committed more of the offences under scrutiny will be most at risk of offending in school.

School peer delinquency and offending in school

Pupils who have delinquent peers in school are more likely to have reported offending in the school context. Table 9.5 confirms this relationship between school peer delinquency and pupils' prevalence of offending behaviour in schools. The table shows that, for all types of offending other than serious offences (where the numbers involved for females make it difficult for statistical significance to be tested) and theft in school, females are more strongly affected by mixing with delinquent peers in school. It also indicates that having delinquent peers in school is more strongly associated with offending in schools than shown by the general delinquent peers measure.

Frequency of offending by pupils in school is related to having delinquent peers in school for overall offending (Table 9.6). This table indicates that the frequency of female offending is more affected by

Table 9.5 School offending by school peer delinquency and sex

School offending	School peer delinquency*			Sig.	Gamma
	Low (%)	Medium (%)	High (%)		
Population					
Theft	1.4	6.6	20.8	0.000	0.72
Assault	4.0	17.9	31.8	0.000	0.64
Vandalism	1.1	8.0	23.2	0.000	0.75
Serious offences	0.2	1.1	4.8	0.000	0.74
Overall offending	6.2	26.5	52.2	0.000	0.70
Male					
Theft	1.0	8.9	21.1	0.000	0.72
Assault	5.8	23.7	37.0	0.000	0.60
Vandalism	1.5	9.1	23.0	0.000	0.70
Serious offences	0.3	2.1	5.9	0.000	0.69
Overall offending	8.1	34.1	55.1	0.000	0.67
Female					
Theft	1.6	4.2	20.0	0.000	0.65
Assault	2.5	11.8	20.9	0.000	0.64
Vandalism	0.8	6.9	23.5	0.000	0.79
Serious offences	0.1	0.2	2.7	n.s.	–
Overall offending	4.6	18.5	46.1	0.000	0.69

Note:

* School peer delinquency scores grouped into low (scores 0–2), medium (scores 3–6) and high (scores 7–10).

school delinquent peers than the frequency of male offending in terms of assaults, vandalism and overall offending in school. No significant relationship was found between school delinquent peers and the frequency of theft. This could indicate that theft in schools is an activity that may not necessarily occur in groups.

Table 9.6 Frequency of offending in school by school delinquent peers, means, significance and eta²

School peer delinquency*	School theft	School assault	School vandalism	Overall school offending
Population				
Low	2.1	1.8	2.6	2.1
Medium	2.7	1.9	2.3	2.7
High	2.9	2.9	3.3	4.7
Sig.	n.s.	0.000	0.003	0.000
Eta²	–	0.08	0.07	0.10
Males				
Low	2.2	1.9	2.8	2.3
Medium	2.8	2.1	2.3	2.9
High	2.8	3.1	3.0	4.8
Sig.	n.s.	0.000	n.s.	0.000
Eta²	–	0.07	–	0.08
Females				
Low	2.1	1.6	2.2	1.8
Medium	2.4	1.6	2.3	2.3
High	3.0	2.5	3.8	4.4
Sig.	n.s.	0.011	0.004	0.000
Eta²	–	0.08	0.16	0.15

Note:
* School peer delinquency scores grouped into low (scores 0–2), medium (scores 3–6) and high (scores 7–10).

Substance use

The third scale used in the lifestyle risk measure relates to pupils' substance use. Before discussing the substance use scale, this section will investigate the prevalence and frequency of substance use in school both in terms of individual differences and between-school differences. Questions in the survey asked how many cigarettes the subject smoked a day (if they did smoke), how many times in the year they had smoked cannabis, and how many times in the last 12 months they had been drunk (these questions were not specifically school-based). The school-based questions concerned cannabis use and inhalants use (i.e. glue sniffing).

General substance use

Table 9.7 indicates that approximately two in three pupils reported having been drunk at least once in the last year, with one in five pupils reporting having been drunk more than six times. There is a very slight difference between males and females, with a higher proportion of females reporting being drunk than males, and also a greater proportion reporting a greater frequency of drunkenness.

Three in ten pupils reported using cannabis in the last 12 months. Approximately one in three males reported having smoked cannabis. Of these, approximately one in seven report having used it over six times in the last 12 months. Females reported using cannabis less than males. Approximately one in four females report using cannabis and one in fourteen reported using it six times or more. Two in three

Table 9.7 Prevalence and frequency of general substance abuse

| | Prevalence (%) | Frequency of times used | | |
		1–2 (%)	3–5 (%)	6+ (%)
General				
Alcohol (drunk)	65.3	29.7	16.0	19.6
Cannabis	27.2	12.3	4.3	10.5
Overall use*	66.9			
Males				
Alcohol (drunk)	63.6	30.1	14.9	18.6
Cannabis	31.5	13.2	4.5	13.8
Overall use*	66.4			
Females				
Alcohol (drunk)	67.1	29.3	17.1	20.7
Cannabis	22.6	11.3	4.2	7.1
Overall use*	67.4			

Note:
* Both cannabis and alcohol use.

pupils in Cardiff have either used cannabis or been drunk in the period the survey related to. This is true for both sexes.

Substance use in school

Table 9.8 shows that one in five pupils have used cannabis or used inhalants. Approximately one in six reported using cannabis in school, whereas one in twelve reported using inhalants in school. One in 20 pupils reported using cannabis six times or more in school, and one in 50 have used inhalants more than six times.

Approximately one in four males report substance use in school compared with one in five females. One in five males reported using cannabis compared with one in seven females. Males report using cannabis six or more times in schools twice as much as females. Prevalence of inhalant use in schools is fairly similar for both sexes.

Substance use in schools: between-school differences

Tables 9.9 and 9.10 show the prevalence and frequency of cannabis use and inhalants abuse among pupils, broken down by school. The tables indicate between-school variation in both frequency and prevalence rates of pupils' substance abuse in school. Table 9.9 shows the following:

Table 9.8 Substance use in school, overall and by sex

Substance use	Prevalence (%)	Once or twice (%)	A few times (3–5 times) (%)	Yes, many times (6+ times) (%)
Population				
Cannabis	16.6	8.9	2.7	4.9
Inhalants	8.2	5.7	1.2	1.3
Overall use	20.6			
Boys				
Cannabis	19.1	9.9	2.6	6.6
Inhalants	8.3	5.5	1.0	1.9
Overall use	23.2			
Girls				
Cannabis	14.0	7.9	2.9	3.2
Inhalants	8.1	5.8	1.4	0.8
Overall use	17.9			

- In the school that experiences the highest level of pupils who report cannabis abuse, one in four reported having used cannabis in school. This is in comparison with one in 50 at the school that experiences the lowest rate of cannabis use.

Table 9.10 shows the following:

- Schools range between 1.1 per cent and 14.4 per cent in terms of the percentage of pupils who report inhalant use in schools.
- The two schools that experience the greatest prevalence of inhalants use also experience the greatest prevalence of pupils who have abused inhalants six or more times.

This section has shown sex differences and between-school differences concerning substance use among Year 10 pupils in Cardiff's schools.

Table 9.9 Prevalence and frequency of pupils' cannabis use in school, by school

School	Prevalence (%)	Overall rank	Once or twice (%)	A few times (3–5 times) (%)	Yes, many times (6+ times) (%)
Thomas	25.0	(2)	12.5	0.0	12.5
Parker	19.4	(6)	8.3	5.6	5.6
Ruddock	25.8	(1)	15.9	2.3	7.6
Shanklin	18.3	(9)	7.8	3.9	6.7
Robinson	24.8	(3)	12.0	4.3	8.5
Morris	15.6	(12)	5.2	2.6	7.8
Henson	12.4	(14)	6.2	4.4	1.8
Bennett	11.8	(15)	7.3	0.9	3.6
Jenkins	22.6	(5)	13.7	4.8	4.0
Phillips	24.5	(4)	12.2	5.4	6.8
Owen	13.0	(13)	5.6	3.1	4.3
Charvis	18.8	(7)	10.2	2.0	6.6
Jones	17.6	(10)	9.2	2.9	5.4
Peel	18.4	(8)	11.8	1.6	4.9
Williams	11.0	(17)	6.6	1.1	3.3
Davies	16.2	(11)	7.1	2.0	7.1
Luscombe	10.5	(18)	7.0	2.6	0.9
Llewellyn	11.2	(16)	8.3	1.8	1.2
Sweeney	8.3	(19)	3.2	1.9	3.2
Cockbain	2.1	(20)	2.1	0.0	0.0

Table 9.10 Prevalence and frequency of inhalant use in schools, by school

School	Prevalence (%)	Overall rank	Once or twice (%)	A few times (3–5 times) (%)	Yes, many times (6+ times) (%)
Thomas	9.1	(10)	7.3	1.8	0.0
Parker	11.2	(4)	7.5	1.9	1.9
Ruddock	9.2	(9)	6.2	2.3	0.8
Shanklin	13.9	(2)	6.1	2.2	5.6
Robinson	14.4	(1)	8.5	2.5	3.4
Morris	5.2	(15)	3.9	1.3	0.0
Henson	6.2	(14)	4.5	0.9	0.9
Bennett	4.5	(16)	2.7	0.9	0.9
Jenkins	9.8	(6)	7.4	1.6	0.8
Phillips	9.5	(8)	6.8	1.4	1.4
Owen	6.8	(13)	5.0	0.6	1.2
Charvis	12.2	(3)	7.7	1.5	3.1
Jones	7.5	(12)	5.9	1.3	0.4
Peel	8.2	(11)	6.2	0.7	1.3
Williams	3.4	(18)	2.2	1.1	0.0
Davies	11.2	(4)	10.2	1.0	0.0
Luscombe	4.4	(17)	3.5	0.9	0.0
Llewellyn	1.2	(19)	1.2	0.0	0.0
Sweeney	9.7	(7)	7.1	1.3	1.3
Cockbain	1.1	(20)	1.1	0.0	0.0

Those who use one substance also tend to use others

Table 9.11 shows that there are fairly strong correlations between the frequencies of use of different types of substances. A strong relationship is indicated for the number of cigarettes smoked a day and cannabis use, both in school and in general. Another strong relationship is that between having been drunk and use of cannabis in general. Unsurprisingly, there is a fairly strong relationship between those who use cannabis in general and those who use it in school.

The substance use scale

These variables were summed resulting in a scale ranging from 0 to 15, with 15 indicating a very high level of substance use. Figure 9.3 shows that the distribution of substance use in Cardiff is highly skewed towards low frequency use (0 on the scale). There are very few individuals who are high-frequency substance users.

Table 9.11 Zero-order correlations: frequencies of substance abuse categories

	Cigarettes (no. a day)	Alcohol (drunk)	Cannabis (general)	Cannabis (school)	Inhalants (school)
Cigarettes (no. a day)	1.00				
Alcohol (drunk)	0.37	1.00			
Cannabis (general)	0.52	0.46	1.00		
Cannabis (school)	0.52	0.35	0.64	1.00	
Inhalants (school)	0.27	0.19	0.27	0.36	1.00

Note:
All correlations are significant at 0.01 level or better.

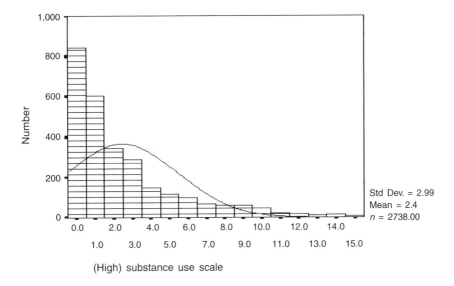

Std Dev. = 2.99
Mean = 2.4
n = 2738.00

(High) substance use scale

Figure 9.3 Substance use scale: distribution

Pupils' substance use is quite closely related to whether they mix with delinquent peers in school ($r = 0.49$, $p = 0.000$, as shown previously). This is true for both males ($r = 0.49$, $p = 0.000$) and females ($r = 0.49$, $p = 0.000$). This association may not be surprising as using substances, such as alcohol, cigarettes and cannabis, is usually a social activity.

The substance use scale and offending in schools

There are statistically significant relationships for both males and females between substance use and offending (see Table 9.12). In most cases, high substance use has a stronger relationship with female prevalence of offending in schools than for males. This is particularly the case for assault and vandalism in school (as indicated by the gamma measures of association).

Table 9.13 shows that high substance use is related to a greater frequency of offending in schools for the whole population. It shows that, for overall pupil offending in schools, the relationship with high substance use explains 14 per cent of the variance. In terms of frequency of offending for all types of offending in schools, it appears that males have a slightly stronger relationship between offending

Table 9.12 (High) substance use by offending prevalence in schools by population and sex

School offending	(High) substance use*				
	Low (%)	Medium (%)	High (%)	Sig.	Gamma
Population					
Theft	4.0	13.8	32.9	0.000	0.66
Assault	10.7	26.5	39.1	0.000	0.53
Vandalism	4.3	17.4	42.0	0.000	0.71
Serious offences	0.5	2.8	12.9	–	–
Overall offending	15.6	44.8	70.0	0.000	0.68
Male					
Theft	5.3	17.2	38.5	0.000	0.65
Assault	15.9	33.3	46.2	0.000	0.49
Vandalism	5.7	20.5	41.0	0.000	0.68
Serious offences	1.0	3.5	23.1	–	–
Overall offending	21.7	55.0	76.9	0.000	0.67
Female					
Theft	2.8	10.3	25.8	0.000	0.67
Assault	5.6	19.1	30.0	0.000	0.62
Vandalism	3.0	14.0	43.3	0.000	0.76
Serious offences	0.1	1.9	0.0	–	–
Overall offending	9.7	33.8	61.3	0.000	0.70

Note:

* Substance use scores grouped into low (scores 0–5), medium (scores 6–10) and high (scores 11–15).

Table 9.13 (High) substance use by frequency of offending in school by population and sex, means, significance and eta^2

Substance use*	Theft	Assault	Vandalism	Overall offending
Population				
Low	2.3	1.9	2.3	2.6
Medium	2.7	2.5	3.1	3.7
High	4.1	3.6	3.3	6.7
Sig.	0.001	0.000	0.009	0.000
Eta^2	0.10	0.08	0.06	0.14
Males				
Low	2.3	2.1	2.2	2.7
Medium	3.0	2.6	3.2	3.9
High	4.2	4.3	2.9	7.8
Sig.	0.002	0.000	0.043	0.000
Eta^2	0.12	0.11	0.06	0.16
Females				
Low	2.4	1.4	2.5	2.2
Medium	2.1	2.4	3.0	3.3
High	3.9	2.0	3.8	5.2
Sig.	n.s.	0.008	n.s.	0.000
Eta^2	–	0.09	–	0.14

Note:
* Substance use scores grouped into low (scores 0–5), medium (scores 6–10) and high (scores 11–15).

frequency and substance use. The relationship between frequency of substance use and theft by males in school is fairly strong. Wikström (2002) made a similar finding in the Peterborough Youth Study concerning substance use and theft in general.

The overall lifestyle risk measure

The lifestyle risk measure is a composite scale based on the measures of general peer delinquency, school peer delinquency and substance use described above. For each of these measures the third lowest scores are recoded to the value –1, the middle third are recoded to the value of 0 and the highest third of scores to the value +1.

These scores were then summed giving the lifestyle risk measure which varies from –3 to +3, with +3 indicating a lifestyle where the subject mixes with frequent and serious offenders generally; mixes with fellow pupils who have a high prevalence of school misconduct and offending in school; and who use substances frequently both in general and in school. These behaviours are all indicative of someone who is likely to lead a high-risk lifestyle. The distribution of the pupils in terms of their lifestyle risk scores is shown in Figure 9.4.

Figure 9.4 illustrates that most pupils in the Cardiff School Study report leading relatively low-risk lifestyles. This is particularly true for females who seem, in general, to have lower risk lifestyles than males.

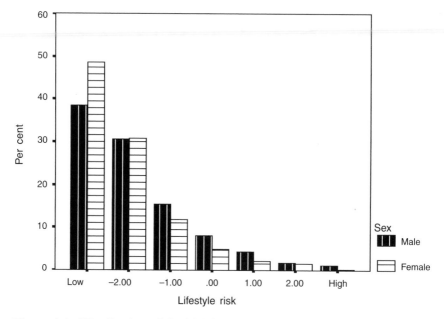

Figure 9.4   Distribution of (high) lifestyle risk scores

Those who lead high-risk lifestyles do not spend much time at home

A question in the survey asked pupils to specify whether they 1) spent most of their time at home; 2) spent quite a lot of time at home; 3) did not spend very much time at home; and 4) almost never spent time at home. The hypothesis in this chapter is that those pupils who lead lifestyles where they mix with delinquent others and use substances are at high risk of offending in schools. Pupils with high-risk lifestyles will be more likely to encounter more high-risk behaviour settings, especially if they are using substances and hanging around with delinquent peers. It is hypothesised that those students who lead high-risk lifestyles will almost never spend time at home, as they will be out and about leading a high-risk lifestyle. This hypothesis is confirmed in Figure 9.5, which clearly shows a difference between time spent at home by those who lead high-risk lifestyles and those who do not. From this it can be inferred that it is likely that, if pupils who lead high-risk lifestyles do not spend time at home, it is more likely that they will be in less safe environments outside the home. Such a conclusion has been indicated by Wikström (2002) who, in his space-time budget analysis, found that those who display high peer-centredness spend more time in high-risk situations, which in turn was indicative of high offending rates.

Lifestyle risk in relation to other constructs

The relationships between area of residence structural risk, family social position risk, pupil relations risk, school climate risk and the

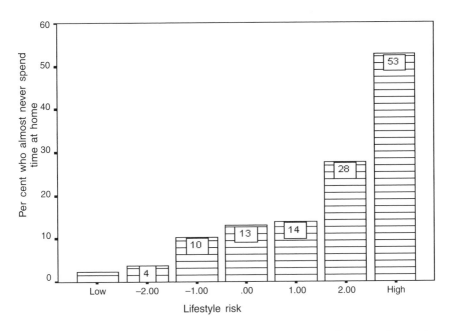

Figure 9.5 Percentage of pupils who 'almost never spend time at home' by (high) lifestyle risk

individual risk-protective score with pupils' lifestyle risk is examined in detail in Table 9.14. There is no statistically significant relationship between a pupil's lifestyle risk and the area in which he or she resides. A weak and statistically significant relationship is shown between family social background and lifestyle risk. Pupil relations in school are shown to explain some variance in lifestyle risk. However, school climate seems to have a relatively stronger relationship, with pupils' lifestyle risk explaining 9 per cent of the variance. The strongest relationship, though, is seen between an individual's risk-protective characteristics and his or her lifestyle risk. In this relationship, individual risk-protective characteristics explain 25 per cent of the variance in pupils' individual lifestyle risk. This relationship exists for both sexes (males: $eta^2 = 0.27$; females: $eta^2 = 0.21$).

Individual risk-protective characteristics are much more important in relation to pupils' lifestyle risk than the type of area they live in, the family background they are from or the school context they experience. This finding in a cross-sectional study may not be surprising, though it must be remembered that area, family and school are likely to have an influence on the development of pupils' individual characteristics over time. This is something that cannot be addressed in a cross-sectional study such as this, but is certainly of interest for future studies that employ longitudinal research designs. It is a central argument that family backgrounds, areas and school contexts in which people live, evolve and develop will affect their individual social situations and dispositions, which in turn will affect their lifestyles and the choices they make in everyday life.

Lifestyle risk and offending behaviour in schools

Table 9.15 shows that, for most offence types, lifestyle risk is more strongly associated with female offending than with male offending in schools. Lifestyle risk has strong associations with all types of offending behaviour in school.

Frequency of offending is associated with pupils' high lifestyle risk, with those males and females who lead riskier lifestyles being far more frequent offenders in school. This is illustrated by Table 9.16, which shows strong significant relationships between lifestyle risk, for males and females, and overall offending in school and assault in school. Lifestyle risk can be seen to have a strong relationship with male theft; however, for females there is no significant relationship.

Table 9.14 Lifestyle risk: means, significance and eta² by other constructs

Construct	Lifestyle mean
Area of residence structural risk	
Low	−2.0
Medium	−2.0
High	−1.9
Sig.	n.s.
Eta²	−
Family social background risk	
Low	−2.1
Medium	−1.9
High	−1.8
Sig.	0.000
Eta²	0.01
Pupil relations risk	
Low	−2.1
Medium	−1.8
High	−1.2
Sig.	0.000
Eta²	0.02
School climate risk	
Low	−2.5
Medium	−2.0
High	−0.5
Sig.	0.000
Eta²	0.09
Individual risk-protective characteristics	
Protective	−2.5
Balanced	−1.6
Risk	0.4
Sig.	0.000
Eta²	0.25

Table 9.15 School offending by lifestyle risk, population and sex

| School offending | (High) lifestyle risk* | | | | |
	Low (%)	Medium (%)	High (%)	Sig.	Gamma
Population					
Theft	2.3	14.0	39.4	0.000	0.78
Assault	8.4	25.6	43.9	0.000	0.60
Vandalism	2.9	15.7	40.9	0.000	0.75
Serious offences	0.4	1.9	13.6	0.000	0.77
Overall offending	11.8	42.0	75.8	0.000	0.72
Male					
Theft	2.8	16.7	36.6	0.000	0.75
Assault	12.4	31.2	56.1	0.000	0.56
Vandalism	3.6	18.2	36.6	0.000	0.72
Serious offences	0.6	3.2	17.1	0.000	0.76
Overall offending	16.3	49.9	75.6	0.000	0.69
Female					
Theft	1.8	10.1	44.0	0.000	0.79
Assault	4.9	17.5	24.0	0.000	0.61
Vandalism	2.4	12.1	48.0	0.000	0.76
Serious offences	0.2	0.0	8.0	–	–
Overall offending	7.9	30.6	76.0	0.000	0.72

Note:
* (High) lifestyle risk scores grouped into low (scores –3 to –2), medium (scores –1 to +1) and high (scores +2 to +3).

Lifestyle risk, other explanatory factors and pupil offending in school: multiple regression analysis

This section examines the various explanatory factors investigated so far and their relative predictive power regarding pupils' offending behaviour in school. Table 9.17 reports a multiple logistic regression that examines all the key explanatory factors employed in the book in relation to prevalence of offending behaviour in school. It shows the following:

- Pupil relations appear to be a significant predictor of overall offending prevalence in schools, but lose significance for other types of offending category. Thus, how pupils perceive their relations with other pupils may be important in determining overall offending prevalence in schools.

Table 9.16 Frequency of offending in school by lifestyle risk, means, significance and eta^2

Lifestyle risk*	School offending frequency (mean)			
	Theft	Assault	Vandalism	Overall
Population				
Low	2.5	1.8	2.3	2.3
Medium	2.4	2.4	2.9	3.4
High	3.8	4.1	3.3	6.8
Sig.	0.003	0.000	0.039	0.000
Eta^2	0.08	0.14	0.04	0.16
Males				
Low	2.5	1.9	2.3	2.5
Medium	2.6	2.5	2.7	3.5
High	4.0	4.4	3.1	7.6
Sig.	0.024	0.000	n.s.	0.000
Eta^2	0.08	0.16	–	0.16
Females				
Low	2.5	1.5	2.3	2.0
Medium	2.1	1.9	3.2	3.0
High	3.6	3.0	3.7	5.5
Sig.	n.s.	0.033	n.s.	0.000
Eta^2	–	0.07	–	0.17

Note:
* (High) lifestyle risk scores grouped into low (scores –3 to –2), medium (scores –1 to +1) and high (scores +2 to +3).

- The main significant predictors of all types of pupil offending behaviour in school are pupils' individual risk-protective characteristics and lifestyles. The interaction between these factors is of great importance regarding all types of pupil offending prevalence in schools.

- Individual perceptions of school climate and pupil relations (school context), once pupils' individual characteristics and lifestyles are controlled for, do not appear to be significant predictors of pupil offending in schools (the exception being pupil relations and overall offending). This is probably due to the fact that the analysis cannot take into account the impact of contextual factors on affecting the development of individual characteristics and lifestyles.

Table 9.17 Multiple logistic regression: prevalence of overall offending, theft, assault and vandalism in schools by sex and key explanatory factors

Overall	Overall		Theft		Assault		Vandalism	
	Exp. (B)	Sig.	Exp. (B)	Sig.	Exp. (B)	Sig.	Exp. (B)	Sig.
Female	0.48	0.000	0.66	0.029	0.40	0.000	0.83	n.s.
Family risk	1.14	0.042	0.98	n.s.	1.22	0.008	0.98	n.s.
Area risk	1.05	n.s.	1.12	n.s.	0.98	n.s.	1.09	n.s.
School climate risk	1.08	n.s.	1.23	n.s.	1.13	n.s.	1.19	n.s.
Pupil relations risk	1.22	0.002	0.97	n.s.	1.09	n.s.	1.14	n.s.
Individual risk	1.48	0.000	1.43	0.020	1.44	0.000	1.46	0.011
Lifestyle risk	2.64	0.000	2.58	0.000	1.95	0.000	2.64	0.000
Family* area	1.01	n.s.	1.11	n.s.	1.05	n.s.	0.84	n.s.
Family* climate	1.02	n.s.	1.01	n.s.	1.08	n.s.	0.85	n.s.
Family* relations	0.94	n.s.	0.98	n.s.	0.91	n.s.	0.91	n.s.
Family* individual	1.05	n.s.	1.11	n.s.	0.95	n.s.	1.41	0.001
Family* lifestyle	0.94	n.s.	0.93	n.s.	0.95	n.s.	0.86	n.s.
Area* climate	0.93	n.s.	0.94	n.s.	0.92	n.s.	0.94	n.s.
Area* relations	1.04	n.s.	1.16	n.s.	1.10	n.s.	1.01	n.s.
Area* individual	1.01	n.s.	0.79	n.s.	1.09	n.s.	1.01	n.s.
Area* lifestyle	1.05	n.s.	1.17	n.s.	0.99	n.s.	1.15	n.s.
Climate* individual	1.09	n.s.	1.15	n.s.	1.04	n.s.	1.08	n.s.

Climate* lifestyle	0.89	n.s.	0.93	n.s.	1.00	n.s.	0.88	n.s.
Climate* relations	1.08	n.s.	1.08	n.s.	1.07	n.s.	1.11	n.s.
Relations* individual	0.97	n.s.	1.03	n.s.	0.95	n.s.	1.02	n.s.
Relations* lifestyle	0.91	n.s.	1.00	n.s.	0.93	n.s.	0.85	n.s.
Individual* lifestyle	0.81	0.001	0.82	0.015	0.82	0.002	0.85	0.047
Chi-square (prob.)	552 (0.000)		212 (0.000)		307 (0.000)		274 (0.000)	
−2 log	2052		939		1701		1011	
Cox and Snell R^2	0.20		0.08		0.11		0.10	
Nagelkerke R^2	0.31		0.23		0.21		0.26	

Note:
*Denotes interaction term.

- Being female appears to lessen the likelihood of having offended in schools, for all offending categories with the exception of vandalism.

Table 9.18 reports an OLS multiple regression model which examines the relationships between all the explanatory factors employed in the book in relation to offending frequency in schools. It shows the following:

- As with offending prevalence, by far the most important predictors of pupil offending frequency in schools are pupils' individual risk-protective characteristics and lifestyle risk and the interaction between them.
- When other factors are controlled for, the measures of school context examined previously lose their significance as predictors of offending frequency in schools.
- The explanatory factors employed in this research explain 25 per cent of pupil differences in overall offending behaviour in schools, 13 per cent regarding theft, 15 per cent regarding assault and 11 per cent regarding vandalism.

Thus, pupils' individual risk-protective characteristics, lifestyles and the interaction between the two are the key explanatory factors of pupils' offending behaviour in schools. This confirms the view that measurements closest to an individual's social action will be most influential in the prediction of offending. However, other factors more distant from social action have been shown to be influential in forming individual risk-protective characteristics and lifestyles. The rest of this chapter will investigate the interaction between pupils' lifestyles and individual risk-protective characteristics in relation to offending in schools. This will build towards some categorisation of pupils in school based on that proposed by Wikström (2002) in relation to adolescent offenders in general.

The interaction between individual risk-protective factors and lifestyle risk and offending in schools

This section will investigate the relationship between pupils' individual risk-protective characteristics and lifestyle risk in relation to pupils' prevalence and frequency of offending in schools. This analysis is

Table 9.18 OLS multiple regression: frequencies of overall offending, theft, assault and vandalism in schools, by sex and key explanatory factors

Variable	Overall offending Beta	Prob.	Theft Beta	Prob.	Assault Beta	Prob.	Vandalism Beta	Prob.
Sex	−0.08	0.000	−0.04	0.041	−0.12	0.000	0.01	n.s.
Family social position risk	0.04	n.s.	0.02	n.s.	0.03	n.s.	0.02	n.s.
Area risk	0.02	n.s.	0.01	n.s.	0.02	n.s.	0.02	n.s.
School climate risk	0.04	n.s.	0.03	n.s.	0.05	0.048	0.01	n.s.
Pupil relations risk	0.03	n.s.	0.03	n.s.	0.01	n.s.	0.01	n.s.
Individual risk	0.06	0.019	0.01	n.s.	0.07	0.013	0.06	0.041
Lifestyle risk	0.26	0.000	0.17	0.000	0.18	0.000	0.21	0.000
Family* area risk	0.00	n.s.	0.01	n.s.	−0.01	n.s.	0.01	n.s.
Family* school climate risk	−0.04	n.s.	−0.02	n.s.	0.01	n.s.	−0.05	0.049
Family* relations risk	−0.01	n.s.	−0.01	n.s.	−0.01	n.s.	−0.01	n.s.
Family* individual risk	0.08	0.002	0.04	n.s.	0.04	n.s.	0.09	0.001
Family* lifestyle risk	0.00	n.s.	−0.06	n.s.	−0.01	n.s.	0.01	n.s.
Area* school climate risk	0.02	n.s.	0.03	n.s.	−0.01	n.s.	0.01	n.s.
Area* relations risk	0.02	n.s.	0.03	n.s.	0.02	n.s.	−0.00	n.s.
Area* individual risk	−0.04	n.s.	−0.08	0.005	0.02	n.s.	−0.02	n.s.
Area* lifestyle risk	0.04	n.s.	0.06	0.008	−0.03	n.s.	0.03	n.s.
School climate* individual risk	0.00	n.s.	0.02	n.s.	0.04	n.s.	−0.04	n.s.
School climate* lifestyle risk	0.05	n.s.	0.04	n.s.	−0.02	n.s.	0.04	n.s.
Relations* individual risk	0.00	n.s.	0.02	n.s.	−0.04	n.s.	0.05	n.s.
Relations* lifestyle risk	0.02	n.s.	0.10	0.000	−0.02	n.s.	−0.05	0.04
School climate* relations risk	0.03	n.s.	0.02	n.s.	0.02	n.s.	0.03	n.s.
Individual* lifestyle risk	0.16	0.000	0.10	0.001	0.11	0.000	0.08	0.000
Multiple $R^2 \times 100$ =	25		13		15		11	

Note:
Interaction terms were calculated by first centring each of the two variables and then multiplying them.

based on, and seeks to explore further, the interaction effect reported previously in the regression-based models. First, overall prevalence of offending in schools will be investigated. Table 9.19 illustrates that lifestyle exerts a statistically significant and strong effect on the three groups of pupils defined by their individual risk-protective characteristics. The relationship between lifestyle and having protective characteristics is the strongest, with 34 per cent of pupils who display protective individual characteristics and medium lifestyle risk having offended in school. However, there are no pupils who display high-risk lifestyles and protective individual characteristics (this is theoretically consistent, as it would seem unlikely that pupils who have good bonds, who are well monitored, with high levels of self-control, pro-social values and a sense of shame would lead high-risk lifestyles). The table also indicates how strong a predictor this interaction between lifestyle risk and individual characteristics is regarding offending in schools. Fewer than 1 in 10 who display individual protective characteristics and have a low lifestyle risk report offending in schools, in comparison with 8 in 10 pupils who lead a high-risk lifestyle and have high-risk individual characteristics who report having offended in school. This indicates that, as shown in Table 9.17 (logistic regression above), the interaction between these characteristics is very important in determining whether a pupil has offended or not in school.

Pupils' offending frequency in school

Table 9.20 shows the interaction between individual characteristics and lifestyle risk and pupils' frequency of overall offending in schools. This illustrates that the interaction between individual risk-protective

Table 9.19 The interaction between lifestyle risk and individual risk characteristics in relation to prevalence of overall offending in schools

| Lifestyle risk | Individual risk-protective characteristics | | | | | |
	Protective (%)	Balanced (%)	Risk (%)	Sig.	Gamma	n
Low	7.9	18.2	45.5	0.000	0.45	1,972
Medium	34.8	42.4	55.0	0.024	0.21	618
High	–	71.8	80.0	n.s.	–	64
Sig.	0.000	0.000	n.s			
Gamma	0.72	0.57	0.45			
n	1,413	1,145	96			

characteristics and lifestyle risk on frequency of offending, for the protective and balanced individual risk-protective characteristic groups, is statistically significant. The strength of these associations varies widely. For the protective group, the association with lifestyle risk is fairly weak. The variance explained between lifestyle and frequency of offending for the balanced groups is much greater. This suggests that those with balanced individual risk-protective characteristics may be more readily influenced or dependent upon their lifestyle in determining their frequency of offending. The relationship between lifestyle risk and frequency of offending for those displaying high-risk individual risk characteristics is stronger still. There are 11 pupils who display high-risk individual characteristics and a low-risk lifestyle; 60 who display high-risk individual characteristics and medium-risk lifestyle; and 25 who display a high lifestyle risk and high-risk individual characteristics. This latter 25 can be seen to offend at an average frequency of 7.5 offences over the period. This relationship is illustrated in Figure 9.6.

The interaction effect between lifestyle risk and individual risk-protective characteristics on pupils' overall offending frequency in school has been shown. Next, three of the offences included in the overall offending scale will be investigated to see if the same effects exist by offending type. For theft, analysis indicates that belonging to the high-risk lifestyle group has a strong effect on those who display high-risk individual characteristics (sig. = 0.000, eta^2 = 0.18). The next strongest relationship is for those in the balanced individual characteristics group (sig. = 0.000, eta^2 = 0.06). For those in the protective individual characteristic group, lifestyle has a weak relationship with frequency of theft offending (sig. = 0.000, eta^2 = 0.02).

Table 9.20 The interaction between individual risk-protective characteristics, lifestyle risk and frequency of offending in school, means, significance and eta^2

| Lifestyle risk | Individual risk-protective characteristics | | |
	Protective	Balanced	Risk
Low	0.2	0.4	0.9
Medium	0.7	1.4	2.0
High	–	3.5	7.5
Sig.	0.000	0.000	0.000
Eta^2	0.04	0.11	0.24
n	1,413	1,145	96

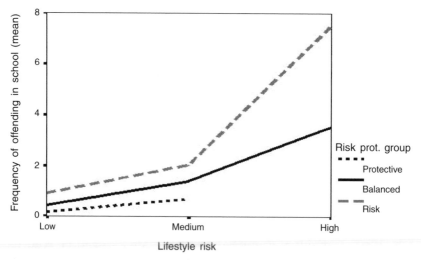

Figure 9.6 Mean overall offending frequency in school by combinations of groups of lifestyle risk and individual risk-protective characteristics

Concerning the frequency of assault in school, the strongest influence by lifestyle risk is for the high-risk group (sig. = 0.000, eta² = 0.14), followed by the balanced group (sig. = 0.000, eta² = 0.04) and then the protective group (sig. = 0.000, eta² = 0.02).

The strongest influence by lifestyle risk on frequency of vandalism in school is for the balanced individual risk characteristic group (sig. = 0.000, eta² = 0.05), followed by the protective group (sig. = 0.000, eta² = 0.01). The influence on the high-risk individual characteristic group just misses statistical significance (sig. = 0.056, eta² = 0.06).

Table 9.21 examines the sex differences in this interaction effect by comparing zero-order correlations between offending in school and lifestyle risk for the three main groups of individual risk-protective score. This shows no great differences between the sexes. The strongest influence on offending in school by lifestyle risk appears to be for those in the high-risk individual risk-protective characteristic group followed by the balanced group. This is consistent for both sexes.

The analysis of this interaction effect between lifestyle risk and individual risk-protective characteristics suggests the following:

- Lifestyle risk has a strong effect on frequency of offending in schools by adolescents who have high-risk individual risk-protective characteristics.

- Lifestyle risk has a strong effect on pupils who display balanced individual risk-protective characteristics.

- Lifestyle risk does not have much of an influence on those pupils who display protective individual characteristics.

Pupils who lead high-risk lifestyles and have weak bonds to society and poorly adjusted dispositions are more likely to offend more frequently in school. Perhaps the most interesting group in terms of crime prevention in school is the balanced individual risk-protective group. If high-risk lifestyles are discouraged, this may significantly reduce the frequency of offending in school among this group.

Table 9.21 Zero-order correlations between offending frequency in school and lifestyle risk score by main groups for the total sample and by sex

Type of offence	Individual risk protective group		
	Protective	Balanced	Risk
Total			
Overall offending	0.19	0.32	0.45
Theft	0.12	0.23	0.40
Assault	0.12	0.20	0.36
Vandalism	0.11	0.22	0.20
n =	1,413	1,145	96
Males			
Overall offending	0.20	0.31	0.44
Theft	0.14	0.23	0.36
Assault	0.14	0.22	0.41
Vandalism	0.09	0.20	(0.10)
n =	610	636	62
Females			
Overall offending	0.18	0.33	0.49
Theft	0.10	0.22	0.45
Assault	0.10	0.15	(0.25)
Vandalism	0.15	0.24	0.05
n =	803	509	34

Note:
Figures in brackets indicate a non-significant relationship. All other correlations are significant at the 0.05 level or better.

Pupils' lifestyle risk in relation to parental monitoring

Previously, it has been shown that adolescents who lead high-risk lifestyles also tend to spend a great deal less time at home. One could hypothesise that those who lead high-risk lifestyles are also more likely to experience poorer levels of parental monitoring. This is confirmed in Figure 9.7, for both males (sig. = 0.000, eta^2 = 0.20) and females (sig. = 0.000, eta^2 = 0.20). The influence of parental monitoring on frequency of overall offending in school is similar for all individual-risk characteristic groups (see Table 9.22), although the relationship is non-significant for the high-risk group (this is probably due to a small n, rather than any other more substantive reason).

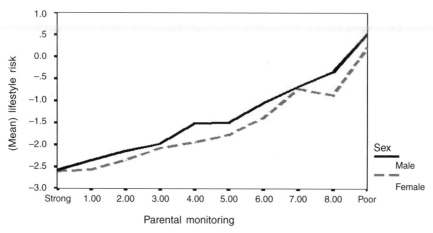

Figure 9.7 Mean lifestyle risk score by level of (poor) parental monitoring

Table 9.22 Overall offending frequency in school by level of (poor) parental monitoring: bivariate regressions for main groups of individual risk-protective characteristics

Risk-protective group	b	Beta	Sig.	$R^2 \times 100$	n
Protective	0.11	0.10	0.003	1	1,506
Balanced	0.45	0.08	0.001	1	1,284
Risk	0.52	0.11	n.s.	–	110

Replicating Wikström's (2002) typology for pupil offending in schools

The findings presented so far in the chapter are similar to Wikström's (2002) in the Peterborough Youth Study, which focused on general juvenile criminality. He argued that a possible interpretation of his results which, as has been shown, can also be applied to offending in schools, is that there are three types of adolescent in relation to offending. He based his heuristic typology on a history of longitudinal research which has indicated that there may be two main groups of offenders. One group is small in size, offends for a long period of time, at a great frequency, and is responsible for a large proportion of a cohort's crime. This group may be deemed to be chronic in their offending habits (see Blumstein *et al.* 1986; Piquero *et al.* 2003). The other group is larger in size and offends for a relatively short duration with a low frequency (see Wolfgang *et al.* 1972; Wikström 1987; Farrington 1998). Moffit (1993) refers to these groups as adolescence-limited and life-course persistent offenders. In contrast to this developmental or life-course view of stability in offending for chronic offenders, Gottfredson and Hirschi (1990) argued that the age effect on offending is invariant. All offenders, regardless of stable between-individual differences, will offend less frequently as they age. Thus, the age–crime debate is divided into two specific camps. The criminal career paradigm suggests that there is a small group of persistent offenders who will maintain offending at a high rate throughout the life course, whereas others, such as Gottfredson and Hirschi, believe that as the chronic group ages they will diminish in their offending frequency. Sampson and Laub (2003) state that longitudinal research attempts seeking to resolve the age–crime debate and the 'offender group' question have suffered three main limitations:

1 Criminal careers are usually examined over circumscribed portions of the life-course.

2 Trajectories of offending are typically identified retrospectively, based on the outcome, rather than prospectively, based on the causal factors presumed to differentiate groups of offenders.

3 When estimating desistance from offending, incapacitation and death are usually not accounted for.

Sampson and Laub (2003: 556) thus state:

Post-hoc typologies of offenders are thus ubiquitous in criminology; prospective categorisation of risk typologies and valid criminal trajectories over the long run that support or invalidate them are not. This is understandable, for long-term studies that follow the same individuals over time are as rare as they are difficult to carry out.

Sampson and Laub (2003) provide evidence which suggests even the most serious offending group, based on a reanalysis and update of the Gluecks' dataset used in *Unravelling Juvenile Delinquency* (1950), diminish in their offending frequency with age. They also provide evidence that questions the efficacy of developmental typologies. Their evidence suggests that categorisations such as 'life-course persister' may not be wholly true in reality. However, they argue typologies and groups are useful in managing data and reducing complexity. This is an argument that has a sound basis. The purpose of producing and confirming the efficacy of Wikström's (2002) typology is that it is a useful tool from which to make policy recommendations and in helping to target problems so that effective prevention strategies can be implemented. The typology is a simplified version of reality and indicates broadly three groups of juveniles in both Peterborough and Cardiff. Both these studies are cross-sectional in nature so it is not possible to draw solid conclusions in terms of individual life-course trajectories, nor is it possible to determine which pupils may follow adolescence-limited or life-course persistent trajectories, or indeed other types of trajectory. However, the fact that the following typology has been replicated suggests that, for 14–15-year-old young people, these categorisations may be valid and representative of reality, from which it may be possible to construct and implement successful offending prevention initiatives.

The typology presented, Wikström (2002) argues, mostly contributes to knowledge regarding the aetiology of offending by the group of offenders labelled by Moffit as adolescence limited. The three groups are identified as follows:

1 *Propensity induced* (youths at the risk end of the individual risk-protective score).

2 *Lifestyle dependent* (youths who have balanced individual risk-protective scores).

3 *Situationally limited* (youths at the protective end of the individual risk-protective distribution).

These three broad groupings have been shown to exist in terms of pupils' offending frequencies in Cardiff's schools in relation to pupils' individual risk-protective characteristics and lifestyle risk characteristics. The propensity-induced group have been shown to offend the most frequently on average in schools in Cardiff. This group is small in number (in this study, $n = 110$), but is responsible for a large amount of offending in Cardiff's schools (see Table 9.25, where this small group is shown to be responsible for approximately as great a percentage (or more) of offences that occurred in Cardiff's schools (as reported by the Year 10 population) as the entire situationally limited (protective) group). These pupils are poorly adjusted in terms of dispositions and have very weak bonds to conventional society. They have a high offending prevalence even when they have relatively low-risk lifestyles. However, having a high-risk lifestyle leads to a situation where four in five in this group have offended in school. This group report having offended on average seven times more frequently in school than their counterparts who have a low-risk lifestyle. It appears that lifestyle risk is quite important for frequency of offending in school for this group. This may be because this study primarily focuses on offending in schools rather than on offending in general. Schools may exert a controlling influence on those pupils who have high-risk individual risk-protective characteristics, which may not be the case when looking at offending in general. However, those pupils who lead high-risk lifestyles may be less susceptible to the schools' controlling influence, possibly explaining their high frequency of offending in schools. Those pupils with lower-risk lifestyles, but who have high-risk individual risk-protective characteristics, may be more susceptible to the schools' controlling influence, which may help explain their reduced frequency of offending. This group are, however, likely to have offended in school regardless of how low-risk their lifestyles are. Table 9.23 indicates that this group are not so strongly affected by school peer delinquency or substance use; however, they are influenced by general peer delinquency.

The lifestyle-dependent offenders in this study, as in the Peterborough Youth Study, are youths who display balanced dispositions and medium-strength bonds to conventional society. This group is lifestyle dependent regarding their likelihood of offending in school (prevalence) and also in terms of their average frequency of offending. Those who lead high-risk lifestyles are more likely to offend and also more likely to offend more frequently in schools. This could be a very important group on which to focus crime prevention strategies. Schools and parents should focus on discouraging high-

Table 9.23 Overall offending frequency in school by main lifestyle risk constructs: multiple regressions for main groups of individual risk-protective characteristics

| Lifestyle risk construct | Individual risk-protective group | | | | | |
| | Protective | | Balanced | | Risk | |
	Beta	Sig.	Beta	Sig.	Beta	Sig.
General peer delinquency	0.04	n.s.	0.10	0.001	0.24	0.019
School peer delinquency	0.21	0.000	0.21	0.000	0.13	n.s.
Substance use	0.07	0.009	0.21	0.000	0.20	0.054
Multiple $R^2 \times 100 =$	6		15		18	

risk lifestyles among these pupils. This can be achieved through better and more rigorous supervision and monitoring. This group is particularly influenced by mixing with delinquent peers in school, mixing with delinquent peers in general and abusing substances in determining their offending habits (see Table 9.23).

The situationally limited group, who display protective individual risk-protective characteristics, are individually well adjusted youths with sound dispositions and bonds to conventional society. Pupils in this group may offend occasionally in schools if they have a medium-level lifestyle risk. None in this group leads a high-risk lifestyle, which is in keeping with their protective individual risk-protective characteristics. In terms of offending in school, having delinquent school peers may be the strongest influence on them, followed by substance use (see Table 9.23). General peer delinquency has no significant influence on this group. This goes hand in hand with the fact that they lead low-risk lifestyles and are unlikely to mix with delinquent peers outside school, due perhaps to higher levels of parental monitoring. (Tables 9.24 and 9.25 report the percentage in the main lifestyle risk group by main individual risk-protective score group, and the percentage of pupils and percentage of offences reported by pupils by main risk-protective groups, respectively.)

Summary

This chapter has focused on examining the influence of lifestyle risk on pupil offending behaviour in schools. Theoretically, the case has been made that future criminological research should focus on developing lifestyle explanations of offending behaviour and also on developing

Table 9.24 Per cent in main lifestyle risk group by main individual risk-protective score group

| Risk-protective group | Lifestyle risk group | | | | |
	Low	Medium	High	Total	n
Protective	89	11	–	100	1,413
Balanced	61	35	3	100	1,145
Risk	12	62	26	100	96

Table 9.25 Per cent pupils and per cent of offences (overall offending and main types of offence) reported by pupils by main risk-protective groups

| Risk-protective group | Per cent subjects | Percent of offences committed by group | | | | |
		Overall offending	Theft	Assault	Vandalism	Serious offences
Protective	51.9	18.9	21.1	21.1	9.4	8.5
Balanced	44.3	61.8	58.0	61.4	72.4	52.1
Risk	3.8	19.1	20.9	17.5	18.2	39.5
$n =$	3,103	1,705	412	764	457	72

empirical measures of lifestyle, rather than focusing on spurious explanations provided by traditional 'subcultural' theorists. It is argued that, far from denying the existence of varying 'subcultures' in society, the notion of lifestyle accepts they are present, but that people throughout the life course will dip in and out of various subcultures and that these alone will not provide sound and useful explanations as to why individuals offend or not.

The chapter has employed a measure of lifestyle risk which can be improved on in future studies (for example, through employing time-space budgets), but which shows how important the concept can be in predicting individual pupil offending behaviour. The measure, made up of three scales measuring school peer delinquency, general peer delinquency and substance use, is shown to be strongly related to the amount of time pupils spend at home. Analysis showed that pupils who hang around with delinquent peers in school, in general and use substances are far more likely to spend little time at home. Further analysis also indicates a strong relationship between pupils' lifestyle risk and truancy from school in the last year (population $r = 0.44$, $p = 0.000$; males $r = 0.45$, $p = 0.000$; females $r = 0.44$,

$p = 0.000$). This suggests that such pupils are likely to spend a greater amount of time in unsupervised settings, where they are more likely to encounter risk situations. It is also likely that pupils who lead high-risk lifestyles are more likely to find themselves in riskier settings on the school premises because, if they are likely to truant, they are also probably more likely to try to stay away from supervised settings; this may help somewhat in understanding the offending–victimisation link. Pupils leading high-risk lifestyles may find themselves in risk settings where supervision is minimal and, as a result, be more likely to offend and also be at a greater risk of victimisation than fellow pupils who report leading low-risk lifestyles.

Analyses in the chapter provide further evidence that the strongest predictors of individual offending in school are the pupils' individual risk-protective characteristics and lifestyle risk and the interaction between these two measures. These factors are more immediate to individual social action and decision-making. Community, family and school factors are likely to influence the development of individual risk-protective characteristics and lifestyle risk. Further longitudinal research should contribute to knowledge regarding this contextual–individual link and how context influences individual development. An analysis of the interaction between the individual risk-protective measure and lifestyle risk has provided a basis from which a discussion of a heuristic typology of pupils has been discerned in relation to offending in school, which is a replication of a similar finding in another research project (see Wikström 2002). The fact this finding is similar between two city samples of 14–15-year-old adolescents suggests the rigour of these groupings, which may have great utility in the designation of focused crime prevention strategies both in and out of school.

Chapter 10

Between-school differences

This chapter will investigate between-school differences in pupil prevalence and frequency of offending in relation to compositional measures of school context for each school, based on the pupils' average scores in each school. The chapter will explore the interaction between individual-level pupil characteristics and context-level school characteristics. This is particularly important as it will illustrate how different school contexts affect different types of individual in different ways. Such analysis has wide utility in the policy sphere because it illustrates how different types of contexts influence different types of individuals differently. This approach is likely to lead to better targeted and more successful prevention initiatives and better standards of behaviour in schools. The approach should also address an area long overlooked in criminological research regarding schools, by including how the individual pupil interacts with his or her school environment. One of the strengths of this study is that both school-level data and individual-level data can be analysed to further our understanding and explanation of pupil offending in schools.

Creating a measure of school context risk

The individual (pupil) will be influenced by the school context in terms of how it is organised, managed, its climate and the relations between pupils, and also by the milieu the pupils bring with them. Therefore, the family backgrounds of other pupils, the areas from which they come, the individual characteristics of other pupils, the views of school context held by other pupils and the lifestyles of other pupils will all influence the context in which the individual (pupil) finds him or herself. Following the analytical approach pursued in the rest of this book, the measure of aggregate school context employed in this chapter will, as closely as possible, resemble the actual reality of school context in each school by taking all these factors into account in constructing the measure.

Aggregating pupils by school created the measure of school context risk; thus, each school is attributed an overall school context risk score. Each pupil is assigned the aggregate school score (a measure of context) based on the pupils who attend their schools' mean. The school scores were then categorised into risk categories, using one standard deviation from the mean as a basis. For example, mean pupil (by school) family social position was scored –1, indicating low-risk features, 0 indicating balanced features and +1 indicating high-risk features. Once this process was achieved, all six explanatory factors were summed, resulting in a scale ranging from –6 to +6. A score of –6 means that the school has pupils from protected family backgrounds, protected areas of residence risk, who display protective individual characteristics and protective lifestyles, and who perceive school climate and pupil relations as being good. The distribution of this measure of school context can be seen in Figure 10.1.

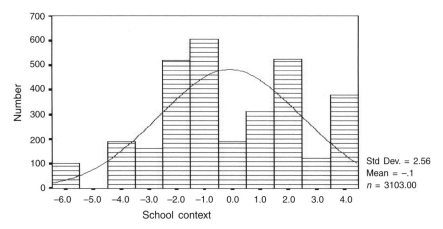

Figure 10.1 School context risk score (based on pupil mean (by school) individual risk-protective characteristics, lifestyle risk, family social position risk, area of residence structural risk, school climate and pupil relations)

Most pupils in Cardiff attend schools with balanced environments or better (i.e. the distribution in Figure 10.1 is skewed towards negative). For the purposes of later analyses, it was decided to refine this school context measure by creating four categories of school context, once again by using standard deviations from the mean as a basis for selection (on this occasion one standard deviation from the mean score on the −6 to +6 school context measure just described). The distribution of schools in this scale is represented in Figure 10.2.

This figure illustrates that most school contexts in Cardiff are similar, considering their relative deviations from the mean based on the explanatory variables previously mentioned. There is only one school that is in the very low-risk category (represented by 0), which contains 101 pupils. In the low-risk group (represented by 1) there are two schools (n = 351 pupils). In the medium-risk group (represented by 2) there are 13 schools (n = 2,150) and in the high-risk group (represented by 3) there are four schools with a total pupil population of 501 pupils.

School context risk by pupils' offending behaviour in schools

Table 10.1 indicates that school context, in terms of the mean lifestyle and individual risk-protective characteristics of pupils, the mean pupils' view of school climate and pupil relations and the mean

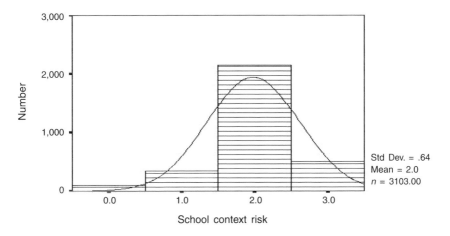

Figure 10.2 School context risk score: distribution of pupils

Table 10.1 School context risk (grouped by schools) by pupils' offending prevalence

| | School context risk (aggregate measure)* | | | | | |
	Very low (%)	Low (%)	Medium (%)	High (%)	Sig.	Gamma
Population						
Theft	1.1	3.3	5.8	9.8	0.000	0.33
Assault	9.5	6.6	13.7	17.2	0.000	0.24
Vandalism	1.1	5.4	7.0	7.7	n.s.	–
Serious offences	0.0	0.3	1.2	2.1	n.s.	–
Overall offending	10.5	12.0	20.9	25.8	0.000	0.24
Males						
Theft	2.9	3.8	8.4	8.2	n.s.	–
Assault	22.9	10.7	18.7	23.5	0.015	0.18
Vandalism	2.9	6.9	8.6	8.6	n.s.	–
Serious offences	0.0	0.6	2.1	2.8	n.s.	–
Overall offending	25.7	17.0	27.3	32.3	0.010	0.18
Females						
Theft	0.0	2.9	3.1	11.3	0.000	0.52
Assault	1.7	2.9	8.3	10.9	0.006	0.34
Vandalism	0.0	4.0	5.3	6.8	n.s.	–
Serious offences	0.0	0.0	0.2	1.4	n.s.	–
Overall offending	1.7	7.4	14.1	19.3	0.000	0.32

Note:

* School context grouped according to standard deviations from the mean. Very low = 1 school, Low = 2 schools, Medium = 13 schools, High = 4 schools.

pupils' family social background and area of residence structural risk of pupils, is related to the amount of offending prevalence a school experiences. For males and females together the aggregate school context measure is statistically significantly related to prevalence of theft, assault and overall offending. For males, associations exist between type of aggregate school context risk and prevalence of assault and overall offending. For females, associations can be clearly seen between theft, assault and overall offending. Girls in high-risk schools are over twice as likely to report having offended in school than their counterparts in low-risk schools (this is over nine times if one considers the difference between high-risk and very low-risk schools). These differences are not so clear cut for males, which are illustrated by the weaker associations when statistical significance is achieved. The composition of pupils lifestyles and individual characteristics, their view of school climate and pupil relations and their family and community backgrounds, by school, can make a difference in terms of offending prevalence in schools. Schools that serve pupils from disadvantaged backgrounds, who display high-risk individual characteristics and lifestyles, and which serve pupils who view their school contexts in a negative way, are more likely to experience higher rates of pupil offending.

Table 10.2 examines whether these factors influence pupils' frequency of offending. For the population, the school context is

Table 10.2 School context risk (groups of schools) by pupils' offending frequency, means, significance and eta^2

	Overall offending	Theft	Assault	Vandalism
Population				
Very low	0.22	0.01	0.15	0.06
Low	0.35	0.08	0.11	0.14
Medium	0.59	0.13	0.27	0.16
High	0.74	0.22	0.34	0.17
Sig.	0.003	0.011	0.002	n.s.
Eta^2	0.004	0.004	0.005	0.001
Male				
Very low	0.55	0.03	0.37	0.16
Low	0.50	0.12	0.14	0.20
Medium	0.82	0.20	0.39	0.17
High	0.82	0.16	0.48	0.15
Sig.	n.s.	n.s.	0.019	n.s.
Eta^2	–	–	0.006	–
Female				
Very low	0.02	0.00	0.02	0.00
Low	0.20	0.52	0.07	0.08
Medium	0.33	0.06	0.13	0.14
High	0.66	0.28	0.19	0.18
Sig.	0.000	0.000	n.s.	n.s.
Eta^2	0.013	0.019	–	–

Note:

* School context grouped according to standard deviations from the mean. Very low = 1 school, Low = 2 schools, Medium = 13 schools, High = 4 schools.

related to frequency of overall offending, theft and assault in schools. Frequency of assault reported by males is the only offence category that is significantly explained by school context while, for females, frequency of overall offending and theft is associated with school context risk. However, where statistical significance is achieved the amount of variance in pupils' offending frequency explained is very slight (being under 2 per cent for females and under 1 per cent for males and for the total population). Females are more likely to offend in contexts where fellow pupils display, on average, high-risk individual characteristics and lifestyles, where fellow pupils are from disadvantaged backgrounds and where pupils, generally, view the school climate and pupil relations in the school negatively.

Pupils with protective individual risk-protective characteristics are significantly affected by their school context

Table 10.3 shows the relationship between the school context of the schools in the research and the individual risk-protective characteristics of the pupils who attend those schools. It can be hypothesised that school context will have the strongest influence on individuals who have a low propensity to offend (it has been shown in Chapter 8 that pupils with protective individual risk-protective characteristics are likely to have a low propensity to offend). This is a similar hypothesis to that espoused by Wikström and Sampson

Table 10.3 School context risk by pupils' individual risk-protective scores: overall pupil offending prevalence in schools

| Individual risk-protective characteristics | School context risk (aggregate measure)* | | | | | | |
	Very low	Low	Medium	Risk	Sig.	Gamma	n
Protective	4.8	6.6	11.4	14.8	0.024	0.26	1,467
Balanced	25.0	19.3	29.1	28.0	n.s.	–	1,220
Risk	0.0	57.1	54.8	73.9	n.s.	–	104
Sig.	0.016	0.000	0.000	0.000			
Gamma	0.70	0.60	0.55	0.52			
n	92	328	1,946	425			

*School context grouped according to standard deviations from the mean. Very low = 1 school, low = 2 schools, medium = 13 schools, high = 4 schools.

(2003), who state: 'We specifically hypothesise that the community strength of impact on motivation to offend varies inversely by the individual propensity to offend.'

It can be argued that pupils who have developed a strong propensity to offend (those who display high-risk individual characteristics) are less likely to be affected by the contexts and behaviour settings they encounter. This is because they already have a high propensity to offend and the context in which they do offend may not be as important for them. However, for protected and balanced pupils, the contexts and the opportunities they supply, in terms of criminogenic behaviour settings, may be more important in guiding their offending behaviour.

Table 10.3 indicates that this hypothesis is valid. Pupils who display protective individual characteristics are most influenced by the context of the school around them (in terms of their fellow pupils' backgrounds, lifestyles, individual risk-protective characteristics and views of climate and pupil relations). There is a statistically significant relationship between pupils who display individual protective characteristics, the risk level of their school context and offending prevalence. Pupils displaying protective individual characteristics are almost three times as likely to report having offended in high-risk school contexts than their counterparts in very low-risk schools. There are no such statistically significant relationships identified for pupils displaying balanced and risk individual characteristics by level of school context risk.

Overall, the table indicates that pupils' individual risk-protective characteristics are more important in determining offending prevalence than the type of school individuals find themselves in. Once again, though, it must be stated that pupils' individual risk-protective characteristics are likely to be formed and developed over time by the family, school and community contexts in which they find themselves.

Summary

School context appears to be particularly important for pupils who display individual protective characteristics. No other study of offending in schools has examined this relationship, making it difficult for comparisons to be made. Future research should certainly continue developing this avenue, which is likely to be fruitful in the development of offending prevention strategies and indeed in raising the intellectual achievement of pupils. Studies in the communities and crime tradition have shown some support for this notion – that context may have stronger impacts on individuals who display protective characteristics (i.e. lower propensities to offend). Wikström and Loeber (2000) have shown that community levels of disadvantage had the strongest effect on adolescent onset in serious offending for the most well adjusted subjects while, for the other subjects, no significant community differences by disadvantage were found. Wikström (2002) reports similar findings for prevalence of adolescent offending in the Peterborough Youth Study.

A move towards a greater understanding of how school contexts affect different types of individuals differently should provide a sound basis for better targeting of strategies and resources, which can improve the lives and outcomes of pupils in schools. The interaction between context and individual is critical. More research is still needed as this remains one of the most complex areas in social science today.

Chapter 11

Key findings and implications

The Cardiff School Study represents one of the most in-depth investigations of pupil offending behaviour undertaken to date in schools in the UK. Very few studies, since *Fifteen Thousand Hours* (Rutter *et al.* 1979), have given attention to this important issue in the UK (see Rutter *et al.* 1998). The survey included all Year 10 pupils (ages 14–15) in all the state secondary schools in Cardiff – a time in an individual's life when involvement in crime has been shown to peak (see Farrington and Wikström 1994). It is likely that, during this period, offending behaviour in schools will also peak (although, to the author's knowledge, no research has been conducted relating to this issue). The study represents an aetiological investigation of pupil offending focusing on pupils' individual and lifestyle characteristics as well as assessing their family and neighbourhood backgrounds and their perceptions of school context.

One important limitation of the study is that, because it is cross-sectional in nature, little can be said regarding how pupils have developed (cognitively and morally) over time to the point at which they completed the survey. It is, therefore, impossible to provide any information regarding how their individual differences concerning involvement in crime in schools have evolved over time. It is also not possible to discuss their future development or involvement in crime in general, once they have left school. However, it is entirely reasonable to use findings from previous criminological research, particularly longitudinal studies, to help in the interpretation of the findings regarding pupil offending behaviour in schools. Ideally, a future research project would investigate pupil offending behaviour in schools employing longitudinal techniques. This would provide extensive knowledge regarding pupils' offending patterns over time as well as the development of the factors that cause it. Ultimately, research of this nature can provide a greater understanding and explanation of why some pupils offend in schools and why some schools experience more crime than others. As knowledge and understanding of the causes of the crime phenomenon in schools increases it is likely that prevention initiatives and strategies which are knowledge based can be employed that may have greater utility than the often piecemeal approaches that are currently pursued.

In this study, the measures of community and school context relate to pupils' contexts of action. The findings in this study show that, once individual risk-protective characteristics and lifestyle are controlled for, these contextual measures are generally insignificant predictors of pupils' offending in schools. However, it has been shown that different school contexts influence different types of pupils (in terms of their individual characteristics) in different ways – suggesting the importance of contexts in influencing individual action. There is a high likelihood that, in cross-sectional analysis (such as the multiple regression-based analyses used in earlier chapters), contextual effects will be underestimated in relation to their influence on pupils' offending behaviour. This is because the analysis does not recognise the importance of contextual factors in shaping individual characteristics over time. The analysis, therefore, can be said to underestimate how contextual factors have influenced individuals' development, in terms of their individual risk-protective characteristics and lifestyles. Future longitudinal research could address this issue by focusing on how context influences individual development. In order to do this effectively, further refinements of measures of community and, indeed, school context are necessary.

Pupils' involvement in school crime

Chapter 4 indicates that offending among pupils in schools is usually restricted to less serious offences, with assault, theft and vandalism being the most common types of offending reported (however, there were only a limited number of offences included in the questionnaire survey), with very few (particularly females) reporting having broken into school or having committed robbery in school. Findings indicate that males are more involved in offending behaviour, in schools, than females. Almost twice as many males in comparison with females report offending in schools.

The study, in keeping with a breadth of criminological research, indicates that frequent offenders in schools also tend to be versatile in their offending habits, reporting an array of offences on the school premises. This suggests that future research should focus on factors which cause pupils to offend in schools, rather than just focusing on particular crime types in schools. For instance, if pupils who offend frequently commit a variety of offences including theft in schools, it is likely to be a fruitless strategy just to focus on the causes of theft in schools when the causes of pupil theft in schools may well be similar for pupil vandalism in school (for instance, pupils' lifestyles, individual risk-protective characteristics, etc.).

Chapter 4 indicates that pupils who offend in school are also more likely to be victimised in school. Wikström (2002) suggests a possible reason for this link for general offending and victimisation among adolescents which can be applied to school pupils. He hypothesises that youths with high individual risk-protective characteristics and risky lifestyles more often get into 'trouble', which occasionally results in them committing an offence but sometimes results in them being victimised. Wikström (2002: 231) argues that an implication of this is that 'when we talk about high frequency adolescent offenders, we are likely to talk about adolescents that are also repeatedly victimised and, therefore, the offender and victim roles for this group may be somewhat blurred'.

Between-school differences

Chapter 4 indicates wide differences in pupils' prevalence and frequency of offending rates between schools. Such differences indicate that the school a child goes to may significantly affect his or her chances of exposure to crime. The fact of such variation suggests that not all schools have similar problems in relation to pupil offending. However, those that do have significant problems may benefit from strategies to reduce pupil offending. The variation also suggests that a clearly thought out and targeted strategy involving schools who have high rates of offending may be more effective than an overall generalist policy that includes all schools.

Explanatory factors

Pupils' neighbourhood of residence is weakly associated with offending behaviour in schools

Chapter 5 shows that pupils' area of residence is significantly associated with some types of pupil offending behaviour in schools. However, these associations, both for prevalence and frequency, tend to be weak in the cases where significant differences are found. Regression analyses performed in relation to area and sex explain a small proportion of variance in relation to the types of offending in school examined. Such a finding is common and has been shown previously in research investigating the influence of communities on individual offending (see Martens 1993). However, in later chapters, analysis indicates that pupils' area of residence is related to factors such as the pupils' individual risk-protective scores. This suggests that area of residence may have an indirect effect on pupil offending which is played out through mediating factors such as the pupils' individual risk-protective characteristics.

Future studies should focus on developing more sophisticated measures of neighbourhoods and should expand the field of 'ecometrics', as called for by Raudenbush and Sampson (1999). Raudenbush and Sampson (1999: 640) argue: 'the development of ecometric research procedures and statistical methods for the study of ecological and other macrolevel units is in its infancy.' Future development is necessary, as presently, as employed in this study, large census tracts are usually used that are artificially delimited and which may have little meaning for the people who live in those areas. Longitudinal studies should also pay attention to the communities' role as contexts of individual development, which may indirectly affect individual differences in offending behaviour, as well as focusing on the community as a context of action, where some contexts may well be more criminogenic in their nature than others.

Pupils' family social position is weakly associated with pupil offending behaviour

Chapter 6 demonstrated that pupils' family socioeconomic status is not significantly associated with prevalence of offending in schools. This suggests that the view that pupil offending in school is directly associated with pupils from lower-class backgrounds is flawed. Pupils' family structure (parental composition) is associated with overall offending in schools and with assault. Pupils who are in foster care, staying with relatives or in care are more likely to have reported offending than other pupils, as were pupils from single-parent families and from families where one parent is a step-parent, in comparison with pupils who live with two biological parents. However, pupils' socioeconomic background and family structure (parental composition) are not strongly directly associated with pupil offending behaviour in school. Pupils' family size, in keeping with previous research, proves to have moderate associations with pupil offending in schools, although this effect appears to be more strongly associated with females than males. A possible explanation for this is that pupils from bigger families may get less time and attention from their parents. Pupils' family ethnic background (both immigrant status and ethnicity) showed no statistically significant associations with pupil offending behaviour in schools.

When examining pupils' family socioeconomic status, parental composition and family size together in a risk scale, weak associations were found for the pupil population with assault, vandalism, serious offences and overall offending prevalence in schools. Analysis in Chapter 8 illustrates how important pupils' family social position (particularly in relation to socioeconomic status) is in affecting pupils' individual risk-protective scores. This confirms an argument made throughout the book that suggests that structural characteristics have a distant and indirect effect on pupils' offending behaviour, with measures closer to pupils' social action being more important in determining their offending behaviour. Structural measures, including family social position, tend to lose their significance as predictors of offending in the regression-based analyses, once pupils' individual risk-protective characteristics and lifestyles are controlled for.

Pupils' view of school context is significantly related to offending in school

Chapter 7 examined how a number of newly developed scales relating to pupils' perceptions, attitudes and experiences of their schools were related to their offending behaviour. Parental interest in schooling, pupils' view of school ethos, pupils' social capital, school disorder and pupils' respect for school authority were all found to have significant and, in some cases, fairly strong associations with pupils' offending behaviour in school.

Following a factor analysis, these scales were reduced into two risk scales, with each scale measuring a different aspect of school context. The first scale related to school climate (based on school ethos, respect for authority and parental school interest); the second related to pupil relations (based on pupils' social capital and school disorder). Both these scales were shown, independently, to exert strong and significant associations with pupils' involvement in crime in schools. Regression analyses indicated that these two constructs, alongside sex, explained 6 per cent of the variance for overall offending in school. However, the analysis indicates that, of the two constructs, school climate has the strongest predictive power. This suggests that how individual pupils view their school climate is of greater importance than how they see their relationships with other pupils in influencing their offending behaviour.

Strategies that may reduce pupil offending in the school context could benefit by focusing on 1) building better and stronger links between the school and parents; 2) improving the pupils' respect for school authority; and 3) improving the general ethos of the school. Through improving social trust and capital (see Bryk and Schneider 2002 for a discussion of the importance of trust in educational institutions) in the school between pupils, teachers, managers and parents it may be possible to help reduce the rates of pupil offending in schools.

Pupils know the difference between right and wrong

Findings in Chapter 8 indicate that the majority of pupils in Cardiff's schools know the difference between right and wrong, in terms of their perceptions of a host of deviant and criminal activity. The great majority of pupils have pro-social values, and analysis indicates that there are no differences in pupils' levels of pro-social values by family social position or area of residence structural risk (see Chapter 8, Table 8.4, for this latter analysis). This finding, alongside Wikström's (2002) similar finding among a similar-aged sample of youths in the Peterborough Youth Study, provide evidence indicating that there are no social-class or neighbourhood-disadvantaged-based 'subcultures' of crime and delinquency.

However, the measure of pro-social values used in this study is a strong predictor of pupil offending in schools. Pupils with anti-social values (as measured by the pro-social values scale) tend to offend more prevalently and frequently than those with pro-social values.

Pupils' social situations and dispositions are strong predictors of their risk of offending behaviour in school

Chapter 8 indicates that pupils' individual social situations and dispositions are important predictors of offending behaviour in school.

Pupils' bonds to family and school and levels of parental monitoring were all shown to have significant associations with offending prevalence. However, in the multiple regression-based analyses, when pupils' self-control and aspects of their morality (pro-social values and (sense of) shaming) were controlled for, pupils' bonds to school and family became insignificant in predicting frequency of offending in schools. The strongest predictors of pupil offending in schools (out of social situational and dispositional characteristics) were pupils' pro-social values and self-control. Thus, pupils who are impulsive and have anti-social values are deemed more likely to offend in school. These models also controlled for the pupils' family social position. All this confirms the view that, as one measures aspects that are closer to forming individuals' action, one finds that predictive power increases.

Chapter 8 suggests that all the pupils' social situational and dispositional characteristics are fairly closely related and may be interpreted as a risk-protective dimension, which is a very powerful predictor of pupil offending in schools in relation to the pupils' family social position and area of residence structural risk characteristics. The findings suggest that, the more risk characteristics a pupil displays, the greater the likelihood he or she will have to offend, to offend frequently and to be versatile in his or her habits. Those who display many protective individual characteristics are less likely to report offending of any type in schools.

So far it has been indicated that pupils' family backgrounds are not directly related to pupil offending behaviour; rather, they influence pupils' individual risk-protective characteristics, which have been shown to be good predictors that account for individual pupil differences in offending behaviour in school. Pupils vary widely in their social situations and dispositions. However, there may be strategies that schools can employ to help prevent pupils' offending based on these findings. One such strategy may be to try to strengthen pupils' bonds to schools, for example. Early interventions, before pupils reach secondary school, may also be of great importance in helping to increase levels of self-control, sense of shame and pro-social values among young pupils.

The importance of lifestyle

Chapter 9 indicates the importance that pupils' peers, both in general and in school, have on pupils' delinquency. The chapter also illustrated the importance of substance use in relation to delinquent activity. Having delinquent peers in school and generally and using substances are indicative of a high-risk lifestyle. These factors were combined to create a lifestyle risk score, which was strongly associated with pupil offending in schools. This lifestyle risk score was also shown to be strongly related to the amount of time pupils spent at home, with those leading high-risk lifestyles spending hardly any of their waking time at home. This finding suggests that pupils with high-risk lifestyles may receive less monitoring and, as a result, have less of a controlling influence in their lives.

The analysis examined an interaction between adolescents' lifestyle risk and individual risk-protective characteristics, which goes a long way towards replicating Wikström's (2002) typology of adolescent offenders. This interaction showed that pupils with high-risk individual characteristics were more likely than others to have offended in school regardless of their lifestyle risk; however, those pupils with both high-risk lifestyles and high-risk individual risk-protective characteristics are, by some distance, the group that offend most frequently in Cardiff's schools. The group who displayed balanced individual risk characteristics appear to be most affected by their lifestyle risk. These findings, combined with the work of Wikström (2002) and based on previous knowledge from longitudinal research (see Moffitt 1993; Moffitt *et al.* 2001), provide evidence for the possible existence of three main broad groups of pupil offenders in schools (or three types of adolescent offenders), as proposed by Wikström (2002). These are as follows.

1. Propensity induced

This group of pupils who offend in schools are very small in number but, as Chapter 9 indicates, they are responsible for a great percentage of offending in schools in comparison with their small size. These pupils have high-risk individual risk-protective scores and are likely to have offended regardless of lifestyle; however, those with particularly bad lifestyles are likely to offend at a great frequency. For this group, peer relations in school and substance use appear to be unimportant in relation to their offending behaviour. However, outside school they tend to be influenced by delinquent peers. This may be because they spend very little time at home and probably receive very little attention from parents.

2. Lifestyle-dependent pupil offenders

These pupils display balanced individual risk-protective characteristics and are lead greatly in their offending behaviour in schools by their lifestyle risk. As illustrated in Chapter 9, this is a group for whom hanging around with the wrong sort of peers and abusing substances may greatly influence their offending habits.

3. Situationally limited

This group of pupils displays protective individual risk-protective characteristics. This group is unlikely ever to lead a high-risk lifestyle and these pupils are only likely to offend in schools occasionally, with a very low frequency. Interestingly, this group of pupils is not affected by their delinquent peers, generally, in determining their offending behaviour. They are, however, influenced by delinquent peers and substance use in schools. This suggests that strong peer influences in schools may occasionally contribute to pupils in this group offending in schools.

Pupils with protective individual risk-protective characteristics are more likely to report offending in schools that display many contextual risk factors

Chapter 10 examined between-school differences in pupil offending rates by categorising schools into four groups based on means of pupil composition scores by each of the explanatory constructs used in this book. This analysis clearly showed that schools that have a high mean regarding pupil composition (in terms of pupils' individual risk-protective characteristics, pupils' lifestyles, pupils' family social position, pupils' area of residence structural risk, pupils' view of school climate and pupil relations, in school) were found to have a higher prevalence of pupils who reported offending. This suggests that school context does have an influence regarding pupil offending.

This aggregate school context measure was examined by controlling for pupils' individual risk-protective characteristics. This illustrated that pupils who display protective individual risk-protective characteristics were most likely to be influenced by school context in relation to their offending behaviour. The balanced and high-risk groups were shown not to be significantly influenced by the type of school they attend in terms of their offending behaviour. This all suggests that the typology of offenders discussed above is highly relevant to pupil offending in schools. Those pupils with protective individual characteristics who attend schools with high-risk contexts may more often come into contact with delinquent peers at school and encounter more risk situations as a result. This could explain their higher rate of offending in risk contexts as opposed to their counterparts in schools that display more protective characteristics.

A final summary

Schools are central in the production of well-rounded citizens. They mould the future and their effective functioning is essential in the maintenance and evolution of civilisation. The young people who attend schools will go on to be the leaders and workers of tomorrow. If they are to be educated properly and safely, the context in which the process of education occurs should be safe. The Cardiff School Study represents an analytical investigation which highlights factors that influence individual and between-school differences in offending behaviour in the school context. The study has demonstrated that school context does influence pupil behaviour and that schools vary quite widely in pupils' self-reported offending. Future research would benefit from investigating further the way context has varying influences on different types of individuals. Such research can go a long way in informing successful evidence-based strategies that can be implemented to help both those who offend and those who do not offend in schools.

Knowledge is essential if strategies that make pupils feel safer, offend less and achieve the goals of education are to succeed.

References

Anderson, C. (1982) 'The search for school climate: a review of the research', *Review of Educational Research*, 52: 368–420.

Anderson, S., Kinsey, R., Loader, I. and Smith, C. (1994) *Cautionary Tales: Young People, Crime and Policing in Edinburgh*. Aldershot: Avebury.

Baerveldt, C. (1992) 'Schools and the prevention of petty crime: search for a missing link', *Journal of Quantitative Criminology*, 8: 79–94.

Baldwin, J. and Bottoms, A.E. (1976) *The Urban Criminal*. London: Tavistock.

Barker, R.G. (1968) *Ecological Psychology: Concepts and Methods for Studying the Environment of Human Behaviour*. Stanford, CA: Stanford University Press.

Barker, R.G. and Gump, P.V. (1964) *Big School, Small School*. Stanford, CA: Stanford University Press.

Belson, W.A. (1975) *Juvenile Theft: The Causal Factors*. London: Harper & Row.

Bissel, C. (1996) *Improving Security in Schools. Department for Education and Employment Guide* 4. London: HMSO.

Blumstein, A., Cohen, J., Roth, J. and Visher, C. (eds) (1986) *Criminal Careers and 'Career Criminals'*. Washington, DC: National Academy Press.

Bottoms, A.E. (1993) 'Recent criminological and social theory: the problem of integrating knowledge about individual criminal acts and careers and areal dimensions of crime', in D.P. Farrington *et al.* (eds) *Integrating Individual and Ecological Aspects of Crime*. Stockholm: Allmanna Forlaget.

Bottoms, A.E., Claytor, A. and Wiles, P. (1992) 'Housing markets and residential community crime careers: a case study from Sheffield', in D.J. Evans *et al.* (eds) *Crime, Policing and Place: Essays in Environmental Criminology*. London: Routledge.

Bottoms, A.E. and Wiles, P. (1997) 'Environmental criminology', in M. Maguire *et al.* (eds) *The Oxford Handbook of Criminology* (2nd edn). Oxford: Clarendon Press.

Braithwaite, J. (1979) *Inequality, Crime and Public Policy*. London: Routledge.

Braithwaite, J. (1981) 'The myth of social class and criminality reconsidered', *Amercian Sociological Review*, 46: 36–57.

Brantingham, P. and Brantingham, P. (1989) *Environmental Criminology*. Beverly Hills, CA: Sage.

Bronfenbrenner, U. (1979) *The Ecology of Human Development*. Cambridge, MA: Harvard University Press.

Brooks-Gunn, G.J., Duncan, G.J. and Aber, J.L. (1997) *Neighbourhood Poverty (vols 1 and 2)*. New York, NY: Russell Sage.

Bryk, A.S. and Driscoll, M.E. (1988) *The School as Community: Theoretical Foundations, Contextual Influences, and Consequences for Students and Teachers*. Madison, WI: University of Wisconcin, National Center of Effective Secondary Schools.

Bryk, A.S., Lee, V.E. and Holland, P.B. (1993) *Catholic Schools and the Common Good*. Cambridge, MA: Harvard University Press.

Bryk, A.S. and Schneider, B. (2002) *Trust in Schools: A Core Resource for Improvement*. New York, NY: Russell Sage Foundation.

Bryk, A.S. and Thum, Y.M. (1989) 'The effects of high school organisation on dropping out: an exploratory investigation', *American Educational Research Journal*, 26: 353–83.

Bunge, M. (1999) *Social Science under Debate: A Philosophical Perspective*. Toronto: University of Toronto Press.

Bunge, M. (2004) 'How does it work? The search for explanatory mechanisms', *Philosophy of the Social Sciences*, 34: 1–29.

Butterworth, D., Wikstrom, P.-O. H. and Parmar, A. (forthcoming) 'The low rate of offending by Asian females: exploring the interaction between gender and ethnicity.'

Canter, R.J. (1982) 'Family correlates of male and female delinquency', *Criminology*, 20: 149–67.

Cardiff Research Centre (2002) *Deprivation in Cardiff*. Cardiff: Cardiff County Council.

Cernkovich, S.A. and Giordano, P.C. (1987) 'Family relationships and delinquency', *Criminology*, 25: 295–321.

Chaney, D. (1996) *Lifestyles*. London: Routledge.

Cohen, L.E. and Felson, M. (1979) 'Social change and crime rate trends: a routine activity approach', *American Sociological Review*, 44: 588–608.

Coleman, J.S. (1990) *Foundations of Social Theory*. Cambridge, MA: The Belknap Press of Harvard University Press.

Coleman, J.S., Campbell, E.Q., Hobson, C.J., McPartland, J., Mood, A.M., Weinfeld, F.D. and York, R.L. (1966) *Equality of Educational Opportunity (2 vols)*. Washington, DC: Office of Education, US Department of Health Education, and Welfare, US Government Printing Office.

Cowie, H., Jennifer, D. and Sharp, S. (2003) 'School violence in the United Kingdom: addressing the problem', in P.K. Smith (ed.) *Violence in Schools: The Response in Europe*. London: RoutledgeFalmer.

Department of Education and Science (1967) *Children and their Primary Schools* (the Plowden Report). London: HMSO.

Department for Education and Skills (2002) *Education and Skills: Delivering Results. A Strategy to 2006*. London: HMSO.

Dunaway, R.G., Cullen, F.T., Burton, J.R. and Evans, D.T. (2000) 'The myth of social class and crime revisited: an examination of class and adult criminality', *Criminology*, 38: 589–631.

Earls, F. and Buka, S. (2000) 'Measurement of community characteristics', in J.P. Shonkoff and S.J. Meisels (eds) *Handbook of Early Childhood Intervention* (2nd edn). Cambridge: Cambridge University Press.

Elliot, D., Huizinga, D. and Ageton, S. (1985) *Explaining Delinquency and Drug Use*. Beverly Hills, CA: Sage.

Elliot, D.S., Hamburg, B.A. and Williams, K.R. (1998) *Violence in American Schools*. Cambridge: Cambridge University Press.

Entner Wright, B.R., Caspi, A., Moffit, T.E., Miech, R.A. and Silva, P.A. (1999) 'Reconsidering the relationship between SES and delinquency: causation but not correlation', *Criminology*, 37: 175–95.

Espiritu, R., Huizinga, D., Crawford, A.M. and Loeber, R. (2001) 'Epidemiology of self-reported delinquency', in R. Loeber and D.P. Farrington (eds) *Child Delinquents. Development, Intervention and Service Needs*. London: Sage.

Farrington, D.P. (1972) 'Delinquency begins at home', *New Society*, 21: 495–97.

Farrington, D.P. (1977) 'The effects of public labelling', *British Journal of Criminology*, 17: 112–25.

Farrington, D.P. (1992) 'Explaining the beginning, progress and ending of anti-social behaviour from birth to adulthood', in J. McCord (eds) *Facts, Frameworks and Forecasts*. New Brunswick, NJ: Transaction.

Farrington, D.P. (1993) 'Have any individual, family or neighbourhood influences on offending been demonstrated conclusively?', in D.P. Farrington *et al.* (eds) *Integrating Individual and Ecological Aspects of Crime*. Stockholm: Allmanna Forlaget.

Farrington, D.P. (1997) 'Human development and criminal careers', in M. Maguire *et al.* (eds) *The Oxford Handbook of Criminology*. Oxford: Oxford University Press.

Farrington, D.P. (1998) 'Individual differences and offending', in M. Tonry (ed.) *The Handbook of Crime and Punishment*. Oxford: Oxford University Press.

Farrington, D.P. (2001) *What has been Learned from Self-reports about Criminal Careers and the Causes of Offending? A Report for the Home Office*. London: Home Office. Research, Development and Statistics Bureau.

Farrington, D.P., Jolliffe, D., Hawkins, D.J., Catalano, R.F., Hill, K.G. and Kosterman, R. (2003) 'Comparing delinquency careers in court records and self-reports', *Criminology*, 41: 953–58.

Farrington, D.P., Sampson, R.J. and Wikstrom, P.-O.H. (1993) *Integrating Individual and Ecological Aspects of Crime*. Stockholm: Allmanna Forlaget.

Farrington, D.P. and Wikstrom, P.-O.H. (1994) 'Criminal careers in London and Stockholm: a cross national comparative study', in E.G.M. Weitekamp and H.J. Kerner (eds) *Cross-national Longitudinal Research on Human Development and Criminal Behaviour*. Dordrecht: Kluwer Academic.

Felson, R.B., Liska, A.E., South, S.J. and McNulty, T.L. (1994) 'The subculture of violence and delinquency: individual vs. school context effects', *Social Forces*, 73: 155–73.

Flood-Page, C., Campbell, S., Harrington, V. and Miller, J. (2000) *Youth Crime: Findings from the 1998/99 Youth Lifestyles Survey. Home Office Research Study 209*. London: Home Office.

Garbarino, J. and Ganzel, B. (2000) 'The human ecology of early risk', in J.P. Shonkoff and S.J. Meisels (eds) *Handbook of Early Childhood Intervention* (2nd edn). Cambridge: Cambridge University Press.

Garbarino, J. and Sherman, D. (1980) 'High-risk neighbourhoods and high-risk families: the human ecology of child maltreatment', *Child Development*, 51: 188–98.

Garofalo, J. (1986) 'Lifestyles and victimisation: an update', in A.E. Fattah (ed.) *From Crime Policy to Victim Policy – Reorienting the Justice System*. London: Macmillan.

Garofalo, J., Siegel, L. and Laub, J. (1987) 'School related victimisations among adolescents: an analysis of national crime survey narratives', *Journal of Quantitative Criminology*, 3: 321–38.

Gibson, H., Morrison, S. and West, D.J. (1970) 'The confession of known offences in response to a self-reported delinquency schedule', *British Journal of Criminology*, 10: 277–80.

Glueck, S. and Glueck, E.T. (1950) *Unravelling Juvenile Delinquency*. Cambridge, MA: Harvard University Press.

Glueck, S. and Glueck, E.T. (1952) *Delinquents in the Making: Paths to Prevention*. New York, NY: Harper & Brothers Publishers.

Gold, M. (1978) 'Scholastic experience, self esteem and delinquent behaviour: a theory for alternative schools', *Crime and Delinquency*, 24: 290–308.

Gottfredson, D.C. (2001) *Schools and Delinquency*. Cambridge: Cambridge University Press.

Gottfredson, D.C., McNeil III, R.J. and Gottfredson, G.D. (1991) 'Social area influences on delinquency: a multi-level analysis', *Journal of Research in Crime and Delinquency*, 28: 197–226.

Gottfredson, G.D. and Gottfredson, D.C. (1985) *Victimisation in Schools*. New York, NY: Plenum Press.

Gottfredson, G.D., Gottfredson, D.C., Gottfredson, N.C. and Jones, E.M. (2002a) 'Community characteristics, staffing difficulty, and school disorder in a national sample of secondary schools.' Paper presented at the American Society of Criminology annual conference, Chicago.

Gottfredson, G.D., Gottfredson, D.C., Payne, A.A. and Gottfredson, N.C. (2002b) 'School climate predictors of school disorder: results from the National Study of Delinquency Prevention in Schools.' Paper presented at the American Society of Criminology annual conference, Chicago.

Gottfredson, M. and Hirschi, T. (1990) *A General Theory of Crime*. Stanford, CA: Stanford University Press.

Graham, J. (1988) *Schools, Disruptive Behaviour and Delinquency: A Review of Research*. Home Office Research Study 96. London: Home Office.

Graham, J. and Bowling, B. (1995) *Young People and Crime*. Home Office Research Study 145. London: HMSO.

Graham, J. and Utting, D. (1996) 'Families, schools and criminality prevention', in T. Bennett (ed.) *Preventing Crime and Disorder: Targeting Strategies and Responsibilities*. Cambridge: Institute of Criminology, University of Cambridge.

Grasmick, H.G., Tittle, C.R., Bursik, R.J. Jnr and Arnekley, B.J. (1993) 'Testing the core empirical implications of Gottfredson and Hirschi's general theory of crime', in *Journal of Research in Crime and Delinquency*, 30: 5–29.

Greenberg, D.F. (1979) *Mathematical Criminology*. New Brunswick, NJ: Rutgers University Press.

Hagan, F.E. (1993) *Research Methods in Criminal Justice and Criminology* (3rd edn). New York, NY: Macmillan.

Halpern, D. (2001) 'Moral values, social trust and inequality: can values explain crime?', *British Journal of Criminology*, 41: 236–51.

Hand, M. (2004) 'On the desirability of education: a reply to John Wilson', *British Journal of Educational Studies*, 52: 1.

Hargreaves, D. H. (2001) 'A capital theory of school effectiveness and improvement', *British Educational Research Journal*, 27: 487–503.

Hargreaves, D.H., Hester, S.K. and Mellor, F. (1975) *Deviance in Classrooms*. London: Routledge & Kegan Paul.

Hauser, R.M., Sewell, W.H. and Alwin, D.F. (1976) 'High school effects on achievement', in W.H. Sewell *et al.* (eds) *Schooling and Achievement in American Society*. New York, NY: Academic Press.

Hawkins, J.D., Catalano, R.F., Morrison, D.M., O'Donnell, J., Abbott, R.D. and Day, L.E. (1992) 'The Seattle Social Development Project: effects of the first four years on protective factors and problem behaviours', in J. McCord and R.E. Tremblay (eds) *Preventing Antisocial Behaviour: Interventions from Birth Through Adolescence*. New York, NY: Guilford Press.

Heath, A. and Clifford, P. (1980) 'The seventy thousand hours that Rutter left out', *Oxford Review of Education*, 6: 3–19.

Hedstrom, P. and Swedberg, R. (1998) *Social Mechanisms: An Analytical Approach to Social Theory*. Cambridge: Cambridge University Press.

Hellevik, O. (1984) *Introduction to Causal Analysis. Exploring Survey Data by Crosstabulation*. London: Allen & Unwin.

Hellman, D.A. and Beaton, S. (1986) 'The pattern of violence in urban public schools: the influence of school and community', *Journal of Research in Crime and Delinquency*, 23: 102–27.

Herrenkohl, T.I., Hawkins, D.J., Ick-Joong, C., Hill, K.G. and Battin-Pearson, S. (2001) 'School and community risk factors and interventions', in R. Loeber and D.P. Farrington (eds) *Child Delinquents: Development, Intervention and Service Needs*. London: Sage.

Hindelang, M., Gottfredson, M.R. and Garofalo, J. (1978) *Victims of Personal Crime: An Empirical Foundation for a Theory of Personal Victimisation*. Cambridge, MA: Ballinger.

Hindelang, M., Hirschi, T. and Weis, G. (1981) *Measuring Delinquency*. Beverly Hills, CA: Sage.

Hirschi, T. (1969) *Causes of Delinquency*. Berkeley, CA: University of California Press.

Hirschi, T. (1991) 'Family structure and crime', in B.J. Christensen (ed.) *When Families Fail: The Social Costs*. Lanham, MD: University Press of America.

Hirschi, T. and Gottfredson, M. (1993) 'Commentary: testing the general theory of crime', *Journal of Research in Crime and Delinquency*, 30: 47–54.

Hirschi, T. and Gottfredson, M. (2002) 'The generality of deviance', in J.H. Laub (ed.) *Travis Hirschi: The Craft of Criminology*. London: Transaction Publishers.

Hoffmann, J.P. and Johnson, R.A. (2000) 'Multilevel influences on school disorder: a comment on Welsh, Greene, and Jenkins', *Criminology*, 38: 1275–88.

Huizinga, D. and Elliot, D.S. (1986) 'Reassessing the reliability and validity of self-report delinquent measures', *Journal of Quantitative Criminology*, 2: 293–327.

Ingoldsby, E.M. and Shaw, D.S. (2002) 'Neighbourhood contextual factors and early-starting antisocial pathways', *Clinical Child and Psychology Review*, 5: 21–55.

Jencks, C.S., Smith, M., Acland, H., Bane, M.J., Cohen, D., Gintis, H., Heyns, B. and Michelson, S. (1972) *Inequality: A Reassessment of the Effect of Family and School in America*. New York, NY: Basic Books.

Jenkins, P. (1997) 'School delinquency and the school social bond', *Journal of Research in Crime and Delinquency*, 34: 337–68.

Junger-Tas, J. and Marshall, I. (1999) 'The self-report methodology in crime research', in M. Tonry (ed.) *Crime and Justice: A Review of Research. Volume 25*. Chicago, IL: University of Chicago Press.

Kennedy, D.S. (1993) *South Glamorgan Health and Social Care Profile*. Cardiff: South Glamorgan Health Authority.

Klein, M.W. (1984) 'Offence specialisation and versatility among juveniles', *British Journal of Clinical Psychology*, 24: 185–94.

Klein, M.W. (1994) 'Communities change, too', in E.G.M. Weitekamp and H.J. Kerner (eds) *Cross National Longitudinal Research on Human Development and Criminal Behaviour*. Dordrecht: Kluwer.

Kornhauser, R. (1978) *Social Sources of Delinquency*. Chicago, IL: University of Chicago Press.

Kuperschmidt, J.B., Griesler, P.C., DeRosier, M.E., Patterson, C.J. and Davis, P.W. (1995) 'Childhood aggression and peer relations in the context of family and neighbourhood factors', *Child Development*, 66: 360–75.

Laub, J.H. and Lauritsen, J.L. (1998) 'School violence, neighbourhood and family conditions', in D.S. Elliot *et al.* (eds) *Violence in American Schools*. Cambridge: Cambridge University Press.

Lauritsen, J.L., Sampson, R.J. and Laub, J.H. (1991) 'The link between offending and victimisation among adolescents', *Criminology*, 29: 265–91.

Lear, J. (1995) *Aristotle: The Desire to Understand*. Cambridge: Cambridge University Press.

LeBlanc, M. (1997) 'A generic control theory of the criminal phenommena: the strucural and dynamic statements of an integrative multi-layered control theory', in T.P. Thornberry (ed.) *Developmental Theories of Crime and Delinquency*. New Brunswick, NJ: Transaction Press.

Lindström, P. (1993) *School and Delinquency in a Contextual Perspective*. Sweden: National Council for Crime Prevention.

Lindström, P. (1995) *School Context and Delinquency. The impact of Social Class Structure and Academic Balance. Project Metropolitan 41*. Stockholm:Department of Sociology, University of Stockholm.

Lindström, P. (1996) 'Family interaction, neighbourhood context and deviant behaviour', *Studies in Crime and Crime Prevention*, 5: 113–19.

Lindström, P. (1997) 'Patterns of school violence. A replication and empirical extension', *British Journal of Criminology*, 37: 121–30.

Lindström, P. (2001) 'School violence: a multi-level perspective', *International Review of Victimology*, 8: 141–58.

Lizotte, A.J., Thornberry, T.P., Krohn, M.D., Chard-Wierschem, D. and McDowall, D. (1994) 'Neighbourhood context and delinquency: a longitudinal analysis', in E.G.M. Weitekamp and H.J. Kerner (eds) *Cross-national Longitudinal Research on Human Development and Criminal Behaviour*. Dordrecht: Kluwer.

Loeber, R. and Farrington, D.P. (2001) 'Executive summary', in R. Loeber and D.P. Farrington (eds) *Child Delinquents: Development, Intervention and Service Needs*. London: Sage.

Loeber, R. and Stouthamer-Loeber, M. (1986) 'Family factors as correlates and predictors of juvenile conduct problems and delinquency', in M. Tonry and N. Morris (eds) *Crime and Justice: An Annual Review of Research*. Chicago, IL: University of Chicago Press.

Loeber, R., Stouthamer-Loeber, M., Farrington, D.P., Lahey, B.B., Keenan, K. and White, H.R. (2002) 'Editorial introduction: three longitudinal studies of children's development in Pittsburgh: the Developmental Trends Study, the Pittsburgh Youth Study, and the Pittsburgh Girls Study', *Criminal Behaviour and Mental Health*, 12: 1–23.

MacBeath, J. and Mortimore, P. (2001) *Improving School Effectiveness*. Buckingham: Open University Press.

Martens, P.L. (1993) 'An ecological model of socialisation in explaining offending', in D.P. Farrington *et al.* (eds) *Integrating Individual and Ecological Aspects of Crime*. Stockholm: Allmanna Forlaget.

Martens, P.L. (1997) 'Parental monitoring and deviant behaviour among juveniles', *Studies on Crime and Crime Prevention*, 6: 224–44.

Mawby, R. (1980) 'Sex and crime: the results of a self-report survey', *British Journal of Sociology*, 31: 525–43.

McDonald, L. (1969) *Social Class and Delinquency*. London: Faber & Faber.

McPartland, J.M. and McDill, E.L. (1977) 'Research on crime in schools', in J.M. McPartland and E.L. McDill (eds) *Violence in Schools*. Lexington, MA: Lexington Books.

McQuoid, J. (1994) 'The self-reported delinquency study in Belfast, Northern Ireland', in J. Junger-Tas *et al.* (eds) *Delinquent Behaviour among Young People in the Western World*. Amsterdam: Kugler.

Meithe, T. and Meier, R. (1994) *Crime and its Social Context*. Binghampton, NY: State University of New York Press.

Merton, R.K. (1938) 'Social structure and anomie', *American Sociological Review*, 3: 672–82.

Moffit, T.E. (1993) 'Adolescence-limited and life-course persistent anti-social behaviour: a developmental taxonomy', *Psychological Review*, 100: 674–701.

Moffit, T.E., Caspi, A., Rutter, M. and Silva, P.A. (2001) *Sex Differences in Antisocial Behaviour. Conduct Disorder, Delinquency and Violence in the Dunedin Longitudinal Study*. Cambridge: Cambridge University Press.

Mortimore, P., Sammons, P., Ecob, R., Stoll, L. and Lewis, D. (1988) *School Matters: The Junior Years*. Salisbury: Open Books.

National Assembly For Wales (2000) *Welsh Index of Multiple Deprivation*. Cardiff: HMSO.

Nuttall, D., Goldstein, H., Prosser, R. and Rasbash, J. (1989) 'Differential School Effectiveness', *International Journal of Educational Research*, 13: 769–76.

Osgood, W.D., Wilson, J.K., O'Malley, P.M., Bachman, J.G. and Johnston, L.D. (1996) 'Routine activities and individual deviant behaviour', *American Sociological Review*, 61: 635–55.

Park, R.E., Burgess, E.W. and Mackenzie, R.T. (1925) *The City*. Chicago, IL: University of Chicago Press.

Piquero, A.R., Farrington, D.P. and Blumstein, A. (2003) 'The criminal career paradigm: background and recent developments', in M. Tonry (ed) *Crime and Justices: An Annual Review of Research. Vol. 30*. Chicago, IL: University of Chicago Press.

Power, M.J., Benn, R.T. and Morris, J.N. (1972) 'Neighbourhood, school and juveniles before the courts', *British Journal of Criminology*, 12: 111–32.

Pratt, T.C. and Cullen, T.F. (2000) 'The empirical status of Gottfredson and Hirschi's general theory of crime: a meta-analysis', *Criminology*, 38: 931–65.

Raudenbush, S.W. and Sampson, R.J. (1999) 'Ecometrics: toward a science of assessing ecological settings, with application to the systematic social observation of neighbourhoods', *Sociological Methodology*, 29: 1–41.

Reiss, A.J. Jnr. (1986) 'Why are communities important in understanding crime?', in A.J. Reiss Jnr and M. Tonry (eds) *Crime and Justice 8: Communities and Crime*. Chicago, IL: University of Chicago Press.

Reiss, A.J. (1988) 'Co-offending and criminal careers', in M. Tonry and N. Morris (eds) *Crime and Justice 10: An Annual Review of Research*. Chicago, IL: University of Chicago Press.

Reiss, A.J. Jnr and Rhodes, A.L. (1961) 'The distribution of juvenile delinquency in the social class structure', *American Sociological Review*, 26: 720–32.

Reynolds, D. (1992) 'School effectiveness and school improvement: an updated review of the British literature', in D. Reynolds and P. Cuttance (eds) *School Effectiveness: Research, Policy and Practice*. London: Cassell.

Riley, D. (1987) 'Time and crime: the link between teenager lifestyle and delinquency', *Journal of Quantitative Criminology*, 3: 339–54.

Riley, D. and Shaw, M. (1985) *Parental Supervision and Juvenile Delinquency*. London: HMSO.

Rutter, M. and Giller, H. (1983) *Juvenile Delinquency: Trends and Perspectives*. Harmondsworth: Penguin Books.

Rutter, M., Giller, H. and Hagell, A. (1998) *Antisocial Behaviour by Young People*. Cambridge: Cambridge University Press.

Rutter, M. and Maughan, B. (2002) 'School effectiveness findings 1979–2002', *Journal of School Psychology*, 40: 451–75.

Rutter, M., Maughan, B., Mortimore, P. and Ousten, J. (1979) *Fifteen Thousand Hours: Secondary Schools and their Effects on Children*. London: Open Books.

Sameroff, A.J., Seifer, R., Barocas, R., Zax, M. and Greenspan, S. (1987) 'Intelligence quotient scores of 4 year-old children: social-environmental risk factors', *Pediatrics*, 79: 343–50.

Sampson, R.J. and Groves, W.B. (1989) 'Community structure and crime: testing social disorganisation theory', *American Journal of Sociology*, 94: 774–802.

Sampson, R.J. and Laub, J.H. (1993) *Crime in the making*. Cambridge, MA: Harvard University Press.

Sampson, R.J. and Laub, J.H. (2003) 'Life-course desisters? Trajectories of crime among delinquent boys followed to age 70', *Criminology*, 41: 555–92.

Sampson, R.J. and Lauritsen, J.L. (1990) 'Deviant lifestyles, proximity to crime, and the offender–victim link in personal violence', *Journal of Research in Crime and Delinquency*, 27: 110–39.

Sampson, R.J., Raudenbush, S.W. and Earls, F. (1997) 'Neighborhoods and violent crime: a multi-level study of collective efficacy', *Science*, 277: 918–24.

Sampson, R.J. and Wooldredge, J.D. (1987) 'Linking the micro- and macro-level dimensions of lifestyle-routine activity and opportunity models of predatory victimization', *Criminology*, 3: 371–93.

Sarnecki, J. (1986) *Delinquent Networks. Report* 1. Stockholm: National Council for Crime Prevention.

Scherer, J. (1978) 'School–community linkages: avenues of alienation or socialisation', in E.A. Wenk and N. Harlow (eds) *School Crime and Disruption*. Washington, DC: National Institute of Education.

Schoggen, P. (1989) *Behaviour Settings: A Revision and Extension of Roger G. Barker's Ecological Psychology*. Stanford, CA: Stanford University Press.

Shapland, J. (1978) 'Self-reported delinquency in boys aged 11 to 14', *British Journal of Criminology*, 18: 255–66.

Shaw, C.R. and McKay, H.D. (1969) *Juvenile Delinquency and Urban Areas* (rev. edn). Chicago, IL: University of Chicago Press.

Shonkoff, J.P. and Phillips, D.A.E. (2000) *From Neurons to Neighbourhoods. The Science of Early Childhood Development*. Washington, DC: National Academy Press.

Simcha-Fagan, O. and Schwartz, J.E. (1986) 'Neighbourhood and delinquency: an assessment of contextual effects', *Criminology*, 24: 667–99.

Skogan, W.G. (1990) *Disorder and Decline: Crime and the Spiral of Decay in American Neighborhoods*. New York, NY: Free Press.

Smith, D., McVie, S., Woodward, R., Shute, J., Flint, J. and McAra, L. (2001) *The Edinburgh Study of Youth Transitions and Crime: Key Findings at Age 12 and 13*. Edinburgh: University of Edinburgh.

Smith, D. and Tomlinson, S. (1989) *The School Effect: A Study of Multi-racial Comprehensives*. London: Policy Studies Institute.

Smith, D.J. and McVie, S. (2003) 'Theory and method in the Edinburgh Study of Youth Transitions and Crime', *British Journal of Criminology*, 43: 169–95.

Sutherland, E.H. (1939) *Principles of Criminology*. Philadelphia, PA: Lippinicot.

Sutherland, E. H. and Cressey, D. (1970) *Principles of Criminology*. Philadelphia, PA: Lippinicot.

Svensson, R. (2004a) *Social Control and Socialisation: The Role of Morality as a Social Mechanism in Adolescent Deviant Behaviour*. Stockholm: Almqvist & Wiksell International.

Svensson, R. (2004b) 'Shame as a consequence of the parent–child relationship: a study of gender differences in juvenile delinquency', *European Journal of Criminology*, 1: 477–504.

Sykes, G.M. and Matza, M. (1957) 'Techniques of neutralization: a theory of delinquency,' in *American Sociological Review*, 22: 664–70.

Thornberry, T.P. and Farnworth, M. (1982) 'Social correlates of criminal involvement: further evidence on the relationship between social status and criminal behaviour', *American Sociological Review*, 47: 505–18.

Thornberry, T.P. and Krohn, M.D. (2000) 'The self-report method for measuring delinquency and crime', in Department of Justice, Office of Justice Programs and National Institute of Justice (eds) *Measurement and Analysis of Crime and Justice. Volume 4*. Washington, DC: US Department of Justice.

Tittle, C.R., Smith, D.A. and Villemez, W.J. (1978) 'The myth of social class and criminality: an empirical assessment of the empirical evidence', *American Sociological Review*, 43: 643–56.

Tittle, C.R., Smith, D.A. and Villemez, W.J. (1982) 'One step forward, two steps back: more on the class/criminality controversy', in *American Sociological Review*, 47: 435–38.

Toby, J. (1995) 'The schools', in J.Q. Wilson and J. Petersilia (eds) *Crime*. San Francisco, CA: ICS Press.

Tonry, M., Ohlin, L.E. and Farrington, D.P. (1991) *Human Development and Criminal Behavior*. New York, NY: Springer Verlag.

Welsh, W.N. (2000) 'The effects of school climate on school disorder', *Annals of American Political and Social Sciences*, 567: 88–107.

Welsh, W.N. (2001) 'Effects of student and school factors on five measures of school disorder', *Justice Quarterly*, 18: 911–47.

Welsh, W.N., Greene, J.R. and Jenkins, P.H. (1999) 'School disorder: the influence of individual, institutional, and community factors', *Criminology*, 37: 73–115.

Welsh, W.N., Stokes, R. and Greene, J.R. (2000) 'A macro-level model of school disorder', *Journal of Research in Crime and Delinquency*, 37: 243–83.

West, D.J. and Farrington, D.P. (1973) *Who Becomes Delinquent?* London: Heinemann.

West, D.J. and Farrington, D.P. (1977) *The Delinquent Way of Life*. London: Heinemann.

Wikström, P.-O.H. (1987) *Patterns of Crime in a Birth Cohort. Sex, Age and Social Class Differences. Project Metropolitan Research Reports 24*. Stockholm: Department of Sociology, University of Stockholm.

Wikström, P.-O.H. (1990) 'The Stockholm Project: an introduction', in P.-O.H. Wikström (ed.) *Crime and Measures against Crime in the City. Report 5*. Stockholm: Allmanna Forlaget.

Wikström, P.-O.H. (1991) 'Housing tenure, social class and offending', *Criminal Behaviour and Mental Health*, 1: 69–89.

Wikström, P.-O.H. (1995) 'Self-control, temptations, frictions and punishment', in P.-O.H. Wikström *et al.* (eds) *Integrating Crime Prevention Strategies: Propensity and Opportunity. Report 5*. Stockholm: Fritzes.

Wikström, P.-O.H. (1996) 'Causes of crime and crime prevention', in T. Bennett (ed.) *Preventing Crime and Disorder: Targeting Strategies and Responsibilities*. Cambridge: University of Cambridge, Institute of Criminology.

Wikström, P.-O.H. (1998) 'Communities and crime', in M. Tonry (ed.) *The Handbook of Crime and Punishment*. New York, NY: Oxford University Press.

Wikström, P.-O.H. and Torstensson, M. (1999) 'Local crime prevention and its national support: organisation and direction', *European Journal on Criminal Policy and Research*, 7: 427–42.

Wikström, P.-O.H. (2002) *Adolescent Crime in Context. A Study of Gender, Family Social Position, Individual Characteristics, Community Context, Lifestyles, Offending and Victimisation*. Cambridge: University of Cambridge, Institute of Criminology (unpublished report for the Home Office).

Wikström, P.-O.H. (2004) 'The social origins of pathways in crime', in D.P. Farrington (ed.) *Testing Integrated Developmental/Life Course Theories of Offending. Advances in Criminological Theory.* New Brunswick, NJ: Transaction.

Wikström, P.-O.H. and Dolmen, L. (2001) 'Urbanisation, neighbourhood social integration, informal social control, minor social disorder, victimisation and fear of crime', *International Review of Victimology*, 8: 121–40.

Wikström, P.-O.H. and Loeber, R. (2000) 'Do disadvantaged neighbourhoods cause well-adjusted children to become adolescent delinquents?', *Criminology* 38: 1201–34.

Wikström, P.-O.H. and Sampson, R. (2003) 'Social mechanisms of community influences on crime and pathways in criminality', in B.B. Lahey *et al.* (eds) *The Causes of Conduct Disorder and Serious Juvenile Delinquency.* New York, NY: Guilford Press.

Wikström, P.-O.H. and Svensson, R. (forthcoming) 'Does gender matter? A study of adolescent criminality and substance use.'

Willcock, H.D. (1974) *Deterrents and Incentives to Crime among Boys and Young Men aged 15–21 years.* London: Office of Population Censuses and Surveys.

Willis, P. (1988) *Learning to Labour.* Aldershot: Gower.

Wilson, J.Q. (1977) 'Crime in society and schools', in J.M. McPartland and E.L. McDill (eds) *Violence in Schools.* Lexington, MA: Lexington Books.

Wilson, J.Q. and Herrnstein, R.J. (1985) *Crime and Human Nature.* New York, NY: Simon and Schuster.

Wittebrood, K. and Nieuwbeerta, P. (1999) 'Wages of sin? The link between offending, lifestyle and violent victimisation', *European Journal on Criminal Policy and Research*, 7: 63–80.

Wolfgang, M.E., Figlio, R.M. and Sellin, T.M. (1972) *Delinquency in a Birth Cohort.* Chicago, IL: University of Chicago Press.

Yinger, J.M. (1960) 'Contraculture and subculture', *American Sociological Review*, 25: 625–35.

Index